Covenants
Not to Compete

A State-by-State Survey

Second Edition

Table of Cases and Indexes

Other BNA Books Authored by the ABA Section of Labor & Employment Law

The Developing Labor Law

Employee Benefits Law

Employee Duty of Loyalty: A State-by-State Survey

Employment Discrimination Law

Equal Employment Law Update

How Arbitration Works

Labor Arbitration: A Practical Guide for Advocates

Labor Arbitrator Development: A Handbook

Occupational Safety and Health Law

The Railway Labor Act

Covenants Not to Compete

A State-by-State Survey

Second Edition

Table of Cases and Indexes

Editor - in - Chief
Brian M. Malsberger

Associate Editors
Arnold H. Pedowitz
Robert W. Sikkel

Employee Rights and Responsibilities Committee

Section of Labor and Employment Law
American Bar Association

The Bureau of National Affairs, Inc., Washington, D.C.

Library of Congress Cataloging-in-Publication Data

Covenants not to compete : a state-by-state survey / editor-in-chief,
    Brian M. Malsberger ; associate editors, Arnold H. Pedowitz, Robert
    W. Sikkel. -- 2nd ed.
        p. cm.
        "Employee Rights and Responsibilities Committee, Section of Labor
    and Employment Law, American Bar Association."
        Vol. 2: Indexes and table of cases.
        ISBN 1-57018-030-X (v. 1 : hb). -- ISBN 1-57018-032-6 (v. 2 : pb)
        1. Covenants not to compete—United States—States.
    I. Malsberger, Brian M. II. Pedowitz, Arnold H. III. Sikkel,
    Robert W. IV. American Bar Association. Committee on Employee
    Rights and Responsibilities in the Workplace.
    KF3463.Z95C68 1996
    344.73'012596--dc20
    [347.30412596]
                                                    96-18836
                                                    CIP

Published by BNA Books
1250 23rd Street, N.W., Washington, D.C. 20037

Typeset by Altaf U. Khan

International Standard Book Number 1-57018-030-X (Main Volume)
1-57018-032-6 (Table of Cases and Indexes)
Printed in the United States of America

Foreword

Since 1945 the ABA Section of Labor and Employment Law has had as its stated purposes (1) to study and report upon continuing developments in the law affecting labor relations, (2) to assist the professional growth and development of practitioners in the field of employment and labor relations law, and (3) to promote justice, human welfare, industrial peace, and the recognition of the supremacy of law in labor-management relations.

Through the publication of books such as *Covenants Not to Compete*, and through annual and committee meeting programs designed to provide a forum for the exchange of ideas, the Section has pursued these stated goals. Gradually, the Section has built a library of comprehensive legal works intended for the use of the Section membership as well as the bar generally.

The Section of Labor and Employment Law is pleased to provide this supplement to its survey of state statutes and case law on covenants not to compete as part of its library of books published by BNA Books, a division of The Bureau of National Affairs, Inc. The initial draft of these chapters was prepared by Editor-in-Chief Brian M. Malsberger, for review by members of the Subcommittee on Individual Responsibilities, Covenants Not to Compete, Trade Secrets, Loyalty, and Conflicts of Interest within the Employee Rights and Responsibilities Committee of the Section of Labor and Employment Law of the American Bar Association, under the direction of subcommittee co-chairs Arnold H. Pedowitz and Robert W. Sikkel.

The Section wishes to express its appreciation to the subcommittee, and in particular to the editor-in-chief, Brian Malsberger of BNA, as well as to the associate editors, Arnold Pedowitz and Robert Sikkel. This group has tried to accomplish two objectives: (1) to be equally balanced and nonpartisan in their viewpoints, and (2) to ensure the book is of significant value to the practitioner, student, and sophisticated nonlawyer. A thank-you is also due to The Bureau of National Affairs, Inc., for making its research facilities available to the Section for this project.

The views expressed herein do not necessarily represent the views of the American Bar Association, or its Section of Labor and Employment Law, or any other organization, but are simply the collective, but not necessarily the individual, views of the authors.

DONALD P. MACDONALD
chair
CHRISTOPHER A. BARRECA
chair-elect
Section of Labor
and Employment Law
American Bar Association

August 1996

Preface

Restrictions on post-employment activities designed to protect legitimate employer interests are relevant today more than ever.

In a service-driven economy, the ability of a business to protect its investment in human resources, customer relationships, and confidential business information is critical to ensuring continued economic viability. In this milieu, businesses increasingly rely upon post-employment covenants not to compete to protect these investments. The growth in the use of such covenants also represents a sound response to increased levels of employee mobility, the globalization of product markets, and rapid advances in technology.

Employees often have access to the proprietary information, trade secrets, and other confidential data of the employer. Certain employees frequently have key relationships with customers and obtain specialized training or technical knowledge, expertise, or skills on the job, often at substantial expense—in terms of both money and time—to the employer. Post-employment restrictions seek to protect employers' interests in such assets and investments by preventing former employees from entering into competitive employment and otherwise eroding the former employer's market share. Such restrictions safeguard interests not protected by trade secret, patent, and copyright statutes, and augment those protections by supplying contractual remedies to which an employer might not otherwise be entitled.

Enforceable covenants not to compete offer obvious benefits to employers: They help to safeguard valuable customer relationships and confidential business information. In addition, they provide an indirect benefit to employees as a class: Given the protections afforded by restrictive covenants, employers can be more confident that the valuable information they impart to their employees, and the crucial customer contacts they develop, will not later be used against them in a competitive endeavor. Employees trusted with such information and contacts are better able to perform their jobs and, in that state, they maintain the viability of the employer and the employer's need for their services. When viewed in this light, even prospective employers can be seen to benefit from the enforcement of reasonable noncompete agreements against prospective employees: Such restrictions help to guarantee a stable business environment and a level playing field—to the extent such firms' own former employees are also competitively restricted. This book is a valuable aid to attorneys for all three classes—employers, employees, and prospective employers of individuals bound by covenants not to compete—because it charts the limits of enforceability of restrictive covenants.

This edition is designed to satisfy attorneys' needs in both the drafting and the counseling context. As a drafting tool, it provides detailed guidance on—and examples of—the statutory and common law limits of covenant enforceability, issues of consideration, and judicial modification of overbroad covenants. Because the cases are very individualized and fact-intensive, the case examples provided are invaluable in this context. To the same extent, however, the book is designed to answer specific questions regarding covenant enforceability in each jurisdiction. Employing a question-and-answer format and including occupation-searchable indexes, it provides a quick assessment of the law in each jurisdiction and, thus, a source of immediate answers to client questions in the counselling context. By using this book, both corporate counsel and private practitioners can answer clients' questions within minutes, and at a fraction of the cost that otherwise might have been incurred.

This edition completely updates the first edition through the end of 1995, alerting counsel to—and explaining the effects of—the many significant statutory and case law developments that relate to issues addressed in the format of the first edition. It also includes the text of profession-specific statutes governing covenants not to compete. Moreover, it discusses nearly 100 issues not analyzed in the first edition, making the treatise an even more valuable aid to employers—whether operating in only one state or in many.

The table of cases and indexes appearing in the soft-cover companion volume help the researcher to determine which occupations, professions, industries, and transactions have been addressed by the covenant case law of each jurisdiction. This enables practitioners and drafters alike to quickly and accurately determine, in conjunction with the main volume, the status of the law on any of an ever-expanding number of critical issues governing the enforceability of postemployment covenants not to compete in the occupation of particular concern to them. The soft-cover volume is to be integrated into annual supplements, with necessary updates.

A work of this scope is necessarily the fruit of joint efforts by many talented individuals. While many of those who contributed to this edition are mentioned elsewhere in the book, the Editor-in-Chief would like to make special mention of two individuals— Altaf U. Khan and Timothy J. Darby, Esq.—and to thank also their families for sparing them the extra time required by this project. Their efforts have assured a thorough, timely, and greatly expanded treatment of the law of covenants not to compete.

Mr. Khan, a veteran of the publishing industry both here and abroad, served as Senior Production Editor and as Master Typesetter for this edition. Formerly a Production Supervisor with *Newsline*, a Karachi-based news magazine, Mr. Khan has also worked with Oxford University Press and is currently a Quality Assurance Editor with BNA's *Environment Reporter Reference File*. Because of his generosity in sharing his technical expertise with the substantive editors, and because of his untiring cooperation, it has been possible to make this edition available to practitioners at the earliest possible moment. His good grace in accepting ever-increasing responsibilities on this project goes very much hand-in-glove with his other contributions to this series, including EM-PLOYEE DUTY OF LOYALTY: A STATE-BY-STATE SURVEY (Washington, D.C.: BNA Books 1995 & Supp. 1996), for which he also serves as Senior Production Editor.

Mr. Darby, an attorney specializing in labor and employment law, also went far beyond the call of duty as BNA Books' Acquisition Manager for this work, becoming both a very valued advisor and an insightful Contributing Editor to this greatly ex-

panded edition. Nearly every innovation appearing in this book—
the inclusion of detailed finding lists, a table of cases, and several
occupation-related indexes—was conceived of by Mr. Darby.
Largely because of him, this edition serves as an even more useful
resource for the practitioner. As is the case for Mr. Khan, Mr.
Darby's participation in this series is not limited to this book: he
also serves as Contributing Editor to Employee Duty of Loyalty
and as Acquisitions Manager for all of the books by the ABA Section of Labor and Employment Law published with BNA Books.

Brian M. Malsberger
Editor-in-Chief

Arnold H. Pedowitz
Robert W. Sikkel
Associate Editors

August 1996

Summary Contents

Appendixes

List of General Questions

Note: Page numbers for answers to the questions below are provided state by state in the finding list beginning at page xix. A list of additional topics exploring issues beyond the general questions below and providing the relevant page numbers for information on those topics appears beginning at page xxx.

1. Is there a state statute of general application that governs the enforceability of covenants not to compete?

    a. What state statutes govern the enforceability of covenants not to compete as regards specific professions?

2. What is an employer's interest and how is that defined?

3. What must the plaintiff be able to show to prove the existence of an enforceable covenant not to compete?

    a. Does the signing of a covenant not to compete at the inception of the employment relationship provide sufficient consideration to support the covenant?

    b. Will a change in the terms and conditions of employment provide sufficient consideration to support a covenant not to compete entered into after the employment relationship has begun?

    c. Will continued employment provide sufficient consideration to support a covenant not to compete entered into after the employment relationship has begun?

    d. What factors will the court consider in determining whether time and geographic restrictions in the covenant are reasonable?

    e. Who has the burden of proving the reasonableness or unreasonableness of the covenant not to compete?

    f.   What type of time or geographic restrictions has the court found to be reasonable? Unreasonable?

    g.   Will the court allow a customer restriction to substitute for, or complement, a geographic restriction?

4. If the restrictions in the covenant not to compete are unenforceable because they are overbroad, are the courts permitted to modify the covenant to make the restrictions more narrow and to make the covenant enforceable? If so, under what circumstances will the courts allow reduction and what form of reduction will courts permit?

5. What must the employer prove to obtain a preliminary injunction enforcing the covenant not to compete?

6. If it is a necessary element of proof, how does the employer establish irreparable harm?

7. What is the standard of review on appeal of a trial judge's decision, following a preliminary injunction hearing, enforcing or refusing to enforce a covenant not to compete?

8. If the employer terminates the employment relationship, is the covenant enforceable?

9. If the court finds the employee has breached the restrictive covenant, will the court measure the period of injunction from the date of termination of employment or from the date of the court order?

10. What damages may an employer recover and from whom for breach of a covenant not to compete?

11. Does a liquidated damage clause for breach of the covenant not to compete preclude injunctive relief to enforce the covenant?

12. What choice of law rules apply to determine which state's law will govern an action seeking to enforce a covenant not to compete?

13. Law review articles that examine the law of covenants not to compete in this state.

14. Illustrative cases

State Abbreviations Used In Finding Lists, Table of Cases, and Indexes*

AL	Alabama	MT	Montana
AK	Alaska	NE	Nebraska
AZ	Arizona	NV	Nevada
AR	Arkansas	NH	New Hampshire
CA	California	NJ	New Jersey
CO	Colorado	NM	New Mexico
CT	Connecticut	NY	New York
DE	Delaware	NC	North Carolina
DC	District of Columbia	ND	North Dakota
FL	Florida	OH	Ohio
GA	Georgia	OK	Oklahoma
HI	Hawaii	OR	Oregon
ID	Idaho	PA	Pennsylvania
IL	Illinois	RI	Rhode Island
IN	Indiana	SC	South Carolina
IA	Iowa	SD	South Dakota
KS	Kansas	TN	Tennessee
KY	Kentucky	TX	Texas
LA	Louisiana	UT	Utah
ME	Maine	VT	Vermont
MD	Maryland	VA	Virginia
MA	Massachusetts	WA	Washington
MI	Michigan	WV	West Virginia
MN	Minnesota	WI	Wisconsin
MS	Mississippi	WY	Wyoming
MO	Missouri		

---

* This list is alphabetical by the full state name, not by the two-letter form. Thus, AL (Alabama) is the first entry on the list, rather than AK (Alaska).

Finding List by Question by State[*]

1. **Is there a state statute of general application that governs the enforceability of covenants not to compete?**

AL	60	IL	351	MT	674	RI	963
AK	95	IN	413	NE	691	SC	974
AZ	104	IA	448	NV	710	SD	997
AR	118	KS	460	NH	728	TN	1009
CA	135	KY	477	NJ	745	TX	1026
CO	170	LA	487	NM	769	UT	1083
CT	185	ME	525	NY	778	VT	1097
DE	206	MD	539	NC	827	VA	1106
DC	227	MA	562	ND	853	WA	1134
FL	242	MI	592	OH	863	WV	1150
GA	293	MN	603	OK	900	WI	1167
HI	333	MS	622	OR	911	WY	1187
ID	340	MO	634	PA	924		

    a. **What state statutes govern the enforceability of covenants not to compete as regards specific professions?**

AL	63	IL	351	MT	676	RI	963
AK	95	IN	413	NE	691	SC	974
AZ	104	IA	448	NV	711	SD	997
AR	118	KS	460	NH	728	TN	1010
CA	143	KY	477	NJ	745	TX	1030
CO	172	LA	494	NM	769	UT	1083
CT	185	ME	525	NY	778	VT	1097
DE	206	MD	539	NC	827	VA	1106
DC	227	MA	562	ND	854	WA	1134
FL	247	MI	594	OH	863	WV	1150
GA	294	MN	603	OK	902	WI	1167
HI	334	MS	622	OR	913	WY	1187
ID	340	MO	634	PA	924		

---

[*] This list is alphabetized by the full state name, not by the two-letter form. Thus, AL (Alabama) is the first entry on the list, and the first chapter in the book, rather than AK (Alaska). For a key to state abbreviations, consult the list of state abbreviations on page xviii. See also page xxx for "Finding List of Additional Topics."

2. What is an employer's interest and how is that defined?

3. What must the plaintiff be able to show to prove the existence of an enforceable covenant not to compete?

a.   **Does the signing of a covenant not to compete at the inception of the employment relationship provide sufficient consideration to support the covenant?**

b.   **Will a change in the terms and conditions of employment provide sufficient consideration to support a covenant not to compete entered into after the employment relationship has begun?**

c. **Will continued employment provide sufficient consideration to support a covenant not to compete entered into after the employment relationship has begun?**

AL	70	IL	372	MT	678	RI	964
AK	98	IN	417	NE	697	SC	978
AZ	106	IA	449	NV	713	SD	999
AR	121	KS	463	NH	732	TN	1013
CA	148	KY	479	NJ	751	TX	1046
CO	174	LA	501	NM	771	UT	1086
CT	190	ME	528	NY	787	VT	1098
DE	211	MD	543	NC	833	VA	1110
DC	230	MA	569	ND	855	WA	1137
FL	252	MI	596	OH	866	WV	1154
GA	299	MN	606	OK	904	WI	1171
HI	335	MS	624	OR	915	WY	1191
ID	342	MO	638	PA	929		

d. **What factors will the court consider in determining whether time and geographic restrictions in the covenant are reasonable?**

AL	70	IL	373	MT	678	RI	964
AK	98	IN	418	NE	698	SC	978
AZ	107	IA	450	NV	714	SD	1000
AR	121	KS	463	NH	732	TN	1014
CA	149	KY	479	NJ	751	TX	1047
CO	175	LA	503	NM	771	UT	1087
CT	191	ME	528	NY	789	VT	1099
DE	212	MD	544	NC	833	VA	1111
DC	231	MA	569	ND	855	WA	1140
FL	252	MI	596	OH	870	WV	1154
GA	300	MN	608	OK	804	WI	1172
HI	336	MS	625	OR	916	WY	1192
ID	342	MO	639	PA	931		

e. Who has the burden of proving the reasonableness or unreasonableness of the covenant not to compete?

AL	71	IL	375	MT	679	RI	965
AK	98	IN	420	NE	699	SC	980
AZ	107	IA	451	NV	714	SD	1000
AR	121	KS	463	NH	733	TN	1014
CA	149	KY	480	NJ	752	TX	1048
CO	175	LA	503	NM	771	UT	1087
CT	191	ME	529	NY	790	VT	1099
DE	212	MD	545	NC	836	VA	1112
DC	231	MA	569	ND	855	WA	1140
FL	253	MI	596	OH	871	WV	1154
GA	303	MN	608	OK	904	WI	1173
HI	336	MS	626	OR	917	WY	1193
ID	343	MO	641	PA	931		

f. What type of time or geographic restrictions has the court found to be reasonable? Unreasonable?

AL	71	IL	375	MT	680	RI	965
AK	98	IN	421	NE	699	SC	980
AZ	108	IA	451	NV	714	SD	1001
AR	121	KS	463	NH	733	TN	1015
CA	150	KY	480	NJ	752	TX	1049
CO	175	LA	503	NM	771	UT	1087
CT	192	ME	529	NY	790	VT	1099
DE	213	MD	546	NC	836	VA	1112
DC	232	MA	569	ND	855	WA	1141
FL	254	MI	596	OH	871	WV	1155
GA	303	MN	608	OK	904	WI	1174
HI	336	MS	626	OR	917	WY	1194
ID	343	MO	641	PA	932		

g. Will the court allow a customer restriction to substitute for, or complement, a geographic restriction?

AL	75	IL	379	MT	681	RI	965
AK	99	IN	423	NE	701	SC	982
AZ	109	IA	452	NV	715	SD	1001
AR	124	KS	464	NH	735	TN	1016
CA	151	KY	481	NJ	752	TX	1053
CO	177	LA	506	NM	772	UT	1088
CT	194	ME	530	NY	794	VT	1100
DE	215	MD	547	NC	840	VA	1116
DC	233	MA	571	ND	855	WA	1141
FL	257	MI	596	OH	875	WV	1156
GA	312	MN	610	OK	905	WI	1176
HI	336	MS	627	OR	918	WY	1195
ID	343	MO	643	PA	937		

4. If the restrictions in the covenant not to compete are unenforceable because they are overbroad, are the courts permitted to modify the covenant to make the restrictions more narrow and to make the covenant enforceable? If so, under what circumstances will the courts allow reduction and what form of reduction will courts permit?

AL	75	IL	381	MT	681	RI	965
AK	99	IN	424	NE	701	SC	982
AZ	109	IA	453	NV	715	SD	1001
AR	124	KS	464	NH	736	TN	1016
CA	151	KY	482	NJ	753	TX	1054
CO	178	LA	506	NM	772	UT	1088
CT	195	ME	531	NY	794	VT	1100
DE	216	MD	548	NC	840	VA	1116
DC	234	MA	571	ND	856	WA	1142
FL	258	MI	597	OH	875	WV	1157
GA	316	MN	611	OK	905	WI	1176
HI	336	MS	627	OR	918	WY	1195
ID	343	MO	643	PA	937		

5. What must the employer prove to obtain a preliminary injunction enforcing the covenant not to compete?

AL	76	IL	385	MT	682	RI	968
AK	100	IN	427	NE	702	SC	984
AZ	110	IA	454	NV	716	SD	1002
AR	125	KS	466	NH	738	TN	1017
CA	152	KY	482	NJ	754	TX	1058
CO	178	LA	508	NM	772	UT	1088
CT	196	ME	531	NY	795	VT	1101
DE	216	MD	550	NC	841	VA	1118
DC	235	MA	572	ND	856	WA	1143
FL	259	MI	597	OH	878	WV	1157
GA	319	MN	612	OK	906	WI	1178
HI	337	MS	628	OR	919	WY	1199
ID	344	MO	644	PA	940		

6. If it is a necessary element of proof, how does the employer establish irreparable harm?

AL	77	IL	389	MT	682	RI	968
AK	100	IN	428	NE	703	SC	984
AZ	111	IA	455	NV	717	SD	1003
AR	127	KS	467	NH	738	TN	1017
CA	153	KY	482	NJ	755	TX	1060
CO	178	LA	509	NM	773	UT	1091
CT	197	ME	532	NY	801	VT	1101
DE	219	MD	551	NC	842	VA	1118
DC	235	MA	574	ND	856	WA	1144
FL	267	MI	598	OH	878	WV	1158
GA	319	MN	613	OK	906	WI	1178
HI	337	MS	628	OR	919	WY	1199
ID	345	MO	646	PA	942		

7. What is the standard of review on appeal of a trial judge's decision, following a preliminary injunction hearing, enforcing or refusing to enforce a covenant not to compete?

AL	77	IL	390	MT	683	RI	968
AK	100	IN	429	NE	703	SC	985
AZ	111	IA	455	NV	717	SD	1003
AR	127	KS	468	NH	738	TN	1017
CA	153	KY	483	NJ	756	TX	1062
CO	178	LA	511	NM	773	UT	1092
CT	199	ME	532	NY	802	VT	1101
DE	219	MD	551	NC	843	VA	1118
DC	236	MA	575	ND	856	WA	1144
FL	270	MI	598	OH	879	WV	1158
GA	319	MN	615	OK	906	WI	1178
HI	337	MS	628	OR	919	WY	1199
ID	345	MO	646	PA	947		

8. If the employer terminates the employment relationship, is the covenant enforceable?

AL	78	IL	392	MT	683	RI	968
AK	100	IN	431	NE	704	SC	985
AZ	111	IA	455	NV	718	SD	1003
AR	127	KS	468	NH	739	TN	1018
CA	154	KY	483	NJ	756	TX	1064
CO	179	LA	511	NM	773	UT	1092
CT	199	ME	533	NY	803	VT	1102
DE	220	MD	551	NC	844	VA	1119
DC	236	MA	575	ND	856	WA	1144
FL	271	MI	598	OH	880	WV	1158
GA	320	MN	616	OK	906	WI	1179
HI	337	MS	628	OR	919	WY	1201
ID	345	MO	648	PA	946		

9. **If the court finds the employee has breached the restrictive covenant, will the court measure the period of injunction from the date of termination of employment or from the date of the court order?**

AL	78	IL	393	MT	684	RI	969
AK	101	IN	432	NE	704	SC	985
AZ	112	IA	455	NV	718	SD	1003
AR	127	KS	468	NH	739	TN	1018
CA	154	KY	483	NJ	756	TX	1065
CO	179	LA	512	NM	773	UT	1092
CT	200	ME	533	NY	804	VT	1102
DE	221	MD	552	NC	845	VA	1120
DC	236	MA	576	ND	857	WA	1145
FL	272	MI	598	OH	880	WV	1159
GA	320	MN	616	OK	907	WI	1179
HI	337	MS	629	OR	919	WY	1203
ID	346	MO	651	PA	947		

10. **What damages may an employer recover and from whom for breach of a covenant not to compete?**

AL	78	IL	393	MT	684	RI	969
AK	101	IN	432	NE	704	SC	985
AZ	113	IA	456	NV	718	SD	1003
AR	128	KS	468	NH	739	TN	1018
CA	155	KY	484	NJ	756	TX	1065
CO	179	LA	512	NM	774	UT	1092
CT	200	ME	533	NY	804	VT	1102
DE	221	MD	552	NC	845	VA	1121
DC	237	MA	576	ND	857	WA	1145
FL	273	MI	599	OH	881	WV	1159
GA	321	MN	617	OK	907	WI	1180
HI	337	MS	630	OR	920	WY	1203
ID	346	MO	653	PA	948		

11. Does a liquidated damage clause for breach of the covenant not to compete preclude injunctive relief to enforce the covenant?

AL	80	IL	394	MT	684	RI	970
AK	101	IN	433	NE	705	SC	987
AZ	113	IA	457	NV	719	SD	1005
AR	128	KS	469	NH	740	TN	1019
CA	156	KY	484	NJ	758	TX	1067
CO	179	LA	513	NM	774	UT	1094
CT	201	ME	534	NY	809	VT	1103
DE	222	MD	553	NC	846	VA	1121
DC	237	MA	576	ND	857	WA	1146
FL	274	MI	599	OH	882	WV	1159
GA	321	MN	618	OK	907	WI	1180
HI	338	MS	630	OR	920	WY	1204
ID	347	MO	654	PA	950		

12. What choice of law rules apply to determine which state's law will govern an action seeking to enforce a covenant not to compete?

AL	80	IL	395	MT	684	RI	971
AK	102	IN	434	NE	705	SC	987
AZ	114	IA	457	NV	719	SD	1005
AR	128	KS	469	NH	741	TN	1019
CA	156	KY	485	NJ	758	TX	1068
CO	180	LA	515	NM	775	UT	1094
CT	201	ME	535	NY	809	VT	1103
DE	222	MD	554	NC	846	VA	1121
DC	237	MA	577	ND	857	WA	1147
FL	275	MI	599	OH	882	WV	1160
GA	322	MN	618	OK	907	WI	1181
HI	338	MS	630	OR	920	WY	1204
ID	347	MO	655	PA	951		

13. Law review articles that examine the law of covenants not to compete in this state.

AL	82	IL	395	MT	684	RI	971
AK	102	IN	434	NE	706	SC	987
AZ	114	IA	457	NV	719	SD	1006
AR	130	KS	469	NH	741	TN	1020
CA	157	KY	485	NJ	758	TX	1070
CO	180	LA	515	NM	775	UT	1094
CT	202	ME	535	NY	809	VT	1103
DE	222	MD	554	NC	846	VA	1122
DC	238	MA	579	ND	858	WA	1147
FL	276	MI	601	OH	883	WV	1160
GA	322	MN	618	OK	907	WI	1182
HI	338	MS	631	OR	920	WY	1205
ID	348	MO	656	PA	951		

14. Illustrative cases

AL	82	IL	396	MT	685	RI	971
AK	102	IN	434	NE	706	SC	988
AZ	114	IA	457	NV	720	SD	1006
AR	130	KS	470	NH	741	TN	1020
CA	158	KY	485	NJ	758	TX	1072
CO	181	LA	516	NM	775	UT	1094
CT	202	ME	535	NY	811	VT	1104
DE	223	MD	554	NC	847	VA	1122
DC	238	MA	579	ND	858	WA	1147
FL	277	MI	602	OH	883	WV	1160
GA	323	MN	618	OK	908	WI	1183
HI	338	MS	631	OR	921	WY	1205
ID	348	MO	656	PA	952		

Finding List of Additional Topics

D

Table of Cases

For the "State" column, see the list of state abbreviations on page xviii in this volume if necessary.

For the "Question Nos." column:

- *See the "List of General Questions" beginning at page xvi of this volume to determine the meaning of question numbers and to determine page numbers of the discussions for particular states in the main volume.*
- *An "AT-" followed by a number (e.g., AT-1) indicates information is contained in a discussion of an Additional Topic; see the "Finding List of Additional Topics" beginning at page xxx of this volume to identify the topic concerned if necessary, and to determine the relevant page numbers of the discussions for particular states in the main volume.*

For the "Citation" column, where the state is noted and it varies from that listed in the "State" column, this indicates a discussion of a case decided in another state.

After locating a case in this table, researchers may locate additional cases involving the same occupation, industry, or transaction by consulting the appropriate index.

Editor's Note: Cases decided by the Texas Court of Appeals before September 1, 1981, are cited as "Tex. Civ. App." After that date, cases are cited as "Tex. Ct. App." The change in the court's name and the rules for proper citation in documents submitted to Texas courts are explained in the Texas Rules of Form.

Case Name	Citation	Occupation or Transaction/ Relationship	Industry	State	Question Nos.
A. Hollander & Son v. Imperial Fur Blending Corp.	2 N.J. 235, 66 A.2d 319 (1949)	Manager (branch)	Fur processing	NJ	6, 10
A. Sulka & Co. v. City of New Orleans	208 La. 585, 23 So.2d 224 (1945)	No covenant	No covenant	LA	4, 14
A.B. Chance Co. v. Schmidt	719 S.W.2d 854 (Mo.App. 1986)	Draftsperson	Pultrusion rods	MO	3, 3d, 3f, 5, AT-68
A.B. Dick Co. v. American Pro-Tech	159 Ill.App.3d 786, 112 Ill.Dec. 649, 514 N.E.2d 45, 4 IER Cases 600 (1st Dist. 1987)	Service technician	Photocopiers, microfiche equipment, and offset printing equipment	IL	2, 5, 6
A.E.P. Indus., Inc. v. McClure	308 N.C. 393, 302 S.E.2d 754 (1983)	Salesperson	Polyethylene products	NC	2, 3, 5, 7, 12
A.E.P. Indus., Inc. v. McClure	308 N.C. 393, 302 S.E.2d 754 (1983)	Salesperson	Polyethylene products	WY	2, 3, 3d
A.J. Dralle, Inc. v. Air Technologies	255 Ill.App.3d 987, 194 Ill.Dec. 353, 627 N.E.2d 690 (2d Dist. 1994)	Vendor/vendee contract	Air filters	IL	AT-95A
A.N. Deringer, Inc. v. Troia	178 A.D.2d 1023, 578 N.Y.S.2d 344 (4th Dep't 1991)	File clerk	Not specified	NY	5, 7
A.T. Hudson & Co. v. Donovan	216 N.J. Super. 426, 524 A.2d 412 (App.Div. 1987)	Consultant	Management	NJ	2, 3a, 14
Abalere Pest Control Serv., Inc. v. Hall	126 Vt. 1, 220 A.2d 717 (1966)	Exterminator	Pest control	VT	2, 3a, 3f, 3g, 9, 14

Case	Citation	Position	Business	State	Sections
Abalene Pest Control Serv., Inc. v. Powell	8 A.D.2d 734, 187 N.Y.S.2d 381 (1959)	Exterminator	Pest control	KS	14
Abbott-Interfast Corp. v. Harkabus	250 Ill.App.3d 13, 189 Ill.Dec. 288, 619 N.E.2d 1337 (2d Dist. 1993)	Salesperson	Fasteners	IL	3, 3f, 3g, 4, AT-55
Abramov v. Royal Dallas, Inc.	536 S.W.2d 388 (Tex.Civ.App. 1976)	Occupation not specified	Diamond wholesaling	KS	14
Acierno v. New Castle County	40 F.3d 645 (3d Cir. 1994)	No covenant	No covenant	PA	5, 6
Ackerman v. Kimball Int'l, Inc.	634 N.E.2d 778 (Ind.App. 1994), *aff'd as modified*, 652 N.E.2d 507 (Ind. 1995)	Corporate officer (vice president)	Wood veneer manufacturing	IN	3d
Ackerman v. Kimball Int'l, Inc.	634 N.E.2d 778 (Ind.App. 1994)	Manager (general)	Wood veneer	IN	2, 3c, 3d
Ackerman v. Kimball Int'l, Inc.	652 N.E.2d 507, 11 IER Cases 153 (Ind. 1995)	Manager (general)	Wood veneer	IN	2, 3c, 3d, 3f, AT-92
Acquafredda v. Messina	408 So.2d 828 (Fla. 5th Dist.Ct.App. 1982)	No covenant	No covenant	FL	7
Adams v. Ohio Dep't of Health	5 Ohio Op.3d 148, 356 N.E.2d 324 (1976)	No covenant	No covenant	OH	7
Adcock v. Speir Ins. Agency	158 Ga.App. 317, 279 S.E.2d 759 (1981)	Salesperson	Insurance	GA	3f, 4
Addressograph Multigraph Corp. v. Kelley	146 Colo. 550, 362 P.2d 184 (1964)	Salesperson	Printing equipment	CO	3f
ADR v. Graves	374 So.2d 699 (La.App 1st Cir.), *writ denied*, 377 So.2d 836 (La. 1979)	Manager (district)	Finance and insurance consulting	LA	1, 12

Case	Citation	Occupation	Industry	State	Notes
Agrimerica, Inc. v. Mathes	170 Ill.App.3d 1025, 120 Ill.Dec. 765, 524 N.E.2d 947 (1st Dist. 1988)	Salesperson	Livestock feed additives	IL	2, 3, 3f, 3g, 5
AGS Computer Servs. v. Rodriguez	592 So.2d 801, 17 Fla. L. Weekly D398 (Fla. 4th Dist.Ct.App. 1992)	Occupation not specified	Computer services	FL	5, 6
Air Ambulance Network, Inc. v. Floribus	511 So.2d 702 (Fla. 3d Dist.Ct.App. 1987)	Occupation not specified	Air ambulance service	FL	6
Air Prods. & Chems., Inc. v. Johnson	296 Pa.Super. 405, 442 A.2d 1114 (1982)	No covenant	No covenant	PA	2
Akey v. Murphy	238 So.2d 94 (Fla. 1970)	Physician (partner)	Health care	FL	5
Akhter v. Shah	199 Ill.App.3d 131, 74 Ill.Dec. 730, 456 N.E.2d 232 (1st Dist. 1983)	Physician	Health care	IL	3, 4
Aladdin v. Krasnoff	214 Ga. 519, 105 S.E.2d 730 (1958)	Occupation not specified	Janitorial supplies	GA	4
Alarm Sec. Protection v. Karasevich	12 Conn. L. Tribune No. 14 at 30 (Super.Ct., Dec. 24, 1985)	Salesperson	Alarms	CT	3c
Albee Homes v. Caddie Homes	417 Pa. 177, 207 A.2d 768 (1965)	Salesperson	Homes	PA	3, 4
Albramson v. Blackman	340 Mass. 714, 166 N.E.2d 729 (1960)	Salesperson	Real estate	MA	14
Aldridge v. Dolbeer	567 So.2d 1267 (Ala. 1990)	No covenant	No covenant	AL	10
Alexander & Alexander v. Danahy	21 Mass.App.Ct. 488, 488 N.E.2d 22 (1986)	Corporate officer (president)	Insurance	MA	3, 3f, 4, 5, 6, 7
Alexander & Alexander v. Simpson	370 So.2d 670 (La.App. 4th Cir.) writ denied, 371 So.2d 836 (La. 1979)	Account executive (assistant)	Commercial property	LA	1, 3g

Case	Citation	Position	Business	State	Sections
Almers v. South Carolina Nat'l Bank of Charleston	265 S.C. 48, 217 S.E.2d 135 (1975)	Corporate officer (vice president)	Bank	SC	3a, 3d, 5, 10, 14, AT-49
Alston Studios, Inc. v. Lloyd V. Gress & Assocs.	492 F.2d 279 (4th Cir. 1979)	Manager, sales (district)	School photographs	VA	3f, 4, 14, AT-21, AT-23
Altana, Inc. v. Schansinger	111 A.D.2d 199, 489 N.Y.S.2d 84 (2d Dep't 1985)	Manager, sales (national)	Pharmaceuticals	NY	3d, 3f, 14
ALW Mktg. Corp. v. McKinney	206 Ga.App. 184, 421 S.E.2d 565 (1992)	Corporate officer (vice president)	Marketing	GA	3d, 3f, 3g, AT-42, AT-53, AT-55
Amdar, Inc. v. Satterwhite	37 N.C.App. 410, 246 S.E.2d 165 (1978)	Instructor	Dance	NC	3f
American Bldg. Servs. v. Cohen	78 Ohio App.3d 29, 603 N.E.2d 432 (Ohio App. 12th Dist. 1992)	Salesperson	Janitorial service	OH	3, 3f, 4
American Broadcasting Cos. v. Wolf	52 N.Y.2d 394, 438 N.Y.S.2d 482, 420 N.E.2d 363 (1981)	Broadcaster	Broadcasting (Television)	AK	3
American Broadcasting Cos. v. Wolf	52 N.Y.2d 394, 438 N.Y.S.2d 482, 420 N.E.2d 363 (1981)	Broadcaster	Broadcasting (Television)	NY	2, 3, 3f, 5, 14
American Claims Serv. v. Boris	137 Ill.App.3d 948, 92 Ill.Dec. 723, 485 N.E.2d 534 (1985)	Manager	Insurance claims adjustment	IL	2
American Credit Bureau v. Carter	11 Ariz.App. 145, 462 P.2d 838 (1969)	Manager, sales	Debt collection	AZ	2, 3, 7, 8, 14
American Credit Bureau v. Carter	11 Ariz.App. 145, 462 P.2d 838 (1969)	Public relations director	Debt collection	AZ	2, 3, 7, 8, 14
American Credit Indemnity Co. v. Sacks	213 Cal.App.3d 622, 262 Cal.Rptr. 92 (1989)	Salesperson	Credit insurance	CA	2, 3g

Case	Citation	Position	Industry	State	Ref.
American Credit Indemnity Co. v. Sacks	213 Cal.App.3d 622, 262 Cal. Rptr. 92 (1989)	Salesperson	Insurance	CA	2, 3g
American Excelsior Laundry Co. v. Derrisseaux	165 S.W.2d 598 (Ark. 1942)	Salesperson (route)	Laundry	AR	3f
American Family Assurance Co. v. Tazelaar	135 Ill.App.3d 1069, 482 N.E.2d 1072 (1985) (applying Georgia law)	Salesperson	Insurance	GA	3g, 3g
American Food Mgmt. v. Henson	105 Ill.App.3d 141, 434 N.E.2d 59 (5th Dist. 1982)	Manager (unit)	Food services	IL	12
American Gen. Life & Accident Ins. Co. v. Fisher	208 Ga.App. 282, 430 S.E.2d 166 (1993)	Salesperson	Insurance	GA	3d, 3f, 3g, 4
American Nat'l Ins. Co. v. Coe	657 F.Supp. 718 (E.D.Mo. 1986)	Manager (district)	Insurance	WY	8
American Paper & Packaging Prods. v. Kirgan	183 Cal.App.3d 1318, 228 Cal.Rptr. 713 (1986)	Salesperson	Packaging material	CA	2, 5, 14
American Precision Vibrator Co. v. National Air Vibrator Co.	764 S.W.2d 274 (Tex.Civ.App.—Houston [1st Dist.] 1988)	No covenant	No covenant	TX	2
American Rim & Brake v. Zoellner	382 N.W.2d 421 (S.D. 1986)	Salesperson	Wheels and brakes (automotive)	SD	3, 3b, 3c, 3f, 5, 7, 14
American Sec. Servs. Inc. v. Vodra	222 Neb. 480, 385 N.W.2d 73 (1986)	Manager (regional)	Security guard service	NE	2, 3, 7
American Sec. Servs., Inc. v. Vodra	222 Neb. 480, 385 N.W.2d 73 (1986)	Manager (regional)	Security guard service	WY	3
American Standard Casualty Co. of Wis. v. Cleveland	124 Wis.2d 258, 369 N.W.2d 168 (1985)	No covenant	No covenant	WI	12
American Yearbook Co. v. St. Pierre	56 A.D.2d 832, 392 N.Y.S.2d 66 (2d Dep't 1977)	Salesperson	School yearbooks	NY	5

Case	Citation	Position	Industry	State	Codes
Amex Distrib. Co. v. Mascari	150 Ariz. 510, 724 P.2d 596 (App. 1986)	Manager	Produce brokerage	AZ	2, 3b, 3d, 3e, 3g, 14
Amex Distrib. Co. v. Mascari	150 Ariz. 510, 724 P.2d 596 (App. 1986)	Manager	Produce brokerage	WY	3f
AMF Tuboscope v. McBryde	618 S.W.2d 105 (Tex.Ct.App. 1981)	Manager, sales	Pipe and tube inspection service (oil field industry)	TX	3f
AMF Tuboscope v. McBryde	618 S.W.2d 105 (Tex.Ct.App. 1981)	Salesperson	Pipe and tube inspection service (oil field industry)	TX	3f
AMP, Inc. Fleischhacker	823 F.2d 1199, 3 IER Cases 73 (7th Cir. 1987)	Manager (division)	Electrical/electronic connector manufacturing	IL	3
Amstell, Inc. v. Bunge Corp.	443 S.E.2d 706 (Ga.App. 1994)	Distributorship agreement	Milk concentrates	GA	3, 3f, 4, 12, AT-23, AT-53A
Anbeck Co. v. Zapata Corp.	641 S.W.2d 608 (Tex.Ct.App. 1982, writ ref'd n.r.e.)	No covenant	No covenant	TX	10
Anchor Alloys, Inc. v. Non-Ferrous Proscessing Corp.	39 A.D.2d 504, 336 N.Y.S.2d 944, lv. to appeal denied, 32 N.Y.2d 612, 346 N.Y.S.2d 1025, 299 N.E.2d 899 (1973)	Corporate officer	Metal smelting and melting	NY	2, 14
Anchor Alloys, Inc. v. Non-Ferrous Proscessing Corp.	39 A.D.2d 504, 336 N.Y.S.2d 944 lv. to appeal denied 32 N.Y.2d 612, 346 N.Y.S.2d 1025, 299 N.E.2d 899 (1973)	Sale of business	Metal smelting and melting	NY	2, 14
Anderson v. Aspelmeier, Fisch, Power, Warner & Engbeg	461 N.W.2d 598 (Iowa 1990)	Attorney (partner)	Law	IN	AT-85

Case	Citation	Position	Industry	State	References
Arpac Corp. v. Murray	226 Ill.App.3d 65, 168 Ill.Dec. 240, 589 N.E.2d 640 (1st Dist. 1992)	Corporate officer (vice president)	Shrink-wrap machine manufacturing	IL	2, 3, 3d, 3f, 3g, 4, 5, 7, 14, AT-6, AT-77
Arrow Chem. Corp. v. Pugh	490 S.W.2d 628 (Tex.Civ.App. 1972)	Salesperson	Chemical cleaners	GA	AT-42
Arrow Chem. Corp. v. Pugh	490 S.W.2d 628 (Tex.Civ.App. 1972)	Salesperson	Janitorial products	GA	AT-42
Arthur Young & Co. v. Black	97 A.D.2d 369, 466 N.Y.S.2d 10 (1st Dep't 1983)	Accountant (partner)	Accounting	NY	2, 3, 6
Arthur Young & Co. v. Galasso	142 Misc.2d 738, 538 N.Y.S.2d 424 (Sup.Ct. 1989)	Accountant (partner)	Accounting	NY	2, 3, 3c
Arthur Murray Dance Studios of Cleveland v. Witter	62 Ohio Laws Abs. 17, 105 N.E.2d 685 (C.P. 1952)	Instructor	Education (Dance)	OH	2, 3, 3d, 3e, 3f, 4, 5, 6, 13, 14
Asheville Assocs. v. Berman	255 N.C. 400,121 S.E.2d 593 (1981)	Salesperson	Insurance	NC	2
Ashland Oil v. Pickard	269 So.2d 714 (Fla. 3d Dist.Ct.App. 1972)	No covenant	No covenant	FL	11
Ashland Oil v. Tucker	768 S.W.2d 595 (Mo.App. 1989)	Manager, sales (district)	Chemical products	MO	3b, 5, 6, 7, 12
Associated Dairies v. Ray Moss Farms, Inc.	205 Tenn. 268, 326 S.W.2d 458 (1959)	Salesperson (route)	Dairy	TN	3c
Associated Surgeons, P.A. v. Wattwood	295 Ala. 229, 326 So.2d 712 (1976)	Physician	Health care (Surgery)	AL	1
Asteco, Inc. v. Smith	172 A.D.2d 1066, 570 N.Y.S.2d 254 (4th Dep't 1991)	Sale of business	Asbestos testing	NY	4

B. Cantrell Oil Co. v. Hino Gas Sales	756 S.W.2d 648 (Tex.Ct.App., Corpus Christi 1988)	Manager	Propane	TX	3b
B.J. Software Sys. v. Osina	827 S.W.2d 543 (Tex.Ct.App.—Houston [1st Dist.] 1992)	Salesperson (primary)	Computer software systems	TX	1, 3, 4
B&Y Metal Painting v. Ball	279 N.W.2d 813 (Minn. 1979)	Sale of business	Metal painting	MN	10
Bagwell v. H.B. Wellborn & Co.	247 Miss. 564, 156 So.2d 739 (1963)	Adjuster	Insurance	MS	3f
Bailey v. King	240 Ark. 245, 398 S.W.2d 906 (1966)	Salesperson (route)	Linen	AR	3a, 3f, 5, 8
Baker v. Battershell	(Tenn.Ct.App. April 19, 1985) (LEXIS, Employ library, Tenn. file)	No covenant	No covenant	TN	7
Baker v. National Credit Ass'n	211 Ga. 635, 88 S.E.2d 19 (1955)	Manager (office)	Not specified	GA	3c
Baker v. Starkey	259 Iowa 480, 144 N.W.2d 889 (1966)	Consultant	Medical/dental office business services	IA	2, 3d, 4
Baker's Aid v. Hussman Foodservice Co.	830 F.2d 13 (2d Cir. 1987)	Manufacturing agreement	Oven manufacturing	PA	6, AT-54.1
Ballenger v. Ballenger	694 S.W.2d 72 (Tex.Ct.App.—Corpus Christi 1985)	No covenant	No covenant	TX	3
Ballesteros v. Johnson	812 S.W.2d 217 (Mo.App. 1991)	Physician	Health care (Cardiology)	MO	2, 3f, 7, 8, AT-39
Baltimore v. Warren Mfg. Co.	59 Md. 96 (1882)	No covenant	No covenant	MD	5
Bancroft-Whitney Co. v. Glen	64 Cal.2d 327, 49 Cal. Rptr. 825, 411 P.2d 921 (Sup.Ct. 1966)	No covenant	No covenant	NJ	14

Bank of the Southwest, N.A., Brownsville v. Halingen Nat'l Bank	662 S.W.2d 113 (Tex.Ct.App.—Corpus Christi 1983)	No covenant	No covenant	TX	3, 5
Barb-Lee Mobile Frame Co. v. Hoot	416 Pa. 222, 206 A.2d 59 (1965)	Repair person	Car repair (automobile frame)	PA	3a, 4
Barberio-Powell v. Bernstein Leibstone Assocs., Inc.	624 So.2d 383, 18 Fla. L. Weekly D2079 (Fla. 4th Dist.Ct.App. 1993)	No covenant	No covenant	FL	6
Barnes Group v. Harper	653 F.2d 175 (5th Cir. 1981), *cert. denied*, 455 U.S. 921 (1982)	Salesperson	Hardware	AK	3
Barnes Group v. Harper	653 F.2d 175 (5th Cir. 1981) *cert. denied*, 455 U.S. 921 (1982)	Salesperson	Hardware	GA	3d
Barnett v. Jabusch	649 So.2d 1158 (La.App. 3rd Cir. 1995)	Sale of business	Flea market	LA	10
Barone v. Marcisck	96 A.D.2d 816, 465 N.Y.S.2d 561 (2d Dep't 1983)	Occupation not specified	Not specified	NY	10
Barrington Trucking Co. v. Casey	117 Ill.App.2d 151, 253 N.E.2d 36 (2d Dist. 1969), *appeal denied*, 42 Ill.2d 586 (1970)	Supervisor	Landfill	IL	4
Barry v. Stanco Communications Prods.	243 Ga. 68, 252 S.E.2d 491 (1979)	Salesperson	Electronic products	GA	3d
Barton v. Travelers Ins. Co.	84 S.C. 209, 66 S.E. 118 (1909)	Salesperson	Insurance	SC	3
Bauer v. P.A. Cutri Co. of Bradford	434 Pa. 305, 253 A.2d 252 (1969)	Sale of business	Insurance agency	PA	10, AT-28
Bauer v. Sawyer	8 Ill.2d 351, 134 N.E.2d 329 (1956)	Physician (partner)	Health care	IL	3d, 3f, 11

Case	Citation	Occupation	Industry	State	Section
Bauer v. Sawyer	8 Ill.2d 351, 134 N.E.2d 329 (1956)	Physician	Health care	NH	10
Baxter Int'l v. Morris	976 F.2d 1189, 7 IER Cases 1377 (8th Cir. 1992)	Scientist	Medical diagnostic kit design	CA	14
Baxter Int'l v. Morris	976 F.2d 1189, 7 IER Cases 1377 (8th Cir. 1992)	Scientist	Microbiological diagnostics research	IL	14
Bayard v. Martin	101 A.2d 329 (1953)	No covenant	No covenant	DE	6
Baybutt Constr. Corp. v. Commercial Union Ins. Co.	455 A.2d 914 (Me. 1983)	No covenant	No covenant	ME	12
Bayly, Martin & Fay v. Pickard	780 P.2d 1168, 5 IER Cases 1616 (Okla. 1989)	Salesperson	Insurance	OK	1, 2, 3g, 4, 5, 14
Beasley v. Banks	90 N.C.App. 458, 368 S.E.2d 885 (1988)	Optometrist	Health care (Optometry)	NC	2, 3d
Becher v. Peress	111 A.D.2d 892, 490 N.Y.S.2d 600 (2d Dep't), *lv. dismissed,* 66 N.Y.2d 605, 499 N.Y.S.2d 1025, 489 N.E.2d 1302 (1985)	Physician	Health care	NY	3
Becker v. Bailey	268 Md. 93, 299 A.2d 835 (1973)	Courier	Automobile tag and title	MD	2, 3, 3f
Beckman v. Cox Broadcasting Corp.	250 Ga. 127, 296 S.E.2d 566 (1982)	Meteorologist	Broadcasting (television)	GA	3f
Beech v. Ragnar Benson, Inc.	587 A.2d 335 (Pa.Super.), *appeal granted,* 592 A.2d 295 (Pa. 1991), *appeal dismissed as improvidently granted,* 613 A.2d 1204 (Pa. 1992)	No covenant	No covenant	PA	10, AT-28
Behnke v. Hertz Corp.	70 Wis.2d 818, 235 N.W.2d 690 (1975)	Counter person	Car rental	WI	3a, 3c, 3f, 14

Case	Citation	Position	Business	State	References
Best Metro. Towel & Linen Supply Co. v. A&P Coat, Apron & Linen	149 A.D.2d 642, 540 N.Y.S.2d 300 (2d Dep't 1990)	No covenant	No covenant	NY	2, 5, 9
Best Maid Dairy Farms v. Houchen	152 Mont. 194, 448 P.2d 158 (1968)	Salesperson (route)	Dairy	MT	2
Bettinger v. C. Berke Assocs.	455 Pa. 100, 314 A.2d 296 (1974)	Recruiter	Employment agency (temporary)	PA	11
Betz v. China Hot Springs Group	657 P.2d 831 (Alaska 1982)	No covenant	No covenant	AK	7
Bicycle Transit Authority v. Bell	214 N.C. 219, 333 S.E.2d 299 (1985)	Sale of business	Bicycle shop	NH	AT-21
Biever, Drees, Nordell v. Coutts	305 N.W.2d 33 (N.D. 1981)	Accountant	Accounting	ND	14
Bigda v. Fischbach Corp.	898 F.Supp. 1004 (S.D.N.Y. 1995)	Attorney (general counsel)	Electrical contracting	NY	AT-49, AT-79
Bigda v. Fischbach Corp.	898 F.Supp. 1004 (S.D.N.Y. 1995)	Attorney	Law	NY	AT-49, AT-79
Bigda v. Fischbach Corp.	898 F.Supp. 1004 (S.D.N.Y. 1995)	Corporate officer (secretary)	Electrical contracting	NY	AT-49, AT-79
Bilec v. Auburn & Assocs. Pension Trust	588 A.2d 538, 6 IER Cases 546 (Pa.Super. 1991)	Draftsperson	Drafting and engineering (industrial) service	PA	2, 3, 3c, 3f, 4, AT-21, AT-49
Birmingham Television Corp. v. DeRamus	502 So.2d 761 (Ala.Civ.App. 1986)	Salesperson	Advertising (television time)	AL	2, 3, 3c, 3f
Blackburn v. Sweeney	637 N.E.2d 1340 (Ind.App. 3d Dist. 1994)	Attorney (partner)	Law	IN	4, 14, AT-5A, AT-85
Blackburn v. Sweeney	53 F.3d 825 (7th Cir. 1995)	Attorney (partner)	Law	IN	AT-5A
Blackburn v. Sweeney	53 F.3d 825 (7th Cir. 1995)	Attorney	Law	IN	AT-5A

Blackwell v. E.M. Helides Jr., Inc.	368 Mass. 225, 331 N.E.2d 54 (1975)	Salesperson	Real estate	MA	2
Blair Design & Constr. v. Kalimon	366 Pa.Super. 194, 530 A.2d 1357 (1987)	Manager (project)	Construction and remodeling (retail space)	PA	3f, 3g, 5, 14
Blalock v. Perfect Subscription Co.	458 F.Supp. 123 (S.D.Ala. 1978), aff'd. 599 F.2d 743 (5th Cir. 1979) (per curiam)	Salesperson	Magazine subscriptions	AL	1, 3f, 10, 12
Blue Ridge Anesthesia & Critical Care v. Gidick	239 Va. 369, 389 S.E.2d 467, 5 IER Cases 292 (1990)	Salesperson	Medical equipment (critical care and anesthesia equipment)	VA	1, 3, 3a, 3d, 3f, 9
Blue Ridge Anesthesia & Critical Care v. Gidick	239 Va. 369, 389 S.E.2d 467, 5 IER Cases 292 (1990)	Serviceperson	Medical equipment (critical care and anesthesia equipment)	VA	1, 3, 3a, 3d, 3f, 9
Board of Regents of Univ. of Okla. v. National Collegiate Athletic Ass'n	561 P.2d 499, 85 A.L.R.3d 953 (Okla. 1977)	No covenant	No covenant	OK	1
Bob Pagan Ford, Inc. v. Smith	638 S.W.2d 176 (Tex.Ct.App.—Houston [1st Dist.] 1982)	Salesperson	Automobiles	TX	3
Boisen v. Petersen Flying Serv.	222 Neb. 239, 383 N.W.2d 29 (1986)	Pilot	Crop spraying (aerial)	NE	2, 3, 3a, 3f, 4, 14
Boldt Mach. & Tools v. Wallace	469 Pa. 504, 366 A.2d 902 (1976)	Salesperson	Machinery and tools (industrial)	PA	2
Bolen Int'l, Inc. v. Meadow	191 So.2d 51 (Fla. 3d Dist.Ct.App. 1966), cert. denied, 200 So.2d 808 (Fla. 1967)	Corporate officer	Building supplies	FL	AT-21

Bolen Int'l, Inc. v. Meadow	191 So.2d 51 (Fla. 3d Dist.Ct.App. 1966), *cert. denied*, 200 So.2d 808 (Fla. 1967)	Corporate officer (director)	Building products manufacturing	FL	AT-21
Booth v. Greber	48 Ill.App.3d 213, 6 Ill.Dec. 477, 363 N.E.2d 6 (1977)	Electrologist	Beauty	IL	2, 5, 8
Booth v. WPMI Television Co.	553 So.2d 209, 3 IER Cases 1799 (Ala. 1988)	Salesperson	Advertising (television time)	AL	2, 3f
Borden, Inc. v. Huey	261 Ark. 313, 547 S.W.2d 760 (1977)	Salesperson	Food products	AR	2, 3f
Borne Chem. Co. v. Dictrow	85 A.D.2d 646, 445 N.Y.S.2d 406 (2d Dep't 1981)	Corporate officer (chief executive officer)	Product packaging	NY	3f, 5, 8, 10
Borne Chem. Co. v. Dictrow	85 A.D.2d 646, 445 N.Y.S.2d 406 (2d Dep't 1981)	Corporate officer (president)	Product packaging	NY	3f, 5, 8, 10
Borne Chem. Co. v. Dictrow	85 A.D.2d 646, 445 N.Y.S.2d 406 (2d Dep't 1981)	Sale of business	Product packaging	NY	3f, 5, 8, 10
Bosley Medical Group v. Abramson	161 Cal.App.3d 284, 207 Cal.Rptr. 477 (1984)	Physician	Health care	CA	1
Boulder Medical Center v. Moore	651 P.2d 464 (Colo.App. 1982)	Physician (partner)	Health care	CO	1, 3f, 5, 10, 14, AT-59
Bouska v. Wright	49 Or.App. 763, 621 P.2d 69 (1980)	Bookkeeper	Service station	OR	3c
Bouska v. Wright	49 Or.App. 763, 621 P.2d 69 (1980)	Consultant	Service station	OR	3c
Bowen v. Carlsbad Ins. & Real Estate	104 N.M. 514, 724 P.2d 223 (1986)	Corporate officer (president)	Insurance	NM	3, 11

Case	Citation	Occupation	Industry	State	Pages
Bowers Window & Door Co. v. Dearman	549 So.2d 1309 (Miss. 1989)	No covenant	No covenant	MS	7
Boyce v. Smith-Edwards-Dunlap Co.	580 A.2d 1382 (Pa. 1990)	Corporate officer (executive)	Typography	PA	10
Boyce v. Franklin Printing Co.	580 A.2d 1382 (Pa.Super. 1990), appeal denied, 593 A.2d 413 (Pa. 1991)	Corporate officer (executive)	Typography	PA	3, 3f, 10, AT-19, AT-41
Boyd v. Davis	897 P.2d 1239 (Wash. 1995)	Sale of business	Health care (Medical practice)	WA	4, 7, AT-9
Boyer v. Piper, Jaffray & Hopwood	391 F.Supp. 471 (D. S.D. 1975)	Occupation not specified	Not specified	SD	12
Bradford v. New York Times Co.	501 F.2d 51 (2d Cir. 1974)	Corporate officer (vice president)	Newspaper	NY	2
Brands v. Sheldon Community School	671 F.Supp. 627 (N.D. Iowa 1987)	No covenant	No covenant	IA	5
Brannon v. Auto Center Mfg. Co.	393 So.2d 75 (Fla. 5th Dist.Ct.App. 1981)	Occupation not specified	Automotive manufacturing	FL	10, 11, 14
Brawning v. Orr	242 Ga. 380, 249 S.E.2d 659 (1978)	Salesperson	Not specified	GA	3
Brazos River Conservation & Reclamation Dist. v. Allen	141 Tex. 208, 171 S.W.2d 842 (1943)	No covenant	No covenant	TX	3, 5
BRB Printing, Inc. v. Buchanan	878 F.Supp. 1049 (E.D.Mich. 1995)	No covenant	No covenant	MI	AT-73A
Brehm v. Johnson	531 P.2d 991 (Colo.App. 1974)	No covenant	No covenant	CO	10
Brewer v. Tracy	198 Neb. 503, 253 N.W.2d 319 (1977)	Garbage collector	Garbage collection	NE	3f

Case	Citation	Position	Industry	State	Ref.
Brewer v. Tracy	198 Neb. 503, 253 N.W.2d 319 (1977)	Garbage collector	Garbage collection	WY	3f
Brewster-Allen-Wichert v. Kiepler	131 A.D.2d 620, 516 N.Y.S.2d 949 (2d Dep't 1987)	Salesperson	Insurance	NY	3f
Brian McDonagh, S.C. v. Moss	207 Ill.App.2d 62, 151 Ill.Dec. 888, 565 N.E.2d 159 (1st Dist. 1990)	Physician (independent contractor)	Health care	IL	11
Briggs v. Boston	15 F.Supp. 763 (N.D. Iowa 1936)	Hostess	Advertising	IA	6, 10
Briggs v. Butler	140 Ohio St. 499, 45 N.E.2d 757 (1942)	Hostess	Advertising	OH	2, 3, 3a, 14
Brignull v. Albert	666 A.2d 82, 11 IER Cases 319 (Me. 1995)	Optometrist	Health care (Optometry)	ME	2, 3, 3c, 3f, 10, 11
Brillhart v. Dannefel	36 Mich.App.359, 194 N.W.2d 63 (1971), leave denied, 387 Mich. 783 (1972)	Sale of business	Restaurant	MI	11
Briskin v. All Seasons Servs., Inc.	615 N.Y.S.2d 166 (App.Div. 4th Dep't 1994)	Salesperson	Vending services	NY	2
Brockley v. Lozier Corp.	241 Neb. 449, 488 N.W.2d 556 (1992)	Corporate officer (vice president)	Store shelving manufacturing	NE	2, 3, 3f, 4, AT-49
Brokaw v. Brokaw	398 N.E.2d 1385 (Ind.App. 1980)	No covenant	No covenant	IN	4
Brooks Distrib. Co. v. Pugh	324 N.C. 326, 378 S.E.2d 31 (N.C. 1989) (per curiam)	Subdistributor	Automotive additives	NC	3b
Brown v. Childers	254 S.W.2d 275 (Mo.App. 1989)	Sale of business	Drug store	MO	9
Brown v. Devine	240 Ark. 838, 402 S.W.2d 669 (1966)	Pilot	Crop spraying (aerial)	AR	3f, 4
Brown v. Kling	101 Cal. 295, 3 P. 995 (1894)	Sale of business	Butchering	CA	3d

Case	Citation	Occupation	Business	State	Sections
Bush v. National School Studios, Inc.	139 Wis.2d 635, 407 N.W.2d 883 (1987)	Photographer	School pictures	WI	4, 12
Bushell v. Wackenhut Int'l	731 F.Supp. 1574 (S.D.Fla. 1990)	No covenant	No covenant	FL	12
Business Inv. Group of Ala. v. Cleveland	571 So.2d 1021 (Ala. 1991)	Franchise	Not specified	AL	AT-49
Buskuhl v. Family Life Ins. Co.	271 Cal.App.2d 514, 76 Cal.Rptr. 602 (1969)	Manager (district)	Insurance	CA	2, 3f
Buskuhl v. Family Life Ins. Co.	271 Cal.App.2d 514, 76 Cal.Rptr. 602 (1969)	Manager (district)	Insurance	ND	1, 14
Buzz Barton & Assocs. v. Giannone	108 Ill.2d 373, 91 Ill.Dec. 636, 483 N.E.2d 1271 (1985)	Occupation not specified	Not specified	IL	5
Byram v. Vaughn	68 F.Supp. 981 (D.D.C. 1946)	Leasing agent	Coin-operated machines	DC	3c, 3f
C. Edgar Wood, Inc. v. Clark	1986 WL 1160 (Del.Ch. 1986)	Salesperson	Insurance	DE	2, 3g, 5
C.G. Caster Co. v. Regan	43 Ill.App.3d 663, 357 N.E.2d 162 (1st Dist. 1976)	Manager (general)	Insurance claims adjustment	IL	8
C.M. Brown & Assocs. v. King	680 S.W.2d 365 (Mo.App. 1984)	Salesperson	Insurance	MO	9
C.R. Bard, Inc. v. Boden	D.C. Mass., No. 89-0088-Z, May 9, 1989	Manager, sales	Medical devices (angioplasty products)	MA	14
C.R. Bard, Inc. v. Boden	D.C. Mass., No. 89-0088-Z, May 9, 1989	Sales director	Medical devices (angioplasty products)	MA	14
C&C Prod. v. Fidelity & Deposit Co.	512 F.2d 1375 (5th Cir. 1975)	Corporate officer (vice president)	Maintenance product manufacturing	AL	1
C&C Prod. v. Fidelity & Deposit Co.	512 F.2d 1375 (5th Cir. 1975)	Salesperson	Maintenance products	AL	1
Cad Cam, Inc. v. Underwood	36 OhioApp.3d 90, 521 N.E.2d 498 (1987)	Occupation not specified	Computer aided design equipment	OH	11, 14

Case	Citation	Occupation	Subject	State	Notes
CAE Vanguard, Inc. v. Newman	246 Neb. 334, 518 N.E.2d 652 (1994)	Manager (plant)	Railroad car axle rebuilding	NE	2, 4
Cafe Assocs. v. Gerngross	406 S.E.2d 162 (S.C. 1991)	Sale of business	Restaurant	SC	3f, 4, AT-21, AT-95
Caine & Estes Ins. Agency v. Watts	278 S.C. 207, 293 S.E.2d 859 (1982)	Salesperson	Insurance	SC	3d, 3g, 14
Caldwell Flexible Staffing v. Mays	1976 WL 1716 (Del.Ch., Nos. 5204 & 5205, Nov. 26, 1976)	Recruiter	Employment agency	DE	8
Calhoun v. Brendle, Inc.	502 So.2d 689 (Ala. 1986)	Occupation not specified	Fire extinguisher sales and service	AL	2, 3, 3e, 3f
Calhoun v. Everman	242 S.W.2d 100 (Ky. 1951)	Delivery person	Laundry	KY	3f
California Intelligence Bureau v. Cunningham	83 Cal.App.2d 197, 188 P.2d 303 (1948)	Salesperson	Investigation service (charitable solicitation scams)	CA	2
Callahan v. L.G. Balfour	179 Ill.App.3d 372, 534 N.E.2d 565 (1st Dist. 1989)	Salesperson	School rings, diplomas and other school items	IL	3, 11, 14
Cam Int'l L.P. v. Turner	1992 WL 74567 (Tenn.App., No. 01-A-01-9203CH00116, 1992)	Salesperson	Automotive parts (after-market)	TN	2, 4
Cambridge Filter Corp. v. International Filter	548 F.Supp. 1301 (D. Nev. 1982) (applying California law)	Salesperson	Air filters (computer, custom-made)	CA	2, 14
Campbell v. Board of Trustees of Stanford Univ.	817 F.2d 499 (9th Cir. 1987)	Psychologist	Vocational aptitude test design	CA	1
Campbell Soup Co v. Giles	47 F.3d 467 (1st Cir. 1995)	Sales director	Soup manufacturing	MA	2, 5
Canady v. Knox	43 Wash. 567, 86 P. 930 (1906)	Sale of business	Butchering	NH	10
Canfield v. Spear	44 Ill.2d 49, 254 N.E.2d 433 (1969)	Physician	Health care	IL	2, 3, 3d, 3f

Case	Citation	Position	Industry	State	References
Cap Gemini Am. v. Judd	597 N.E.2d 1272 (Ind.App. 1st Dist. 1992)	Computer analyst	Computer	IN	2, 3d, 3f
Cap Gemini Am. v. Judd	597 N.E.2d 1272 (Ind.App. 1st Dist. 1992) (applying California law)	Manager (branch)	Computer programming	CA	1, 3f, 12
Cape Mobile Mart v. Mobley	780 S.W.2d 116 (Mo.App. 1989)	Salesperson	Mobile homes	MO	2, 3, 3d, 3f, 7
Capelouto v. Orkin Exterminating Co. of Fla.	183 So.2d 532 (Fla.), *appeal dismissed*, 385 U.S. 11, *reh'g denied*, 385 U.S. 964 (1966)	Exterminator	Pest control	FL	3f
Capelouto v. Orkin Exterminating Co. of Fla.	183 So.2d 532 (Fla.), *appeal dismissed*, 385 U.S. 11, *reh'g denied*, 385 U.S. 964 (1966)	Manager	Pest control	FL	3f, AT-42
Capital Bakers, Inc. v. Leahy	20 Del.Ch. 407, 178 A. 648 (1935)	Manager	Bakery	DE	3a, 3f
Capital Bakers v. Townsend	426 Pa. 188, 231 A.2d 292 (1967)	Salesperson (door-to-door)	Baked goods	PA	3a
Capraro v. Lanier Business Prods.	466 So.2d 212 (Fla. 1985)	Salesperson	Text editing products	FL	1, 5, 6, 14
Capsonic Group v. Swick	181 Ill.App.3d 988, 537 N.E.2d 1378 (2d Dist. 1989)	Engineer	Automated system design	IL	2, 14
Captain & Co. v. Towne	404 N.E.2d 1159 (Ind.App. 1980)	Estimator	Insurance clean-up and reconstruction	IN	2, 3f
Captain & Co. v. Towne	404 N.E.2d 1159 (Ind.App. 1980)	Manager	Insurance clean-up and reconstruction	IN	2, 3f
Car Wash. Sys. of Tex., Inc. v. Brigance	856 S.W.2d 853 (Tex.Ct.App.—Fort Worth 1993)	Manager (service)	Car wash building, supplies, and repair service	TX	3f, 7, AT-21, AT-41

Case	Citation	Position	Industry	State	References
Cellular One, Inc. v. Boyd	653 So.2d 30 (La.App. 1st Cir. 1995)	Salesperson	Cellular phones	LA	1, 3, 3c, 3f, 5, 6, 8, 11, AT-32, AT-40A, AT-51
Cenla Physical Therapy & Rehabilitation Agency v. Lavergne	651 So.2d 461 (La.App. 3d Cir. 1995)	Corporate officer (president)	Health care (physical rehabilitation clinic)	LA	AT-89
Centel Cellular Co. v. Light	899 S.W.2d 343 (Tex.Ct.App.—Tyler 1995)	Salesperson	Cellular phones	TX	AT-90
Centel Cellular Co. v. Light	899 S.W.2d 343 (Tex.Ct.App.—Tyler 1995)	Salesperson	Radio pagers	TX	AT-90
Centorr-Vacuum Indus. v. Lavoie	609 A.2d 1213, 7 IER Cases 982 (N.H. 1992)	Sale of business	Furnace	NH	AT-22
Central Adjustment Bureau v. Ingram Assocs.	622 S.W.2d 681 (Ky.Ct.App. 1981)	Adjuster	Insurance	KY	2, 3, 3a, 3b, 3c, 3d
Central Bancshares of the S. v. Puckett	584 So.2d 829, 6 IER Cases 1076 (Ala. 1991)	Corporate officer (executive)	Bank	AL	3, 3f, 7
Central Water Works Supply, Inc. v. Fisher	240 Ill.App.3d 952, 181 Ill.Dec. 545, 608 N.E.2d 618 (4th Dist. 1993)	Corporate officer (director)	Water/sewer supplies wholesaling	IL	AT-23
Central Credit Collection Control Corp. v. Grayson	7 Wash.App. 56, 499 P.2d 57 (1972)	Debt collector	Debt collection	WA	3f, 11
Central Adjustment Bureau, Inc. v. Ingram	678 S.W.2d 28 (Tenn. 1984)	Manager (collections)	Debt collection	RI	4
Central Adjustment Bureau, Inc. v. Ingram	678 S.W.2d 28 (Tenn. 1984)	Manager (regional)	Debt collection	RI	4

Case	Citation	Position	Industry	State	
Central Adjustment Bureau, Inc. v. Ingram	678 S.W.2d 28 (Tenn. 1984)	Manager (district)	Debt collection	TN	1, 2, 3a, 3b, 3c, 3f, 4, 8, 14
Central Adjustment Bureau, Inc. v. Ingram	678 S.W.2d 28 (Tenn. 1984)	Salesperson	Debt collection	RI	4
Control, Inc. v. Morrow	489 N.W.2d 890 (S.D. 1992)	Consultant (crop and soil)	Agricultural consulting	SD	2, 3b, 3f, 5, 10
Cerami-Kote v. Energywave Corp.	773 P.2d 1143 (Idaho 1989)	No covenant	No covenant	ID	12
Chambers-Dobson, Inc. v. Squier	238 Neb. 748, 472 N.W.2d 391, 6 IER Cases 1127 (1991)	Salesperson	Insurance	NE	2, 3, 3g, 7, 10, AT-66
Champion v. Wright	740 S.W.2d 848 (Tex.Ct.App.—San Antonio 1987)	Manager (office)	Medical record procurement service (legal community)	TX	10
Champion Sports Center, Inc. v. Peters	763 S.W.2d 367 (Mo.App. 1989)	Sale of business	Sporting goods and trophies	MO	3d, 9
Chandler v. Mastercraft Dental Corp.	739 S.W.2d 760 (Tex.Ct.App.—Fort Worth 1987, writ denied)	Sale of business	Dental equipment manufacturing	TX	3f
Chandra v. Gadodia	610 So.2d 15, 17 Fla. L. Weekly D2603 (Fla. 5th Dist.Ct.App. 1992), *review denied*, 621 So.2d 432 (Fla. 1993)	Physician	Health care (Cardiology)	FL	1, 3, 5, 6, 14
Chandra v. Gadodia	610 So.2d 15, 17 Fla. L. Weekly D2603 (Fla. 5th Dist.Ct.App. 1992), *review denied*, 621 So.2d 432 (Fla. 1993)	Physician	Health care (Internal medicine)	FL	1, 3, 5, 6, 14

Case	Citation	Occupation	Industry	State	Ref.
Chapman & Drake v. Harrington	545 A.2d 645, 3 IER Cases 1146 (Me. 1988)	Salesperson	Insurance	ME	2, 3, 3a, 3d, 3f, 3g, 4, 10, 14
Charles P. Young Co. v. Leuser	137 Ill.App.3d 1044, 92 Ill.Dec. 730, 485 N.E.2d 541 (1985)	Corporate officer	Printing (financial)	IL	2
Chavers v. Copy Prods. Co.	519 So.2d 942 (Ala. 1988)	Service technician	Photocopiers	AL	3
Chelsea Indus., Inc. v. Gaffney	389 Mass. 1, 449 N.E.2d 320 (1983)	No covenant	No covenant	MA	2
Chemical Fireproofing Corp. v. Krouse	155 F.2d 422 (D.C.Cir. 1946)	Fireproofing technician	Fireproofing	DC	3d, 3f, 14
Cheney v. Automatic Sprinkler Corp. of Am	377 Mass. 141, 385 N.E.2d 961 (1979)	Manager, sales (district)	Not specified	MA	1
Cherne Indus. v. Grounds & Assocs.	278 N.W.2d 81 (Minn. 1979)	Engineer	Civil engineering	MN	2, 4, 5, 7, 9
Cherry, Bekaert & Holland v. Brown	582 So.2d 502 (Ala. 1991)	Accountant	Accounting	AL	1, 3f, 12,14, AT-49, AT-87, AT-90
Cherry, Bekaert & Holland v. LaSalle	413 So.2d 436 (Fla. 3d Dist.Ct.App. 1982)	Accountant	Accounting	FL	3f
Chicago Towel Co. v. Reynolds	108 W.Va. 615, 152 S.E. 200 (1930)	Occupation not specified	Linen and towel supply	WV	3f
Chicago Pharmacal Co. v. Hood	207 Or. 1, 294 P.2d 613 (1956)	Salesperson	Pharmaceuticals	OR	9
Chick-A-Dilly Properties, Inc. of Camden v. Hilyard	42 Ark.App. 120, 856 S.W.2d 15 (1993) (en banc)	No covenant	No covenant	AR	AT-89
Chrysalis Health Care, Inc. v. Brooks	65 Ohio Misc.2d 32, 640 N.E.2d 915 (Ohio Mun. 1994)	Nurse's aide (geriatric)	Nursing services (geriatric)	OH	3b, 3c, AT-21, AT-39

Clooney v. Scripps-Howard Broadcasting Co. WCPO Television Div.	35 Ohio App.2d 124, 300 N.E.2d 256 (1973)	Broadcaster	Broadcasting (Television)	OH	3f, 7, 14
Clooney v. Scripps-Howard Broadcasting Co. WCPO Television Div.	35 Ohio App.2d 124, 300 N.E.2d 256 (1973)	Host (show)	Broadcasting (Television)	OH	3f, 7, 14
Clooney v. Scripps-Howard Broadcasting Co. WCPO Television Div.	35 Ohio App.2d 124, 300 N.E.2d 256 (1973)	Personality	Broadcasting (Television)	OH	3f, 7, 14
Club Properties v. Atlanta Offices Perimeter	180 Ga.App. 352, 348 S.E.2d 919 (1986)	Manager (office)	Commercial property	GA	3f
Clyde Rudd & Assocs. v. Taylor	29 N.C.App. 679, 225 S.E.2d 602, cert. denied, 290 N.C. 659, 228 S.E.2d 451 (1976)	Salesperson	Not specified	NC	3d, 3f
Coastal Unilube v. Smith	598 So.2d 200, 7 IER Cases 1367, 17 Fla. L. Weekly D1160 (Fla. 4th Dist.Ct.App. 1992)	Salesperson	Automobile lubricating	FL	3c, 7
Cobb Family Dentistry v. Reich	259 Ga. 450, 383 S.E.2d 891, 4 IER Cases 1874 (1989)	Dentist	Health care (Dentistry)	GA	3g, 14
Cockerill v. Wilson	51 Ill.2d 179, 281 N.E.2d 648 (1972)	Veterinarian	Veterinary medicine	IL	2, 3, 3f, 4, 8
Cogley Clinic v. Martini	253 Iowa 541, 112 N.W.2d 678 (1962)	Physician	Health care (Orthopedic surgery)	IA	3f, 14
Cogley Clinic v. Martini	253 Iowa 541, 112 N.W.2d 678 (1962)	Physician	Health care	NV	3f
Cohen v. Lord, Day & Lord	75 N.Y.2d 95, 551 N.Y.S.2d 157, 550 N.E.2d 410 (1989)	Attorney (partner)	Law	IN	AT-85

Collins v. Sears, Roebuck & Co.	164 Conn. 369, 321 A.2d 444 (1973)	No covenant	No covenant	CT	14
Collins Music Co. v. Parent	340 S.E.2d 794 (S.C.App. 1986)	Debt collector	Debt collection	SC	3, 3g, 10, 14
Colonial Life & Accident Ins. Co. v. Kappers	488 P.2d 96 (Colo.App. 1971)	Salesperson	Insurance	CO	3f
Colorado Accounting Machs. v. Mergenthaler	44 Colo.App. 155, 609 P.2d 1125 (1980)	Occupation not specified	Office equipment	CO	2, 3f
Colquitt v. Network Rental	195 Ga.App. 244, 393 S.E.2d 28 (1990)	Manager (store)	Rentals	GA	3d, AT-55
Columbia Ribbon & Carbon Mfg. Co. v. A-1-A Corp.	42 N.Y.2d 496, 398 N.Y.S.2d 1004, 369 N.E.2d 4 (1977)	Salesperson	Office supplies (inked ribbons and carbon paper)	NY	2, 3, 3d, 3f, 5, 14
Columbus Medical Equip. Co. v. Watters	13 Ohio App.3d 149, 468 N.E.2d 343 (1983)	Rental agent	Medical equipment	OH	3b, 3d, 3f, 10, 14
Columbus Medical Equip. Co. v. Watters	13 Ohio App.3d 149, 468 N.E.2d 343 (1983)	Salesperson	Medical equipment	OH	3b, 3d, 3f, 10, 14
Comcast Sound Communications, Inc. v. Hoelke	572 N.Y.S.2d 189 (N.Y.App.Div. 4th Dep't 1991)	Salesperson	Not specified	TN	4
Comet Indus. v. Lawrence	600 So.2d 85 (La.App. 2d Cir. 1992)	Salesperson	Air brakes	LA	3, 3f, 4, 14
Comet Indus. v. Colvin	600 So.2d 89 (La.App. 2d Cir. 1992)	Salesperson	Not specified	LA	14
Comfort, Inc. v. McDonald	1984 WL 8216 (Del.Ch., No. 1066(S), Jun. 1, 1984)	Salesperson	Electrical contracting	DE	3c
Comfort & Fleming Ins. Brokers v. Hoxsey	26 Wash.App. 172, 613 P.2d 138 (1980)	Salesperson	Insurance	WA	8

Case	Citation	Position	Business	State	References
Consolidated Photographic Indus. v. Marks	109 Cal.App.2d 310, 240 P.2d 718 (1952)	Sale of business	Photofinishing	CA	3f
Construction Materials Ltd., Inc. v. Kirkpatrick	631 So.2d 1006 (Ala. 1994)	Construction worker (leased employee)	Construction	AL	1, AT-85A, AT-88, AT-89A, AT-91
Consultants & Designers v. Butler Serv. Group	720 F.2d 1553 (11th Cir. 1983)	Job shopper	Employment agency (technical service firm)	AL	3f
Contempo Communications v. MJM Creative Servs.	182 A.D.2d 351, 582 N.Y.S.2d 667 (1st Dep't 1992)	Manager (project)	Multimedia productions	NY	3f
Continental Car-Na-Var Corp. v. Mosley	24 Cal.2d 104, 148 P.2d 9 (1944)	No covenant	No covenant	CA	2, 9
Continental Group v. Kinsley	422 F.Supp. 838 (D.Conn. 1976)	Engineer	Plastic container	CT	5, 12
Continental Research Corp. v. Scholz	595 S.W.2d 396 (Mo.App. 1980)	Salesperson	Chemical products (industrial maintenance)	MO	2, 3d, 5, 9
Contour Chair Lounge Co. v. Aljean Furniture Mfg. Co.	403 S.W.2d 922 (Mo.App. 1966)	Corporate officer	Chair manufacturing	MO	AT-68
Contour Chair Lounge Co. v. Aljean Furniture Mfg. Co.	403 S.W.2d 922 (Mo.App. 1966)	Designer	Chair	MO	AT-68
Cook v. Johnson	47 Conn. 175 (1879)	Sale of business	Health care (Dental practice)	CT	3
Cook v. Johnson	47 Conn. 175 (1879)	Sale of business	Health care (Dental practice)	NH	3
Cool Insuring Agency, Inc. v. Rogers	125 A.D.2d 758, 509 N.Y.S.2d 180 (3d Dep't 1986), app. dismissed, 69 N.Y.2d 1037, 511 N.E.2d 89 (1987)	Salesperson	Insurance	NY	3f, 5

Case	Citation	Occupation	Industry	State	
Creative Communications Consultants v. Gaylord	403 N.W.2d 654 (Minn.Ct.App. 1987)	Account executive	Advertising	MN	7
Creative Entertainment Inc. v. Lorenz	265 Ill.App.3d 343, 202 Ill.Dec. 571, 638 N.E.2d 217 (1994)	Account executive	Meeting planning	IL	2
Credit Bureau Management Co. v. Huie	254 F.Supp. 547 (E.D. Ark. 1966) (applying Texas law)	Manager	Debt collection	AR	3c, 3f, 4, 12
Crescent Elec. Supply Co. v. Nerison	89 S.D. 203, 232 N.W.2d 76 (1975)	No covenant	No covenant	SD	3f
Criss v. Davis, Presser & LaFaye	494 So.2d 525, *review denied,* 501 So.2d 1281 (Fla. 1st Dist.Ct.App. 1986)	Accountant	Accounting (tax)	FL	3b, 3c
Crowe v. DeGioia	90 N.J. 126, 447 A.2d 173 (1982)	No covenant	No covenant	NJ	5
Crowe v. Manpower Temporary Serv.	256 Ga. 239, 347 S.E.2d 560 (1986)	Occupation not specified	Employment agency (temporary)	GA	3f
Crowell v. Woodruff	245 S.W.2d 447 (Ky.Ct.App. 1952)	Manager (production)	Dry cleaning	KY	3, 3d
Crown Paint Co. v. Bankston	640 P.2d 948 (Okla. 1981), *cert. denied,* 455 U.S. 946 (1982)	Dealership agreement	Paint distribution	OK	1
Cudahy Co. v. American Laboratories, Inc.	313 F.Supp. 1339 (D. Neb. 1970)	No covenant	No covenant	NJ	14
Cukjati v. Burkett	772 S.W.2d 215 (Tex.Ct.App.—Dallas 1989)	Manager (office)	Veterinary medicine	TX	2, 3f
Cukjati v. Burkett	772 S.W.2d 215 (Tex.Ct.App.—Dallas 1989)	Manager (office)	Veterinary medicine	WY	3b
Cukjati v. Burkett	772 S.W.2d 215 (Tex.Ct.App.—Dallas 1989)	Veterinarian	Veterinary medicine	SC	14

Cukjati v. Burkett	772 S.W.2d 215 (Tex.Ct.App.—Dallas 1989)	Veterinarian	Veterinary medicine	TX	2, 3f
Cukjati v. Burkett	772 S.W.2d 215 (Tex.Ct.App.—Dallas 1989)	Veterinarian	Veterinary medicine	WY	3b
Culbreath v. Johnson	427 So.2d 705 (Miss. 1983)	No covenant	No covenant	MS	7
Cullman Broadcasting Co. v. Bosley	373 So.2d 830 (Ala. 1979)	Broadcaster	Broadcasting (Radio)	AL	2, 3f, 5, 10, 11
Curtis v. Amela-Bonsea	137 A.D.2d 944, 525 N.Y.S.2d 69 (3d Dep't 1988)	Electrologist	Beauty	NY	3a, 3d, 3f, 10
Curtis 1000, Inc. v. Suess	24 F.3d 941 (7th Cir. 1994)	Salesperson	Printing	IL	3c, 12
Custom Video v. N.J., Video	Del.Ch., CA No. 9261, Hartnett, V.C. (Sept. 25, 1987) (applying New Jersey substantive law)	Occupation not specified	Video surveillance system sales and service	DE	2
D.W. Trowbridge Ford, Inc. v. Galyen	200 Neb. 103, 262 N.W.2d 442 (1978)	Sale of business	Automobile dealership	NE	10
Dabora, Inc. v. Kline	884 S.W.2d 475 (Tenn.App. 1994)	Salesperson	Advertising (magazine)	TN	3, 3d, 3f, 4, AT-8
Dabora, Inc. v. Kline	884 S.W.2d 475 (Tenn.App. 1994)	Writer	Magazine (horse)	TN	3, 3d, 3f, 4, AT-8
Dahl v. Brunswick Corp.	277 Md. 471, 356 A.2d 221 (1976)	No covenant	No covenant	MD	3c
Dahlberg Bros., Inc. v. Ford Motor Co.	272 Minn. 264, 137 N.W.2d 314 (Minn. 1965)	No covenant	No covenant	MN	2, 5, 7
Daigle v. Stardard Coffee Serv. Co.	479 So.2d 469 (La.App. 3d Cir. 1985)	Salesperson (route)	Coffee	LA	2
Dain Bosworth, Inc. v. Brandhorst	356 N.W.2d 590 (Iowa App. 1984)	Stock broker	Securities	IA	2

Daiquiri's III on Bourbon, Ltd. v. Wandfluh	608 So.2d 222 (La.App. 5th Cir. 1992), *writ denied*, 610 So.2d 801 (La. 1993)	Bartender	Bar	LA	1, 3
Dalton Properties, Inc. v. Jones	683 P.2d 30 (Nev. 1984)	No covenant	No covenant	TN	10
Dana F. Cole & Co. v. Byerly	211 Neb. 903, 320 N.W.2d 916 (1982)	Accountant	Accounting	NE	3b, 3f, 7, 14
Dana F. Cole & Co. v. Byerly	211 Neb. 903, 320 N.W.2d 916 (1982)	Manager (office)	Accounting	NE	3b, 3f, 7, 14
Daniel Boone Clinic, P.S.C. v. Dahhan	734 S.W.2d 488 (Ky.Ct.App. 1987), *disc. rev. denied* (August 26, 1987)	Physician	Health care	KY	11
Daniels v. Thomas, Dean & Hoskins	804 P.2d 359 (Mont. 1990)	Engineer	Civil engineering	MT	1, 3, 3d, 3e, 3f, 7, 14
Danzer v. Professional Insurors	101 N.M. 178, 679 P.2d 1276 (1984)	Salesperson	Insurance	NM	8
Data Management v. Greene	757 P.2d 62, 3 IER Cases 796 (Alaska 1988)	Occupation not specified	Computing service	AK	2, 3, 3a, 3d, 3e, 3f, 4, 11, 14
Data Processing Equip. Corp. v. Martin	Appeal No. 87-230-II (Tenn.Ct.App. Dec. 30, 1987; LEXIS Employ library, Tenn. file)	No covenant	No covenant	TN	2
Data Sys. Computer Centre v. Tempesta	171 A.D.2d 724, 566 N.Y.S.2d 957 (2d Dep't 1991)	Salesperson	Computers	NY	2, 5, 7
Database Sys., Inc. v. C.L. Sys.	640 F.2d 109 (8th Cir. 1981)	No covenant	No covenant	AR	5
Daughtry v. Capital Gas	285 Ala. 89, 229 So.2d 480 (1969)	Manager (branch)	Liquefied petroleum gas/appliance	AL	3a, 3c, 3f, AT-43

Case	Citation	Role	Industry	State	Sections
Davies & Davies Agency v. Davies	298 N.W.2d 127 (Minn. 1980)	Salesperson	Insurance	MN	3b, 3c, 3d, 4
Davis v. Hester	582 So.2d 538 (Ala. 1991)	No covenant	No covenant	AL	7
Daytona Group of Tex. v. Smith	800 S.W.2d 285 (Tex.Ct.App.— Corpus Christi 1990)	Salesperson	Advertising (radio air time)	TX	2, 3, 3c, 3e, 4
De Felice v. Garon	395 So.2d 658 (La. 1981)	No covenant	No covenant	LA	AT-66
Dean Van Horn Consulting Assocs. v. Wold	395 N.W.2d 405, 1 IER Cases 1696 (Minn.Ct.App. 1986)	Consultant	Tax/accounting	MN	4, 10
Dearborn Chem. Co. v. Rhodes	(Tenn.Ct.App. April 19, 1985) (LEXIS, Employ library, Tenn. file)	Manager, sales	Chemicals	TN	3f
Deborah Hope Doelker, Inc. v. Kestly	87 A.D.2d 763, 449 N.Y.S.2d 52 (1st Dep't 1982)	Salesperson	Balloon bouquets	NY	4
Decker, Berta & Co. v. Berta	225 Ill.App.3d 24, 167 Ill.Dec. 190, 587 N.E.2d 72 (4th Dist. 1992)	Accountant (partner)	Accounting	IL	3f, 13, AT-23
DeCristofaro v. Security Nat'l Bank	664 P.2d 167 (Alaska 1983)	Corporate officer (vice president, assistant)	Bank	AK	3
Defco, Inc. v. Decatur Cylinder, Inc.	595 So.2d 1329 (Ala. 1992)	Sale of business	Cylinder manufacturing	AL	AT-90
Delaware Limousine Serv. v. Royal Limousine Serv.	1991 WL 53449 (Del.Super.Ct. April 5, 1991)	No covenant	No covenant	DE	10
Delmar Studios of the Carolinas v. Kinsey	233 S.C. 313, 104 S.E.2d 338 (1958)	Photographer	Photographic services (school yearbook and pictures)	SC	3e, 3f, 5, 14

Case	Citation	Role	Service	State	References
Delmar Studios of the Carolinas v. Kinsey	233 S.C. 313, 104 S.E.2d 338 (1958)	Salesperson	Photographic services (school pictures and yearbook)	SC	3e, 3f, 5, 14
Deloitte & Touche L.L.P. v. Chiampou and Travis	636 N.Y.S.2d 679 (App.Div. 4th Dep't 1995)	Accountant (partner)	Accounting	NY	7
DeMuth v. Miller	652 A.2d 891 (Pa.Super. 1995)	Consultant	Management	PA	3f, 8, AT-38.1, AT-54.1, AT-89.1
DeMuth v. Miller	652 A.2d 891 (Pa.Super. 1995)	Management consultant	Consulting (professional management and accounting)	PA	3f, 8, AT-38.1, AT-54.1, AT-89.1
Denburg v. Parker Chapin, Flattau & Klimpl	184 A.D.2d 343, 586 N.Y.S.2d 107 (1992), *modified and aff'd*, 82 N.Y.2d 375, 604 N.Y.S.2d 900, 624 N.E.2d 995 (1993)	Attorney (partner)	Law	NJ	AT-49, AT-95
Denburg v. Parker Chapin Flattau & Klimpl	184 A.D.2d 343, 586 N.Y.S.2d 107 (1992), *modified and aff'd*, 82 N.Y.2d 375, 604 N.Y.S.2d 900, 624 N.E.2d 995 (1993)	Attorney (partner)	Law	NY	14, AT-30, AT-96
Depositions And . . . Inc. v. Campbell	406 S.E.2d 390, 6 IER Cases 999 (S.C.Ct.App. 1991)	Court reporter	Court reporting	SC	3f, 10, 14
DePova v. Camden Forge Co.	254 F.2d 248 (3d Cir. 1985)	No covenant	No covenant	CT	3b
Derrick, Stubbs & Stith v. Rogers	256 S.C. 395, 182 S.E.2d 724 (1971)	Accountant (partner)	Accounting	SC	8

Case	Citation	Occupation	Industry	State	Ref
Ditus v. Beahm	232 P.2d 184 (Colo. 1951)	Sale of business	Livestock pavilion (partner)	CO	6
Diversified Fastening Sys. v. Rogge	786 F.Supp. 1486 (N.D. Iowa 1991)	Occupation not specified	Fasteners	IA	5
Diversified Human Resources Group v. Levinson-Polakoff	752 S.W.2d 8 (Tex.Ct.App.—Dallas 1988)	Recruiter	Employment agency (data processors)	TX	3f, 4
Dixon v. Royal Cup	386 So.2d 481 (Ala.Civ.App. 1980)	Salesperson	Coffee	AL	3f
Dobbins, DeGuire & Tucker v. Rutherford, McDonald & Olson	218 Mont. 392, 708 P.2d 577 (1985)	Accountant	Accounting	MT	1, 2, 3, 3a, 3d, 3e, 3f, 3g, 14
Dobbins v. Getz Exterminators of Ala.	382 So.2d 1135 (Ala.Civ.App. 1980)	Manager	Pest control	AL	1, 3f, 4, 10
Dobbs v. Guenther	846 S.W.2d 270 (Tenn.App. 1992)	Corporate officer (director)	Automobile dealership	TN	AT-29
Dobbs v. Guenther	846 S.W.2d 270 (Tenn.App. 1992)	Manager (general)	Automobile dealership	TN	AT-29
Dohm & Nelke Div. of Cashin Sys. Corp. v. Wilson Foods Corp.	531 N.E.2d 512 (Ind.App. 1988)	No covenant	No covenant	IN	12
Dominy v. National Emergency Servs.	215 Ga.App. 537, 451 S.E.2d 472 (1994)	Physician	Health care	GA	3f
Dominy v. National Emergency Servs.	215 Ga.App. 537, 451 S.E.2d 472 (1994)	Physician	Health care (Emergency medicine)	GA	3f
Domurat v. Mazzaccoli	138 Conn. 327, 84 A.2d 271 (1951)	Sale of business	Barber shop	CT	14
Donahoe v. Tatum	242 Miss. 253, 134 So.2d 442 (1961)	Recruiter	Employment agency	MS	2, 3, 3f
Donahue v. Permacel Tape Corp.	234 Ind. 398, 127 N.E.2d 235 (1955)	Salesperson	Tapes and adhesives	IN	2, 3, 3d, 3f, 4

Case	Citation	Role	Industry	State	References
Dumont v. Tucker	822 P.2d 96 (Mont. 1991)	Sale of business	Accounting practice	MT	1, 4, AT-2, AT-64
Duncan-Williams v. Barnett	(Tenn.Ct.App. Oct. 24, 1984) (LEXIS, Employ library, Tenn. file)	Salesperson	Securities	TN	3d, 3f, 3g
Dunfey Realty Co. v. Enwright	101 N.H. 195, 138 A.2d 80 (1957)	Salesperson	Insurance and real estate	NH	2, 3d, 3f, 14
Dunn v. Ward	105 Idaho 354, 670 P.2d 59 (1983)	Sale of business	Wood stake wholesaling	WY	10
Dunning v. Tallman	244 Neb. 1, 504 N.W.2d 85 (1993)	Owner (divorce)	Computer supplies sales	NE	AT-63
Durapin v. American Prods.	559 A.2d 1051 (R.I. 1989)	Distributorship agreement	Not specified	RI	3, 4, 14
Durham v. Stand-by Labor of Ga.	230 Ga. 558, 198 S.E.2d 145 (1973)	Occupation not specified	Not specified	GA	2, 3, 3d, 4
Dutch Maid Bakeries v. Schleicher	58 Wyo. 374, 131 P.2d 630 (1942)	Baker	Bakery	WY	3, 3f, 4, 8, 14, AT-93
Dworkin v. Blumenthal	77 Md.App. 774, 551 A.2d 947 (1989)	Dentist	Health care (Dentistry)	MD	2
Dwyer v. Jung	133 N.J. Super. 343, 336 A.2d 498 (Ch.Div.) *aff'd o.b.,* 137 N.J.Super 135, 348 A.2d 208 (App.Div. 1975)	Attorney (partner)	Law	NJ	3, 14
Dyar Sales & Mach. Co. v. Bleiler	106 Vt. 425, 175 A. 27 (1934)	Salesperson	Road machinery	VT	2, 3c, 3d, 3f, 14
Dyson Conveyor Maintenance v. Young & Vann Supply	529 So.2d 212 (Ala. 1988)	Manager (division)	Conveyer belt sales and service	AL	AT-70

Case	Citation	Position	Industry	State	
Ecolab, Inc. v. Gartland	537 N.W.2d 291 (Minn.App. 1995)	Corporate officer (vice president)	Pest control	MN	3, AT-2, AT-21
Ecolab, Inc. v. Morrisette	879 F.2d 325 (8th Cir. 1989) (applying Nebraska law)	Manager	Pest control	NE	2, 3g, 4
Economic Research Analysts v. Brennan	232 So.2d 219 (Fla. 4th Dist.Ct.App. 1970)	Salesperson (independent contractor)	Securities	FL	1
Economy Grocery Stores Corp. v. McMenamy	290 Mass. 549, 195 N.E. 747 (1935)	Manager (meat department)	Grocery	MA	3e, 8
Eden Hannon & Co. v. Sumitomo Trust & Banking Co.	914 F.2d 556 (4th Cir. 1990) (applying Virginia law), cert. denied, 499 U.S. 947 (1991)	Investment contract	Investments	VA	2, 4, AT-85.2
Edgecomb v. Edmonston	257 Mass. 12, 153 N.E. 99 (1926)	Court reporter	Court reporting	MA	6
Edin v. Jostens, Inc.	343 N.W.2d 691 (Minn.Ct.App. 1984)	Salesperson	Not specified	MN	5, 7, 8, 14
Education for Living Seminars v. Leone	558 So.2d 250 (La.App. 1st Cir. 1990)	Psychologist	Seminar production	LA	1, 2, 4
Edward Brown, Inc. v. Astor Supply Co.	4 A.D.2d 177, 164 N.Y.S.2d 107 (1st Dep't 1957)	Salesperson	Cleaning supplies	NY	8
Edwards v. Howe Richardson Scale Co.	237 Ga. 818, 229 S.E.2d 651 (1976)	Mechanic	Scales, industrial	GA	2, 3
Ehlers v. Iowa Warehouse Co.	188 N.W.2d 368 (Iowa 1971)	Manager, sales	Truck leasing	IA	4, 9
Ehlers v. Iowa Warehouse Co.	188 N.W.2d 368, modified, 190 N.W.2d 413 (Iowa 1971)	Manager, sales	Truck leasing	WY	4
El Dorado Laundry Co. v. Ford	174 Ark. 104, 294 S.W. 393 (1927)	Salesperson (route)	Laundry	AR	3f

Case	Citation	Occupation	Industry	State	Notes
Engel v. Ernst	102 Nev. 392, 724 P.2d 215 (1986) (applying Colorado law)	Accountant (partner)	Accounting	NV	11, 12
Engineered Mechanical Servs. v. Langolis	464 So.2d 329 (La.App. 1st Cir. 1984)	Engineer	Mechanical engineering	LA	1
Engineering Assocs., Inc. v. Pankow	258 N.C. 137, 150 S.E.2d 56 (1966)	Engineer	Mechanical (ceramics, tobacco and other industries; designing and manufacturing machines for) engineering	NC	3d
Ensco Int'l v. Blegen	410 N.W.2d 11 (Minn.Ct.App. 1987)	Salesperson	Computers	MN	7
Environmental Defense Fund v. Morton	420 F.Supp. 1037 (D. Mont. 1976)	No covenant	No covenant	MT	6
Equifax Servs. v. Hitz	905 F.2d 1355 (10th Cir. 1990)	Manager (branch)	Insurance industry survey and audit service	KS	4, 5, 6, 12
Erie R.R. v. Tompkins	304 U.S. 64 (1938)	No covenant	No covenant	KS	5, 6
Erikson v. Hawley	56 App.D.C. 268, 12 F.2d 491 (1926)	Orthodontist (apprentice)	Health care (Dentistry)	DC	3e, 3f, 7, 9, 14
Eutectic Welding Alloys Corp. v. West	281 Minn. 13, 160 N.W.2d 566 (1968)	Salesperson	Welders	MN	6
Evans v. Duracote Corp.	13 Ohio App.2d 63, 233 N.E.2d 873 (1968)	Manager, sales, overseas	Airline customers	OH	14
Evans Labs., Inc. v. Melder	262 Ark. 868, 562 S.W.2d 62 (1978)	Occupation not specified	Pest control	AR	3, 3f

Case	Citation	Occupation	Industry	State	References
Evco Distrib. v. Brardau	6 Kan.App.2d 53, 626 P.2d 1192 (1981)	Occupation not specified	Agricultural equipment design and manufacturing	KS	2, 3b
Ex Parte Clements	587 So.2d 317 (Ala. 1991)	Corporate officer (vice president)	Telecommunications equipment manufacturing	AL	AT-9
Excelsior Laundry Co. v. Diehl	32 N.M. 169, 252 P. 991 (1927)	Salesperson (route)	Laundry	NM	3f
Expo Chem. Co. v. Brooks	572 S.W.2d 8 (Tex.Civ.App.—Houston 1st Dist. 1978), rev'd, 576 S.W.2d 369 (Tex. 1979)	No covenant	No covenant	TX	2
Extine v. Williamson Midwest	176 Ohio St.2d 403, 200 N.E.2d 297 (1964) (overruled)	Salesperson	Printing plate materials	OH	3, 3g, 4, 14
F.W. Means & Co. v. Carstens	428 N.E.2d 251 (Ind.App. 1981)	Manager	Laundry	IN	6, 9
Faces Boutique, Ltd. v. Gibbs	455 S.E.2d 707 (S.C.App. 1995)	Esthetician	Beauty (facial spa salon)	SC	2, 3, 3f, 4
Falmouth Ob-Gyn Assocs., Inc. v. Abisla	417 Mass. 176, 629 N.E.2d 291 (1994)	Physician	Health care (Obstetrics and gynecology)	MA	1, 11, AT-21, AT-50, AT-75, AT-94
Famex, Inc. v. Century Ins. Servs.	425 So.2d 1053 (Ala. 1982)	Developer (plan)	Insurance	AL	1
Family Affair Haircutters, Inc. v. Detling	110 A.D.2d 745, 488 N.Y.S.2d 204 (2d Dep't 1985)	Hair stylist	Beauty	NY	3, 5, 14
Farm Bureau Serv. Co. of Maynard v. Kohls	203 N.W.2d 209 (Iowa 1972)	Delivery person	Petroleum	IA	3c, 3f, 4, 9, 14
Farmers Ins. Exch. v. Fraley	80 Or.App. 117, 720 P.2d 770 (1987)	Salesperson	Insurance	OR	3, 3g

Farmers Underwriters Ass'n v. Eckel	185 Neb. 531, 177 N.W.2d 274 (1970)	Salesperson	Insurance	NE	2
Farthing v. San Mateo Clinic	143 Cal.App.2d 385, 299 P.2d 977 (1956)	Physician	Health care (Obstetrics)	CA	1, 10
Faw, Casson & Co. v. Cranston	375 A.2d 463 (Del.Ch. 1977)	Accountant	Accounting	DE	2, 3, 3b, 3c, 3f, 14
Faw, Casson & Co. v. Everngman	99 Md.App. 129, 616 A.2d 426 (1992)	Accountant (partner)	Accounting	MD	14, AT-49
Federal Sanitation Co. v. Frankel	34 Ohio App. 331, 171 N.E. 339 (1929)	Salesperson	Disinfectants (Catholic institution customers)	OH	3f
Federated Mut. Ins. Co. v. Bennett	36 Ark.App. 99, 818 S.W.2d 596 (1991)	Salesperson	Insurance	AR	2, 3, 3f, 4, 14
Federated Mut. Ins. Co. v. Whitaker	232 Ga. 811, 209 S.E.2d 161 (1974)	Salesperson	Insurance	GA	3
Ferraro v. Lattimore Fink Labs.	191 Kan. 53, 379 P.2d 266 (1981)	Physician	Health care (Pathology)	KS	3b
Ferrero v. Associated Materials	923 F.2d 1441 (11th Cir. 1991)	Salesperson	Building supplies	GA	1, 3f, 4, 11, 12
Ferrofluidics Corp. v. Advanced Vacuum Components, Inc.	789 F.Supp. 1201 (D.N.H.), aff'd, 968 F.2d 1463 (1st Cir. 1992)	Manager (product)	Magnetic fluid rotary seal manufacturing	ME	3c
Field v. Alexander & Alexander of Ind.	503 N.E.2d 627 (Ind.App. 1987)	Salesperson	Insurance	IN	3d, 3g, 14
Fields Found. v. Christensen	103 Wis.2d 465, 309 N.W.2d 125 (Wis.Ct.App. 1981)	Physician	Health care (Abortion)	WI	2, 3, 3d, 3f, 7, 11, 14
Financial Guardian, Inc. v. Kutter	630 S.W.2d 197 (Mo.App. 1982)	Salesperson	Insurance	MO	AT-41
Firemen's Ins. Co. of Newark v. Keating	753 F.Supp. 1145 (S.D.N.Y. 1990)	No covenant	No covenant	PA	6, AT-54.1

Case	Citation	Occupation	Business	State	Sections
Foltz v. Struxness	168 Kan. 714, 215 P.2d 133 (1950)	Physician	Health care (Surgery)	KS	2, 3f, 4
Foltz v. Struxness	168 Kan. 714, 215 P.2d 133 (1950)	Physician	Health care	NV	3f
Food Fair Stores v. Greeley	264 Md. 105, 285 A.2d 632 (1972)	Manager	Grocery store	MD	3f, 3g
Forms Mfg. v. Edwards	705 S.W.2d 67 (Mo.App. 1985)	Salesperson	Forms (business)	MO	8, 14, AT-38
Forney Indus. v. Andre	246 F.Supp. 333 (N.D. 1965)	Manager (district)	Welders (electronic arc)	ND	12
Forney Indus. v. Andre	246 F.Supp. 333 (N.D. 1965)	Salesperson	Welders (electronic arc)	ND	12
Forrest Paschal Mach. Co. v. Milholen	27 N.C.App. 678, 220 S.E.2d 190 (1975)	Manager (general)	Brick industry equipment manufacturing	NC	3, 3c, 3f
Forrest v. Kornblatt	328 So.2d 528 (Fla. 3d Dist.Ct.App. 1976), reh'g denied (April 1, 1976)	Occupation not specified	Not specified	FL	12
Forrish v. Kennedy	377 Pa. 370, 105 A.2d 67 (1954)	No covenant	No covenant	PA	AT-21
Fort Smith Light & Traction Co. v. Kelley	94 Ark. 461, 127 S.W. 975 (1910)	Franchise (municipal)	Natural gas	AR	3e
4408, Inc. v. Losure	175 Ind.App. 658, 373 N.E.2d 899 (1978)	Salesperson (route)	Coffee	IN	3d, 3f
Foster v. Realty Title Co.	209 Mont. 183, 680 P.2d 323 (1984)	Occupation not specified	Insurance	MT	11
Foster & Co. v. Snodgrass	333 So.2d 521 (Fla. 2d Dist.Ct.App. 1976)	Salesperson	Hardware	FL	3
Foti v. Cook	220 Va. 800, 263 S.E.2d 430 (1980)	Accountant (partner)	Accounting	VA	3e, 3f, 3g, 10, 14
Fowler v. Printers II	89 Md.App. 448, 598 A.2d 794 (1991)	Salesperson	Printing services	MD	2, 3g, 4, 10, 14

Case	Citation	Occupation	Industry	State	Ref
Freudenthal v. Espey	45 Colo. 488, 102 P.2d 280 (1909)	Physician	Health care	CO	3f
Friddle v. Raymond	575 So.2d 1038, 6 IER Cases 199 (Ala. 1991)	Veterinarian	Veterinary medicine	AL	1, 14
Friddle v. Raymond	575 So.2d 1038, 6 IER Cases 199 (Ala. 1991)	Veterinarian	Veterinary medicine	SC	14, AT-82
Friedman & Fuller, P.C. v. Funkhouser	107 Md. App. 91, 666 A.2d 1298 (1995)	Salesperson	Accounting	MD	AT-86
Frierson v. Sheppard Bldg. Supply Co.	247 Miss. 157, 154 So.2d 151 (1963)	Manager (general)	Building supplies	MS	3, 3c, 3f, 8, 9, 14
Frumkes v. Beasley-Reed Broadcasting of Miami, Inc.	533 So.2d 942 (Fla. 3d Dist.Ct.App. 1988)	Broadcaster	Broadcasting (Radio)	FL	AT-21
Fuller v. Kolb	238 Ga. 602, 234 S.E.2d 517 (1977)	Accountant	Accounting	GA	3, 3g
Fullerton Lumber Co. v. Torborg	270 Wis.2d 133, 70 N.W.2d 585 (1955)	Manager (yard)	Lumber retailing	WI	4
Fumo v. Medical Group of Mich. City	590 N.E.2d 1103 (Ind.App. 3d Dist. 1992)	Physician	Health care (Gastroenterology)	IN	3, 3d, 3f, 5, 6, 7, 14
Furniture Mfg. Corp. v. Joseph	900 S.W.2d 642 (Mo.App. 1995)	Salesperson	Furniture	MO	5, 8, 9, AT-7, AT-18, AT-66
G.T. Michelli Co. v. McKey	599 So.2d 355 (La.App. 1st Cir. 1992)	Occupation not specified	Not specified	LA	10, 11, AT-66
G&W Elec. Co. v. Joslyn Mfg. & Supply Co.	127 Ill.App.3d 44, 468 N.E.2d 449 (3d Dist. 1984)	Occupation not specified	Electrical equipment manufacturing	IL	3f
Gagliardi Bros., Inc. v. Caputo	538 F.Supp. 525 (E.D.Pa. 1982)	Corporate officer (controller)	Meat processing	AK	3

Case	Citation	Occupation	Industry	State	Sections
Gelco Express Corp. v. Ashby	689 S.W.2d 790 (Mo.App. 1985)	Manager (senior regional)	Courier service	MO	3d, 3e
Gelder Medical Group v. Webber	41 N.Y.2d 680, 394 N.Y.S.2d 867, 363 N.E.2d 573 (2d Dep't 1977)	Physician (partner)	Health care	NJ	2, 3
Gelder Medical Group v. Webber	41 N.Y.2d 680, 394 N.Y.S.2d 867, 363 N.E.2d 573 (2d Dep't 1977)	Physician (partner)	Health care	NY	2, 3, 3f, 5, 14
General Elec. Co. v. Keyser	166 W.Va. 456, 275 S.E.2d 289 (1981)	No covenant	No covenant	WV	12
General Medical Corp. v. Koobs	179 Wis.2d 422, 507 N.W.2d 381, 8 IER Cases 1409 (Wis.Ct.App. 1993)	Salesperson	Medical supplies	WI	2, 3, 3f, 3g, 4, 12, 14, AT-89
Geocaris v. Surgical Consultants	100 Wis.2d 387, 302 N.W.2d 76 (Wis.Ct.App. 1981)	Physician	Health care (Surgery)	WI	3, 3e, 3f
George W. Kistler, Inc. v. O'Brien	464 Pa. 475, 347 A.2d 311 (1975)	Manager (service and branch)	Fire prevention equipment	PA	3b, 3c
Giddings Petroleum Corp. v. Peterson Food Mart, Inc.	859 S.W.2d 89 (Tex.Ct.App.—Austin 1993)	No covenant	No covenant	TX	AT-14
Gill v. Computer Equip. Corp.	266 Md. 170, 292 A.2d 54 (1972)	Occupation not specified	Manufacturer's representative	MD	3a, 3g
Gill v. Guy Chipman Co.	681 S.W.2d 264 (Tex.Ct.App.—San Antonio 4th Dist. 1984)	Manager (office)	Real estate brokerage	TX	3, 3a
Gillen v. Diadrill, Inc.	624 S.W.2d 259 (Tex.Ct.App. 1981)	Salesperson	Oil well drill bits, stabilizers, and cement mills	TX	3f
Gillespie v. Carbondale & Marion Eye Centers, Ltd.	251 Ill.App.3d 625, 190 Ill.Dec. 950, 622 N.E.2d 1267 (5th Dist. 1993)	Physician	Health care (Ophthalmology)	IL	2, 3, 3d, 3f, 4, 7

Gilmore Ford, Inc. v. Turner	599 So.2d 29 (Ala. 1992)	Sale of business	Automobile dealership	AL	1
Gimper v. Giacchetta	633 N.Y.S.2d 614 (App.Div. 3d Dep't 1995)	Salesperson	Manufacturer's representative	NY	10
Girard v. Rebsamen Ins. Co.	14 Ark.App. 154, 685 S.W.2d 526 (1985)	Salesperson	Insurance	AR	2, 3, 3c, 3d, 3g, 9, 10, 14
Glatt v. Bank of Kirkwood Plaza	383 N.W.2d 473 (N.D. 1986)	No covenant	No covenant	ND	1
Gobel v. Laing	41 Ohio Op.2d 175, 12 Ohio App.2d 93, 231 N.E.2d 341 (1967)	Recruiter	Employment agency	OH	3f, 5
Godfrey v. Roessle	5 App.D.C. 299 (1895)	Sale of business	Laundry	DC	3e
Goff v. Aamco Auto. Transmissions	313 F.Supp. 667 (Md. 1970)	No covenant	No covenant	MD	12
Goldammer v. Fay	326 F.2d 268 (10th Cir. 1964)	Franchise	Ice cream shop	CO	3
Golden Distribs., Ltd., In re	134 Bankr. 750 (S.D.N.Y. 1991) (applying Massachusetts law)	No covenant	No covenant	MA	2
Golden State Linen Serv. v. Vidalin	69 Cal.App.3d 1, 137 Cal.Rptr. 807 (1977)	Manager (depot)	Laundry	CA	1
Golden State Linen Serv. v. Vidalin	69 Cal.App.3d 1, 137 Cal.Rptr. 807 (1977)	Salesperson (route)	Laundry	CA	1
Gomez v. Chua Medical Corp.	510 N.E.2d 191, 2 IER Cases 490 (Ind.App. 1987)	Physician	Health care	IN	8, 10, 11, 14
Gomez v. Zamora	814 S.W.2d 114, 6 IER Cases 114 (Tex.Ct.App.—Corpus Christi 1991)	Financial eligibility worker	Medical third-party resource service	TX	3d, 3e, 3f, 4, 7
Gonzales v. Zamora	791 S.W.2d 258 (Tex.Ct.App.—Corpus Christi 1990)	Supervisor	Medical third-party resource service	TX	2

Case	Citation	Role	Industry	State	Ref
Goodie Olde Fashion Fudge Co. v. Kuiros	597 A.2d 141 (Pa.Super. 1991)	Confectioner	Confection	PA	5, 7, AT-47, AT-54
Goodman v. Motor Prods. Corp.	9 Ill.App.2d 57, 132 N.E.2d 356 (2d Dist. 1956), aff'd after remand, 22 Ill.App.2d 378, 161 N.E.2d 31 (2d Dist. 1959)	No covenant	No covenant	TN	10
Goodson Bros. Coffee Co. v. Institutional Jobbers Co.	1992 WL 184685 (Tenn.App., No. 03A01-9111-CH-00415, Sept. 11, 1991)	No covenant	No covenant	TN	10
Goodwin v. Coe Pontiac	392 Mich. 195, 220 N.W.2d 664 (1974)	No covenant	No covenant	MI	AT-73A
Gordon v. Wasserman	153 Cal.App.2d 328, 314 P.2d 759 (1957)	Salesperson (door-to-door)	Household goods (installment plan)	CA	2, 3f
Gordon Termite Control v. Terrones	84 Cal.App. 176, 148 Cal.Rptr. 310 (1978)	Exterminator	Pest control	CA	2
Gordon Wahls Co. v. Linde	306 Pa.Super. 64, 452 A.2d 4 (1982)	Recruiter	Employment agency (printing industry)	PA	3g
Gorman Publishing Co. v. Stillman	516 F.Supp. 98 (N.D.Ill. 1980)	Publisher	Magazine	IL	3c
Goselin v. Archibald	121 N.H. 1016, 437 A.2d 302 (1981)	Sale of business	Motel	NH	AT-21
Gottsch v. Bank of Stapleton	235 Neb. 816, 458 N.W.2d 443 (1990)	No covenant	No covenant	NE	7
Gramanz v. T-Shirts and Souvenirs, Inc.	894 P.2d 342 (Nev. 1995)	Shareholders' agreement	Souvenir shop	NV	10

Case	Citation	Occupation	Law / Business	State	Reference
Gray v. Martin	63 Or.App. 173, 663 P.2d 1285, review denied, 295 Or. 541, 668 P.2d 384 (1983)	Attorney (partner)	Law	NJ	AT-49, AT-95
Great N. Ry. v. Melton	193 F.2d 729 (9th Cir. 1952)	No covenant	No covenant	MT	3a
Green v. City of Bennettsville	197 S.C. 313, 15 S.E.2d 334 (1941)	No covenant	No covenant	SC	7
Greenlee v. Tuscaloosa Office Prod. & Supply	474 So.2d 669 (Ala. 1985)	Service technician	Photocopiers	AL	2, 3f
Greenwich Mills Co., Inc. v. Barrie House Coffee Co.	91 A.D.2d 398, 459 N.Y.S.2d 454 (1983)	Salesperson	Coffee and tea	NY	2, 5
Gregory v. Spieker	110 Cal. 150, 42 P. 576 (1895)	Sale of business	Medical compound (kidney, liver and bitters)	CA	3d
Griffin v. Vendegriff	205 Ga. 288, 53 S.E.2d 345 (1949)	Salesperson (route)	Laundry	GA	3e, 3f
Gross v. QMS, Inc.	613 So.2d 331 (Ala. 1993)	Occupation not specified	Not specified	AL	5, 7
Gross, Kelly & Co. v. Bibo	19 N.M. 495, 145 P. 480 (1914)	Creditors' composition agreement	Mercantile business	NM	3
Group Ass'n Plans v. Colquhoun	151 App.D.C. 298, 466 F.2d 469 (1972)	Salesperson	Insurance	DC	10
Guffey v. Shelnut & Assocs.	247 Ga. 667, 278 S.E.2d 371 (1981)	Manager	Insurance	GA	3d, 3g
Guffey v. Shelnut & Assocs.	247 Ga. 667, 278 S.E.2d 371 (1981)	Salesperson	Insurance	GA	3d, 3g

Hainz v. Shopko Stores, Inc.	121 Wis.2d 168, 359 N.W.2d 397 (Wis.App. 1984)	No covenant	No covenant	WI	3c
Hall v. Willard & Woolsey P.S.C.	471 S.W.2d 316 (Ky.Ct.App. 1971)	Physician	Heath care (Internal medicine)	KY	2, 3, 3d, 3f
Hamer Holding Group v. Elmore	202 Ill.App.3d 994, 148 Ill.Dec. 310, 560 N.E.2d 907 (1st Dist. 1990)	Manager	Property management	IL	5, 7, AT-23
Hamer Holding Group v. Elmore	202 Ill.App.3d 994, 148 Ill.Dec. 310, 560 N.E.2d 907 (1st Dist. 1990)	Property manager	Property management	IL	5, 7, AT-23
Hammermill Paper Co. v. Palese	(Del.Ch., C.A. No. 7128, June 14, 1983)	Salesperson	Paper and janitorial supplies	DE	2, 3b, 3f
Hammons v. Big Sandy Claims Serv.	567 S.W.2d 313 (Ky.Ct.App. 1978)	Adjuster	Insurance	KY	2, 3, 3d, 3e, 3f, 4
Hamrick v. Kelley	260 Ga. 307, 392 S.E.2d 518 (1990)	Sale of business	Not specified	GA	4
Hancock v. Fickling & Walker Ins. Agency	248 Ga. 608, 284 S.E.2d 414 (1981)	Manager	Insurance	GA	3f
Handal v. American Farmers Mut. Casualty Co.	79 Wis.2d 67, 255 N.W.2d 903 (1977)	No covenant	No covenant	WI	12
Hanks v. GAB Business Servs.	644 S.W.2d 707 (Tex. 1982)	Sale of business	Not specified	TX	AT-17
Hansen v. Edwards	83 Nev. 189, 426 P.2d 792 (1967)	Physician	Health care (Podiatry)	NV	1, 2, 3, 3a, 3f, 5, 7, 9, 10, 13, 14

Case	Citation	Occupation	Industry	State	References
Hart v. Jackson & Coker (Hart I)	5 IER Cases 1441 (Ga.Super.Ct., DeKalb County, No. 90-5654-3, Sept. 7, 1990)	Recruiter	Employment agency (physicians)	GA	1, 3g, 4, 11
Hart v. Marion A. Allen, Inc. of Ga.	211 Ga.App. 431, 440 S.E.2d 26 (1993)	Salesperson	Insurance	GA	3d, 3f, 14
Hart Forms & Sys. v. Goetsch	1990 WL 195473 (Minn.Ct.App. 1990)	Salesperson	Forms (business)	MN	3c, 3f, 3g, 6
Hart, Nininger, Campbell Assocs. v. Rogers	16 Conn.App. 619, 548 A.2d 758 (1988)	Salesperson	Manufacturer's representative	CT	3a, 3f, 5, 6, 7
Hartford Elec. Light Co. v. Levitz	173 Conn. 15, 376 A.2d 381 (1979)	No covenant	No covenant	CT	6
Hartman v. W.H. Odell & Assocs., Inc.	450 S.E.2d 912 (N.C.App. 1994)	Actuary	Actuarial services	NC	2, 3, 3d, 3e, 3f, 4, 9, AT-23, AT-42
Harvest Ins. Agency v. Inter-Ocean Ins. Co.	492 N.E.2d 686 (Ind. 1986)	Salesperson	Insurance	IN	5, 7
Harwell Enters., Inc. v. Heim	6 N.C.App. 548, 170 S.E.2d 540 (1969)	Occupation not specified	Silk screening	NC	3e
Harwell Enters., Inc. v. Heim	6 N.C.App. 548, 170 S.E.2d 540 (1969), aff'd in part and rev'd in part, 276 N.C. 475, 173 S.E.2d 316 (1970)	Salesperson	Silk screen processing	NC	3e
Hasty v. Rent-A-Driver	671 S.W.2d 471 (Tenn. 1984)	Truck driver	Truck driver leasing	TN	1, 2, 3, 14
Haugen v. Sundseth	106 Minn. 129, 118 N.W. 666 (1908)	Sale of business	Undertaking, furniture	KS	14
Haut v. Rossbach	128 N.J. Eq. 77, 15A.2d 227 (Ch.Div. 1940)	No covenant	No covenant	NJ	14

Hawkins v. Cox	592 So.2d 852 (La.App. 3d Cir. 1991)	No covenant	No covenant	LA	AT-89
Hawkins Chem., Inc. v. McNea	321 N.W.2d 918 (N.D. 1982)	Sale of business	Chemical sales and distribution	ND	14
Hawkins Chem., Inc. v. McNea	321 N.W.2d 918 (N.D. 1982)	Sale of business	Chemicals	ND	4
Hay Group v. Nadel	170 A.D.2d 398, 566 N.Y.S.2d 616 (1st Dep't 1991)	Sale of business	Consulting	NY	3f, 5, 6, AT-56
Hayes v. Altman	424 Pa. 23, 225 A.2d 670 (1967)	Optometrist	Health care (Optometry)	PA	3f, 9, 10
Hayes v. Parkiane Hosiery Co.	24 Conn.Supp. 218, 189 A.2d 522 (Super.Ct. Hartford Cty. 1963)	Sale of business	Hosiery store	CT	14
Hayes-Albion Corp. v. Kuberski	421 Mich. 170, 364 N.W.2d 609 (1984) reh'g denied, 42 Mich. 1202 (1985)	Engineer	Engineering	MI	2, 13
HBD, Inc. v. Ryan	203 A.D.2d 326, 610 N.Y.S.2d 300 (App.Div. 2d Dep't 1994)	Income tax preparer	Income tax preparation	NY	2, AT-30A
Headquarters Buick-Nissan v. Michael Oldsmobile	149 A.D.2d 745, 539 N.Y.S.2d 355 (1st Dep't 1989)	No covenant	No covenant	NY	14
Heatron v. Shackelford	898 F.Supp. 1491, 10 IER Cases 1736 (D. Kan. 1995)	Team leader	Heating element manufacturing	KN	3b, 5
Hebb v. Stump, Harvey & Cook, Inc.	25 Md.App. 478, 334 A.2d 563, cert. denied, 275 Md. 749 (1975)	Salesperson	Insurance	MD	4
Hefelfinger v. David	305 So.2d 823 (Fla. 1st Dist.Ct.App. 1975	Physician	Health care (Pediatrics)	FL	8
Heideck v. Kent Gen. Hosp., Inc.	446 A.2d 1095 (Del.Super. 1982)	No covenant	No covenant	DE	8

Hekimian Laboratories v. Domain Sys.	664 F.Supp. 493, 2 IER Cases 928 (S.D. Fla. 1987)	Corporate officer (director, systems engineering)	Telecommunications testing (remote access)	MD	3, 3f
Hekimian Laboratories v. Domain Sys.	664 F.Supp. 493, 2 IER Cases 928 (S.D. Fla. 1987)	Engineer	Telecommunications testing (remote access)	MD	3, 3f
Helms Boys, Inc. v. Brady	171 W.Va. 66, 297 S.E.2d 840 (1982)	Salesperson	Appliance and furniture retailing	VA	2
Helms Boys, Inc. v. Brady	171 W.Va. 66, 297 S.E.2d 840 (1982)	Salesperson	Furniture and appliances (retail)	VA	2
Helms Boys, Inc. v. Brady	171 W.Va. 66, 297 S.E.2d 840 (1982)	Salesperson	Furniture and appliances (retail)	WV	2, 3, 3f
Hemminger v. Johnson	85-CA-1987-MR, LEXIS, All States, KY (Ky.Ct.App. 1986)	Veterinarian	Veterinary medicine	KY	11
Henshaw v. Kroecke	656 S.W.2d 416 (Tex. 1983)	Consultant (partnership)	Management (medical and dental practices)	TX	3
Herring Gas Co. v. Whiddon	616 So.2d 892 (Miss. 1993)	Sale of business	Liquefied petroleum gas	MS	3d
Herrington v. Hall	624 S.W.2d 148 (Mo.App. 1981)	Operator	Car repair	MO	3d, 10
Herrman & Andreas Ins. Agency v. Appling	800 S.W.2d 312 (Tex.Civ.App., Corpus Christi 1990)	Salesperson (partner)	Insurance	TX	AT-12, AT-40
Hesse v. Grossman	152 Cal.App.2d 536, 313 P.2d 625 (1949)	No covenant	No covenant	CA	10
Hice v. Cole	295 S.W.2d 661 (Tex.Civ.App.— Beaumont 1956)	Sale of business	Liquefied petroleum gas	TX	3f
Higdon Food Serv. v. Walker & Kesterson Meat Co.	641 S.W.2d 750 (Ky. 1982)	Salesperson	Grocery (wholesale)	KY	2, 3, 3a, 3b, 3g, 8, 14

Case	Citation	Occupation	Product/Service	State	Sections
Hiss v. Great N. Am. Cos., Inc.	871 S.W.2d 218 (Tex.Ct.App., Dallas 1993)	Occupation not specified	Office supply telemarketing	TX	7
Hogan v. Bergen Brunswig Corp.	153 N.J. Super. 37, 378 A.2d 1164 (App.Div. 1977) (per curiam)	Salesperson	Dental lab	NJ	3d, 3f, 8
Hogan v. Bergen Brunswig Corp.	153 N.J.Super. 37, 378 A.2d 1164 (App. Div. 1977) (per curiam)	Salesperson	Dental lab supplies	NY	3c
Hollander v. Capon	853 S.W.2d 723 (Tex.Ct.App.—Houston [1st Dist.] 1993)	No covenant	No covenant	TX	AT-17
Hollingsworth Solderless Terminal Co. v. Turley	622 F.2d 1324 (9th Cir. 1980) (applying California law)	Salesperson	Connectors (electrical)	CA	2, 3, 3a, 5, 9, 12, 14
Holloway v. Brown	171 Ga. 481, 155 S.E. 917 (1930)	Sale of business	Restaurant	GA	8
Holloway v. Faw, Casson & Co.	319 Md. 324, 572 A.2d 510 (1990)	Accountant	Accounting	MD	2, 3f, 4, 10, 11, 14
Holloway v. Faw, Casson & Co.	78 Md.App. 205, 552 A.2d 1311 (1989) (Holloway I), cert. granted, 559 A.2d 375, aff'd in part and rev'd in part, 319 Md. 324, 572 A.2d 510 (1990)	Accountant	Accounting	MD	2, 3g, 4, 10, 11, 14
Holloway v. Faw, Casson & Co.	319 Md. 324, 572 A.2d 510 (1990)	Accountant	Accounting	NH	10
Holman v. Korsen Protection Servs.	580 N.E.2d 984 (Ind.App. 2d Dist. 1991)	Engineer	Fire detection and extinguishing equipment	IN	AT-18
Holman v. Korsen Protection Servs.	580 N.E.2d 984 (Ind.App.2d Dist. 1991)	Estimator	Fire detection and extinguishing equipment	IN	AT-18
Holsen v. Marshall & Lisley Bank	52 Wis.2d 281, 190 N.W.2d 189 (1971)	Occupation not specified	Studio (not specified as to type)	WI	3f
Holt v. Holt	751 S.W.2d 426 (Tenn.App. 1988)	No covenant	No covenant	TN	3

Holts Cigar Co. v. 222 Liberty Assocs.	404 Pa.Super. 578, 591 A.2d 743 (1991)	No covenant	No covenant	PA	10, 14
Home Beneficial Ass'n v. White	180 Tenn. 585, 177 S.W.2d 545 (1944)	No covenant	No covenant	TN	3
Home Gas Corp. v. Stafford Fuels	130 N.H. 74, 534 A.2d 390 (1987)	Distributorship agreement	Heating fuel	NH	2, 3g, 5
Hoppe v. Preferred Risk Mut. Ins. Co.	470 So.2d 1161 (Ala. 1985)	Salesperson	Insurance	AL	1, 3
Hopper v. All Pet Animal Clinic, Inc.	861 P.2d 531, 9 IER Cases 554 (Wyo. 1993)	Veterinarian	Veterinary medicine	WY	2, 3, 3a, 3b, 3c, 3d, 3e, 3f, 4, 6, 7, 8, 9, 10, 13, AT-4, AT-21, AT-73, AT-82, AT-93
Hotel Riviera v. Torres	97 Nev. 399, 632 P.2d 1155 (1981)	Chief operating officer	Hotel	NV	2, 3f, 14
House of Vision, Inc. v. Hiyane	37 Ill.2d 32, 225 N.E.2d 21 (1967)	Physician	Health care (Ophthalmology)	IL	2, 3d, 3f, 4
Household Fin. Corp. v. Sutton	130 W.Va. 277, 43 S.E.2d 144 (1947)	Manager (branch)	Finance	WV	3, 9, 10
Howard v. Babcock	6 Cal.4th 409, 863 P.2d 150 (Cal. 1993)	Attorney (partner)	Law	CA	1, 10, 13, 14
Howard v. Babcock	863 P.2d 150 (Cal. 1993)	Attorney (partner)	Law	GA	13

Case	Citation	Position	Industry	State	References
Howard v. Babcock	7 Cal.Rptr.2d 687 (Ct.App. 1992), aff'd in part and rev'd in part, 6 Cal.4th 409, 25 Cal.Rptr. 80, 863 P.2d 150 (1993)	Attorney (partner)	Law	NJ	AT-49, AT-95
Howard Johnson & Co. v. Feinstein	241 Ill.App.3d 828, 182 Ill.Dec. 396, 609 N.E.2d 930 (1st Dist. 1993)	Sale of business	Actuarial	IL	3, AT-23, AT-42
Howard Schultz & Assocs. of the Se. v. Broniec	239 Ga. 181, 236 S.E.2d 265 (1977)	Auditor	Not specified	GA	2, 3, 3d, 3e, 3f, 3g, 4, AT-86A
Hubman Supply Co. v. Irvin	67 Ohio Laws Abs. 119, 119 N.E.2d 152 (C.P. 1953)	Manager, sales (assistant)	Cleaning material	OH	5
Hudgins & Co. v. Cole	247 Ga. 182, 274 S.E.2d 462 (1981)	Supervisor	Building demolition	GA	3
Hughes v. Enterprise Irrigation Dist.	226 Neb. 230, 410 N.W.2d 494 (1987)	No covenant	No covenant	NE	7
Humana Medical Plan v. Jacobson	1992 WL 385412 (Fla. 3d Dist.Ct.App., No. 91-1396, Dec. 29, 1992)	Physician	Health care	FL	11, 14, AT-75
Hunke v. Wilcox	815 S.W.2d 855, 6 IER Cases 1358 (Tex.Ct.App.—Corpus Christi 1991)	Dentist	Health care (Dentistry (pediatric))	TX	1, 2, 3, 9, 11, 14
Hyde Corp. v. Huffines	158 Tex. 566, 314 S.W.2d 763, cert. denied, 358 U.S. 898 (1958)	No covenant	No covenant	TX	2
Hyde Park Prods. Corp. v. Maximilian Lerner Corp.	65 N.Y.S.2d 316, 491 N.Y.S.2d 302, 480 N.E.2d 1084 (1985)	Sale of business	Peat moss sales	NY	5, 10

Case	Citation	Position	Industry	State	
In re Stanford Coffee Serv. Co.	499 So.2d 1314 (La.App. 4th Cir. 1986) *writ denied*, 501 So.2d 232 (La. 1987)	Salesperson (route)	Coffee	LA	1, 2
In re Uniservices	517 F.2d 492 (7th Cir. 1975)	Corporate officer (chief executive officer)	Laundry, uniform rental	IN	2
Independent Metal Strap Co. v. Cohen	96 A.D.2d 830, 465 N.Y.S.2d 579 (2d Dep't 1983)	Salesperson	Not specified	NY	3f
Industrial Corp. v. Marlow	292 Ala. 407, 295 So.2d 396 (1976)	Manager, sales	Not specified	AL	1
Industrial Corp. v. Marlow	292 Ala. 407, 295 So.2d 396 (1976)	Salesperson	Not specified	AL	1
Ingersoll-Rand Co. v. Ciavatta	110 N.J. 609, 542 A.2d 879, 3 IER Cases 1285 (1988)	Engineer	Construction (mining equipment manufacturer) engineering	NJ	2, 3d, 3e, 14
Ingraham v. University of Maine at Orano	441 A.2d 691 (Me. 1982)	No covenant	No covenant	ME	5
Instant Air Freight Co. v. C.F. Air Freight, Inc.	882 F.2d 797 (3d Cir. 1989)	No covenant	No covenant	PA	6
Instrumentalist Co. v. Band, Inc.	134 Ill.App.3d 884, 89 Ill.Dec. 530, 480 N.E.2d 1273 (1985)	Editor	Magazine	IL	2, 3f
Instrumentalist Co. v. Band, Inc.	134 Ill.App.3d 884, 89 Ill.Dec. 530, 480 N.E.2d 1273 (1985)	Manager (advertising)	Magazine	IL	2, 3f
Insulation Corp. v. Brobston	11 IER Cases 170 (Pa. Super., No. 322 Philadelphia 1994, Nov. 3, 1995)	Manager (sales)	Insulation	PA	3, 8

Case	Citation	Position	Industry	Jurisdiction	Sections
Insulation Corp. v. Brobston	1995 Pa.Super. LEXIS 3370, 11 IER Cases 170 (Pa. Super., No. 322 Philadelphia 1994, Nov. 3, 1995)	Sales manager	Insulation	PA	3, 8
Insurance Agents v. Abel	388 N.W.2d 531 (Iowa App. 1983)	Salesperson	Insurance	IA	3c
Insurance Assocs. Corp. v. Hansen (Hansen I)	111 Idaho 206, 723 P.2d 190 (Ct.App. 1986)	Salesperson	Insurance	ID	3c, 3g, 8, 10
Insurance Assocs. Corp. v. Hansen (Hansen II)	116 Idaho 948, 782 P.2d 1230 (1989)	Salesperson	Insurance	ID	2, 10, 11
Insurance Center v. Hamilton	218 Ga. 597, 129 S.E.2d 801 (1963)	Salesperson	Insurance	GA	11
Insurance Center, Inc. v. Taylor	94 Idaho 896, 499 P.2d 1252 (1972)	Salesperson	Insurance	ID	2, 3, 3f, 4
Insurance Center, Inc. v. Taylor	94 Idaho 896, 499 P.2d 1252 (1972)	Salesperson	Insurance	WY	4
Insurance Field Servs. v. White & White Inspection	384 So.2d 303 (Fla. 3d Dist.Ct.App. 1980)	Manager (branch)	Insurance underwriting, inspection, auditing, and loss-control	FL	9
Interfirst Bank Clifton v. Fernandez	853 F.2d 292 (5th Cir. 1988)	No covenant	No covenant	KS	12
International Collection Serv. v. Gibbs	510 A.2d 1325 (Vt. 1986)	Salesperson	Debt collection	VT	12
Investor Access Corp. v. Doremus & Co.	588 N.Y.S.2d 842 (App.Div. 2d Dep't 1992)	Account executive (senior)	Investments	NY	3, 3f
Investors Diversified Servs. v. McElroy	645 S.W.2d 338 (Tex.Ct.App. 1982)	Salesperson	Securities	TX	3f, 3g

Case	Citation	Position	Industry	State	References
Iowa Glass Depot, Inc. v. Jindrich	338 N.W.2d 376 (Iowa 1983)	Manager	Automobile glass installation	IA	2, 3b, 3c, 3d, 3e, 3f, 4, 5
Iredell Digestive Disease Clinic, P.A. v. Petrozza	92 N.C.App. 21, 373 S.E.2d 449 (1988), *aff'd*, 324 N.C. 327, 377 S.E.2d 750 (1989)	Physician	Health care (Gastroenterology and internal medicine)	NC	3, 3d, 3f, 4, 5, 7, 10, 11, 14
Iroquois Indus. Corp. v. Popik	415 N.E.2d 4 (Ill.App. 1980)	Salesperson	Paper and packaging products	IL	2
Isuani v. Manske-Sheffield Radiology Group	798 S.W.2d 346 (Tex.Ct.App.—Beaumont 1990), *reversed*, 802 S.W.2d 235 (Tex.) *on remand*, 805 S.W.2d 602 (Tex.Civ.App., Beaumont 1991)	Physician (partner)	Health care (Radiology)	TX	2, 3f, 4, 7, 14, AT-66
J.D. Marshall Int'l v. Fradkin	87 Ill.App.3d 118, 42 Ill.Dec. 509, 409 N.E.2d 4 (1st Dist. 1980)	Corporate officer (director, division)	Power generator set exporting	IL	2, 3
J.T. Miller Co. v. Madel	176 Mont. 49, 575 P.2d 1321 (1978)	Salesperson	Insurance	MT	1, 3d, 3e, 3f, 14
J.W. Hunt & Co. v. Davis	437 S.E.2d 557 (S.C. 1993)	Accountant (partner)	Accounting	SC	3a, AT-49
Jackes-Evans Mfg. Co. v. Christen	848 S.W.2d 553, 8 IER Cases 469 (Mo.App. 1993)	Manager, sales	Barbecue and fireplace accessories	MO	5, 10, AT-12, AT-21
Jackson v. Caldwell	18 Utah 2d 81, 415 P.2d 667 (1976)	No covenant	No covenant	NE	2
Jackson v. Fair	846 F.2d 811 (1st Cir. 1988)	No covenant	No covenant	MA	14
Jackson & Coker v. Hart (Hart II)	261 Ga. 371, 405 S.E.2d 253, 6 IER Cases 1000 (1991)	Recuiter	Employment agency (physicians)	GA	1, 2, 3, 3d, 3f, 3g, 4, 8, 9, 11, AT-20

Case	Citation	Type	Industry/Occupation	State	Sections
Jenkins v. Jenkins Irrigation	244 Ga. 95, 259 S.E.2d 47 (1979)	Sale of business	Sprinkler systems (underground; sales and installation)	GA	3, 4, AT-23, AT-53A
Jenson v. Olson	144 Mont. 224, 395 P.2d 465 (1964)	Sale of business	Dairy product retailing	KS	14
Jewel Box Stores Corp. v. Morrow	272 N.C. 659, 158 S.E.2d 840 (1968)	Sale of business	Jeweler	NC	3e, 3f
Jewel Tea Co. v. Watkins	26 Colo.App. 494, 145 P. 719 (1915)	Salesperson (route)	Coffee and tea	CO	3f
Jewett Orthopaedic Clinic, P.A. v. White	629 So.2d 922, 18 Fla. L. Weekly D2548 (Fla. 5th Dist.Ct.App. 1993)	Physician	Health care (Orthopedic surgery (hands))	FL	1, 3, 5, 6, AT-75
Jim w. Miller Constr. v. Schaefer	298 N.W.2d 455 (Minn. 1980)	Salesperson	Real estate	MN	2
John Roane, Inc. v. Tweed	33 Del.Ch. 4, 89 A.2d 548 (1952)	Adjuster	Insurance	DE	2, 3f
John F. Matull & Assocs. v. Cloutier	194 Cal.App.3d 1049, 240 Cal.Rptr. 211, 2 IER Cases 1731 (1987)	Attorney	Law (Labor)	CA	2
John F. Matull & Assocs. v. Cloutier	194 Cal.App.3d 1049, 240 Cal.Rptr. 211, 2 IER Cases 1731 (1987)	Consultant	Law (Labor)	CA	2
John Jay Esthetic Salon v. Woods	377 So.2d 1363 (La.App. 4th Cir. 1979)	Hair stylist	Beauty	LA	1, 3g
John G. Bryant Co. v. Sling Testing & Repair	471 Pa. 1, 369 A.2d 1164 (1977)	Salesperson	Industrial material-lifting equipment	PA	2, 3e, 3f, 4, 5, 6, 14
Johnson v. Lee	243 Ga. 642, 423 S.E.2d 49 (Ga.App. 1992)	Hair stylist	Beauty	GA	3d

Case	Citation	Position	Industry	State	Sections
Juliette Fowler Homes, Inc. v. Welch Assocs.	793 S.W.2d 660 (Tex. 1990)	Fund raising contract	Not specified	TX	3, 3d, 3g, 4, 10, AT-91
Junior Salesman of Fla. v. Bogeais	541 So.2d 676 (Fla. 5th Dist.Ct.App. 1989), *reh'g denied* (April 19, 1989)	Salesperson (independent contractor)	Confection	FL	1
Justin Belt Co. v. Yost	502 S.W.2d 681 (Tex. 1973)	Manager (general)	Boot and belt manufacturing	TX	13
Kadis v. Britt	224 N.C. 154, 29 S.E.2d 543 (1944)	Debt collector	Clothing retailing	NC	3, 3b
Kadis v. Britt	224 N.C. 154, 29 S.E.2d 543 (1944)	Delivery person	Clothing retailing	NC	3, 3b, 3e
Kaplan v. Nalpak Corp.	158 Cal.App.2d 197, 322 P.2d 226 (1958)	Sale of business	Hand truck manufacturing	CA	3f
Kari Family Clinic of Chiropractic P.A. v. Bohnen	349 N.W.2d 868 (Minn.Ct.App. 1984)	Chiropractor	Health care (Chiropractic)	MN	3c
Karlin v. Weinberg	77 N.J. 408, 390 A.2d 1161 (1978)	Physician	Health care (Dermatology)	GA	AT-65
Karlin v. Weinberg	77 N.J. 408, 390 A.2d 1161 (1978)	Physician	Health care (Dermatology)	NJ	2, 3, 3b, 3d, 3f
Karpinski v. Ingrasci	28 N.Y.2d 45, 320 N.Y.S.2d 1, 268 N.E.2d 751 (1971)	Dentist	Health care (Oral surgery)	NV	3
Karpinski v. Ingrasci	28 N.Y.2d 45, 320 N.Y.2d 1 268 N.E.2d 751 (1971)	Dentist	Health care (Oral surgery)	NY	2, 3, 3f, 5, 11
Kasco Servs. Corp. v. Benson	831 P.2d 86 (Utah 1992)	Salesperson	Meat cutters and grinders	UT	3, 5, 9, AT-81

				FL	3f
Kenco Chem. & Mfg. Co. v. Railey	286 So.2d 272 (Fla. 1st Dist.Ct.App. 1973)	Occupation not specified	Chemical		
Kennedy v. Kennedy	195 A.D.2d 229, 607 N.Y.S.2d 773 (4th Dep't 1994)	Occupation not specified	Advertising	NY	AT-59
Kennedy v. Wackenhut Corp.	41 Or.App. 275, 599 P.2d 1126, modified, reh'g granted, 42 Or.App. 435, 601 P.2d 474 (1979)	Occupation not specified	Not specified	OR	3f
Kensington Court Assocs. v. Gullo	180 A.D.2d 888, 579 N.Y.S.2d 485 (3d Dep't 1992)	No covenant	No covenant	NY	5
Kersten v. Pioneer Hi-Bred Int'l	626 F.Supp. 647 (N.D. Iowa 1985)	No covenant	No covenant	IA	6
Key Temporary Personnel, Inc. v. Cox	884 P.2d 1213 (Okla. 1994)	Account manager	Employment agency (temporary)	OK	4
Key Temporary Personnel, Inc. v. Cox	884 P.2d 1213 (Okla. 1994)	Manager (account)	Employment agency (temporary)	OK	4
Key v. Perkins	173 Okla. 99, 46 P.2d 530 (1935) (per curiam)	Sale of business	Undertaking, furniture and hardware	OK	1
Keystone Life Ins. Co. v. Marketing Mgmt., Inc.	687 S.W.2d 89 (Tex.Ct.App.—Dallas 1985, no writ)	Independent contractor agreement	Insurance	TX	5
Kimble v. Dell Broadcasting Corp.	592 N.Y.S.2d 195 (App.Div. 4th Dep't 1992)	News director	Broadcasting (radio)	NY	AT-8
King Records, Inc. v. Brown	21 A.D.2d 593, 252 N.Y.S.2d 988 (1964)	Recording artist (musical vocalist)	Record company	NY	2
King Records, Inc. v. Brown	21 A.D.2d 593, 252 N.Y.S.2d 988 (1964)	Singer	Record company	NY	2
Kirschbaum v. Jones	206 Ga. 192, 56 S.E.2d 484 (1949)	Occupation not specified	Not specified	GA	3g

Case	Citation	Occupation	Industry	State	
Knowles Broadcasting Co. v. Oreto	3 Mass.App. 707, 322 N.E.2d 791 (1975)	Occupation not specified	Broadcasting	MA	2, 6
Knowles-Zeswith Music v. Cara	260 A.2d 171 (Del.Ch. 1969)	Salesperson	Musical instruments	DE	2, 3, 3f, 4, 11, 14
Knox Kershaw, Inc. v. Kershaw	598 So.2d 1372 (Ala. 1992)	Sale of business	Railroad track maintenance equipment manufacturing	AL	9, 10, AT-42
Koger Properties v. Adams-Cates Co.	247 Ga. 68, 274 S.E.2d 329 (1981)	Corporate officer (executive)	Developer (office park)	GA	3d, 4, AT-55
Koppers Prods. Co. v. Readio	60 R.I. 207, 197 A. 441 (1938)	Manager (regional)	Tar products	RI	3, 4, 14
Kozuch v. Cra-Mar Video Center, Inc.	478 N.E.2d 110 (Ind.App. 1985)	No covenant	No covenant	IN	7
Kraft Agency, Inc. v. Delmonico	110 A.D.2d 177, 494 N.Y.S2d 77 (4th Dep't 1985)	Sale of business	Insurance agency	NY	4
Krauss v. M. L. Klaster & Sons	434 Pa. 403, 254 A.2d 1 (1969)	Corporate officer	Building supplies	PA	3, 3f, 9, AT-16, AT-42
Krauss v. M. L. Klaster & Sons	434 Pa. 403, 254 A.2d 1 (1969)	Corporate officer (executive)	Building supply	PA	3, 3f, 9, AT-16, AT-42
Krauss v. M. L. Klaster & Sons	434 Pa. 403, 254 A.2d 1 (1969)	Corporate officer (director)	Building supply	PA	3, 3f, 9, AT-16, AT-42
Kreger Glass Co. v. Kreger	49 S.W.2d 260 (Mo.Ap. 1932)	Sale of business	Glass (window and plate installation)	MO	9
Kroger v. Stop & Shop Cos.	13 Mass.App. 310, 432 N.E.2d 566, *further appellate review denied* (1982)	Corporate officer (vice president)	Grocery and discount pharmacy chain retailing	MA	1, 2, 3f, 4, 14

Case	Citation	Role	Industry	State	Factors
Landmark Fin. Servs. v. Tarpley	236 Ga. 586, 224 S.E.2d 736 (1976)	Manager (office)	Financial services	GA	3
Landry v. William B. Reily & Co.	524 So.2d 750 (La.App. 3d Cir. 1988)	Salesperson (route)	Coffee	LA	1, 2, 3, 3a, 3b, 3c, 5, 6
Lane Co. v. Taylor	174 Ga.App. 356, 330 S.E.2d 112 (1985)	Manager	Property management	GA	2, 3, 3d, 3g, 4
Lane Co. v. Taylor	174 Ga.App. 356, 330 S.E.2d 112 (1985)	Property manager	Property management (apartment)	GA	2, 3, 4
Lareau v. O'Nan	355 S.W.2d 679 (Ky.Ct.App. 1962)	Physician	Health care	KY	3e, 6
Larsen v. Walton Plywood Co.	65 Wash.2d 1, 390 P.2d 677, modified on reh'g, 65 Wash.2d 21, 396 P.2d 879 (1964)	No covenant	No covenant	WA	10
Las Vegas Novelty v. Fernandez	106 Nev. 113, 787 P.2d 772 (1990) (per curiam)	Settlement agreement	Souvenir wholesaler	NV	3c, 5, 14
Lassen v. Benton	86 Ariz. 323, 346 P.2d 137, modified, 87 Ariz. 72, 347 P.2d 1012 (1959)	Veterinarian	Veterinary medicine	AZ	3, 3f, 4, 5, 14
Lavey v. Edwards	264 Or. 331, 505 P.2d 342 (1973)	Trader (wood products)	Lumber	OR	3d, 3f, 4
Lawrence v. Cain	144 Ind.App. 210, 245 N.E.2d 663 (1969)	Sale of business	Photography	IN	10
LCI Communications v. Wilson	700 F.Supp. 1390 (W.D.Pa. 1988) (applying Ohio law)	Salesperson	Telecommunications products and services	OH	4
Lea v. Young	168 Wash. 496, 12 P.2d 601 (1932)	No covenant	No covenant	WA	8
Leatherman v. Management Advisors	448 N.E.2d 1048 (Ind. 1983)	Salesperson	Insurance	IN	3c, 3f

Case	Citation	Position	Industry	State	AT-90
Lee v. Levi Strauss & Co.	897 S.W.2d 501 (Tex.Ct.App.—El Paso 1995)	No covenant	No covenant	TX	
Lee Builders, Inc. v. Wells	103 A.2d 918 (Del.Ch. 1954)	No covenant	No covenant	DE	10
Lee O'Keefe Ins. Agency, Inc. v. Ferega	163 Ill.App.3d 997, 114 Ill.Dec. 919, 516 N.E.2d 1313 (1987)	Salesperson	Insurance	IL	2, 4
Lehman v. Standard Forms, Inc.	1995 Del. Ch. LEXIS 11 (Del. Chanc., C.A. No. 13688, Jan. 12, 1995) (applying Virginia law)	Manager (sales)	Printing and graphics	VA	2, 3, 3f, 8, 12
Lehman v. Standard Forms, Inc.	1995 Del. Ch. LEXIS 11 (Del. Chanc., C.A. No. 13688, Jan. 12, 1995) (applying Virginia law)	Sales manager	Business forms	VA	2, 3, 3f, 8, 12
Lehman v. Standard Forms, Inc.	1995 Del. Ch. LEXIS 11 (Del. Chanc., C.A. No. 13688, Jan. 12, 1995) (applying Virginia law)	Sales manager	Printing and graphics	VA	2, 3, 3f, 8, 12
Lehman v. Standard Forms, Inc.	1995 Del. Ch. LEXIS 11 (Del. Chanc., C.A. No. 13688, Jan. 12, 1995) (applying Virginia law)	Salesperson	Business forms	VA	2, 3, 3f, 8, 12
Lehman v. Standard Forms, Inc.	1995 Del. Ch. LEXIS 11 (Del. Chanc., C.A. No. 13688, Jan. 12, 1995) (applying Virginia law)	Salesperson	Graphics and printing	VA	2, 3, 3f, 8, 12
Lehman v. Standard Forms, Inc.	1995 Del. Ch. LEXIS 11 (Del. Chanc., C.A. No. 13688, Jan. 12, 1995) (applying Virginia law)	Salesperson	Printing and graphics	VA	2, 3, 3f, 8, 12
Lemire v. Haley	91 N.H. 357, 19 A.2d 436 (1941)	No covenant	No covenant	NH	4
Lenox v. Sound Entertainment	470 So.2d 77 (Fla. 2d Dist.Ct.App. 1985)	Disc jockey (mobile, independent contractor)	Entertainment	FL	1

Case	Citation	Occupation	Business	State	Factors
Leo Silfen, Inc. v. Cream	29 N.Y.2d 387, 328 N.Y.S.2d 423, 278 N.E.2d 636 (1972)	No covenant	No covenant	NY	2, 3, 3f, 14
Lepel High Frequency Laboratories, Inc. v. Capita	278 N.Y. 661, 16 N.E.2d 392 (1938) (per curiam)	Occupation not specified	Medical equipment (short wave electrical)	NY	2
Lesback v. Town of Torrington	698 P.2d 1141 (Wyo. 1985)	No covenant	No covenant	WY	7
Lessner Dental Laboratories v. Kidney	16 Ariz.App. 159, 492 P.2d 39 (1971)	Dental lab technician	Dental lab	AZ	2, 3a, 3f, 14
Levine v. Beckman	48 Ohio App.3d 24, 548 N.E.2d 267 (1988)	Art supervisor	Heat-applied graphics (transfers)	OH	2, 3, 4, 5, 6, 7
Levy v. Baker	528 S.W.2d 558 (Tenn.Ct.App. 1973)	Salesperson	Hearing aids	TN	2
Lewis v. American Family Ins. Group	555 S.W.2d 579 (Ky.Ct.App. 1977)	No covenant	No covenant	KY	12
Lewmor, Inc. v. Fleming	1986 WL 1244 (Del.Ch. No. 8335, Jan. 29, 1986)	Recruiter	Employment agency	DE	3, 3d, 5
Licocci v. Cardinal Assocs.	432 N.E.2d 556 (Ind.App. 1982)	Salesperson	Fund-raising products	IN	4
Licocci v. Cardinal Assocs.	445 N.E.2d 556 (Ind. 1983)	Salesperson	Fund-raising products	IN	2, 3, 3e, 3f, 4, 14
Lifesource Inst. of Fertility & Endocrinology v. Gianfortoni	18 Va.Cir. 330 (Henrico County 1989)	Physician	Health care (Obstetrics, gynecology, endocrinology and *in vitro* fertilization	VA	3
Light v. Centel Cellular Co.	883 S.W.2d 642 (Tex. 1994)	Salesperson	Cellular phones	TX	1, 3, 3a, 3b, 3c, 14, AT-4
Lincoln Towers Ins. Agency v. Farrell	90 Ill.App.3d 353, 54 Ill.Dec.817, 425 N.E.2d 1034 (1st Dist. 1981)	Salesperson	Insurance	IL	2

Case	Citation	Role	Business	State	Codes
Linville v. Servisoft of Va.	211 Va. 53, 174 S.E.2d 785 (1970)	Salesperson	Not specified	VA	3d, 8
Litigation Reprographics & Support Servs. v. Scott	599 So.2d 922 (La.App. 4th Cir. 1992)	Manager	Litigation support services	LA	3c, 3f, 14, AT-32
Litigation Reprographics & Support Servs. v. Scott	599 So.2d 922 (La.App. 4th Cir. 1992)	Salesperson	Litigation support services	LA	3c, 3f, 14, AT-32
Livingston v. Dobbs	559 So.2d 569 (Ala. 1990)	Sale of business	Restaurant	AL	AT-43
Livingston v. Macher	30 Del.Ch. 94, 54 A.2d 169 (1947)	Manager (store)	Clothing/jewelry	DE	3f
Loescher v. Policky	84 S.D. 447, 173 N.W.2d 50 (1969)	Veterinarian	Veterinary medicine	SD	1, 3c, 4, 14
Logic Assocs. v. Time Share Corp.	124 N.H. 565, 474 A.2d 1006 (1984)	License agreement	Computer equipment	NH	7
Lone Star Gas Co. v. Pippin	620 S.W.2d 922 (Tex.Ct.App.—Dallas 1981)	No covenant	No covenant	TX	2
Long Island Oil Terminals Ass'n, Inc. v. Commissioner of N.Y. State Dept. of Transp.	70 A.D.2d 303, 421 N.Y.S.2d 405 (3d Dep't 1979)	No covenant	No covenant	NY	7
Loral Corp. v. Moyes	174 Cal.App.3d 268, 219 Cal.Rptr. 836 (1985)	Corporate officer (president)	Electronics manufacturing	CA	2, 3d, 14
Loranger Constr. Co. v. C. Franklin Corp.	355 Mass. 727, 247 N.E.2d 391 (1969)	Subcontractor's agreement	Excavation contracting	MA	3f
Lord v. Lord	454 A.2d 830 (Me. 1983)	Owner (divorce)	Insurance agency	ME	2, 3b, 3c, 3d, 3f, 4, 14
Louisiana Office Sys., Inc. v. Bodreaux	298 So.2d 341 (La.App.), remanded 302 So.2d 37 (La. 1974), dismissed 309 So.2d 779 (La.App. 1975)	Service technician	Photocopiers	KS	14

Case	Citation	Service technician	Photocopiers	LA	AT-10
Louisiana Office Sys. v. Bodreaux	298 So.2d 341 (La.App.), remanded, 302 So.2d 37 (La. 1974), dismissed, 309 So.2d 779 (La.App. 1975)	Service technician	Photocopiers	LA	AT-10
Love v. Miami Laundry Co.	118 Fla. 137, 160 So. 32 (1934)	Salesperson (route)	Laundry	FL	3f
Lovelace Clinic v. Murphy	76 N.M. 645, 417 P.2d 450 (1966)	Physician	Health care	NM	2, 3, 3f, 7, 14
Lovelace Clinic v. Murphy	76 N.M. 645, 417 P.2d 450 (1966)	Physician	Health care	NV	3f
Lovell Farms, Inc. v. Levy	641 So.2d 103, 9 IER Cases 435 (Fla. 3d Dist.Ct.App. 1994)	Horticulturist	Nursery	FL	5
Loveridge v. Pendleton Woolen Mills	788 F.2d 914 (2d Cir. 1986)	No covenant	No covenant	CT	10
Lowndes Prods. v. Brower	259 S.C. 322, 191 S.E.2d 761 (1972)	Installer (equipment, factory)	Textiles	SC	7
Lowndes Prods. v. Brower	259 S.C. 322, 191 S.E.2d 761 (1972)	Manager (plant)	Textiles	SC	7
Lowndes Prods. v. Brower	259 S.C. 322, 191 S.E.2d 761 (1972)	Sales promoter	Textiles	SC	7
LSBZ Inc. v. Brokis	237 Ill.App.3d 415, 177 Ill.Dec. 866, 603 N.E.2d 1240 (2d Dist. 1992)	Hair stylist	Beauty	IL	2, 3, 5, 14
Luketich v. Goedecke, Wood & Co.	835 S.W.2d 504, 7 IER Cases 1033 (Mo.App. 1992)	Salesperson	Construction industry supplies and equipment	MO	7, 14, AT-38, AT-91
Lundgrin v. Claytor	619 F.2d 61 (10th Cir. 1980)	No covenant	No covenant	KS	5
Lyle v. Memar	259 Ga. 209, 378 S.E.2d 465 (1989)	Occupation not specified	Medical billing	GA	4

Case	Citation	Position	Industry	State	Issues
Management Recruiters of Boulder v. Miller	762 P.2d 763, 3 IER Cases 1265 (Colo.App. 1988)	Recruiter	Employment agency	CO	1, 2, 3b, 3f, 3g, 4, 7, 8, 10, 11, 14
Management Recruiters Int'l v. Professional Placement Servs.	1992 WL 61542 (Minn.Ct.App. No. C6-91-2055, Mar. 31, 1992)	Recruiter	Employment agency (telecommunications)	MN	2, 3f, 3g, 4, 5, 6, 7
Management, Inc. v. Schassberger	39 Wash.2d 321, 235 P.2d 293 (1951)	Salesperson (route)	Laundry	NH	10
Manpower of Guilford County v. Hedgecock	42 N.C.App. 515, 257 S.E.2d 109 (1979)	Manager	Employment agency (temporary)	NC	3d, 9, 14, AT-42
Manrique v. Fabbri	493 So.2d 437 (Fla. 1986)	No covenant	No covenant	FL	12
Mantek Div. of NCH Corp. v. Share Corp.	780 F.2d 702 (7th Cir. 1986)	Salesperson	Chemical products	IN	12
Manuel Lujan Ins. v. Jordan	100 N.M. 573, 673 P. 1306 (1983)	Salesperson	Insurance and bonds	NM	3c, 3g, 9, 10, 14
Marcam Corp. v. Orchard	885 F.Supp. 294 (D.C. Mass. 1995) (applying Massachusetts law)	Corporate officer (vice president)	Computer software development	MA	2, 3, 3f, 5, 6, 14
Marine Contractors v. Hurley	365 Mass. 280, 310 N.E.2d 915 (1974)	Estimator	Marine contracting	MA	3, 3b, 3c, 3f, 4, 14
Marine Contractors v. Hurley	365 Mass. 280, 310 N.E.2d 915 (1974)	Supervisor (field)	Marine contracting	MA	3b, 3c, 3f, 4
Marine Forwarding & Shipping Co. v. Barone	154 So.2d 528 (La.App. 1963)	Corporate officer (director)	Freight forwarding	LA	1
Marine Forwarding & Shipping Co. v. Barone	154 So.2d 528 (La.App. 1963)	Corporate officer (president)	Freight forwarding	LA	1
Marine Forwarding & Shipping Co. v. Barone	154 So.2d 528 (La.App. 1963)	Manager	Freight forwarding	LA	1

Case	Citation	Position	Product/Industry	State	AT-7
Mashburn v. Tri-State Motor Transit Co.	841 S.W.2d 249 (Mo.App. 1992)	No covenant	No covenant	MO	
Mason Corp. v. Kennedy	286 Ala. 639, 244 So.2d 383 (1968)	Salesperson	Hardware, home improvement products, tools	AL	3f, 4, 5, 14
Massachusetts Indem. & Life Ins. Co. v. Dresser	269 Md. 364, 306 A.2d 213 (1973)	Salesperson	Insurance	MD	11
Masterclean of N.C. v. Gay	82 N.C.App. 45, 345 S.E.2d 692 (1986)	Asbestos-abatement technician	Asbestos abatement	NC	3f, 6, 7, 8, 14
Mastrom, Inc. v. Warren	18 N.C.App. 199, 196 S.E.2d 528 (1973)	Counsellor	Financial management	NC	3b
Matter of Cent. Watch	22 B.R. 561, 9 Bankr.Ct.Dec. 523 (1982)	Corporate officer (president)	Security service	WI	3e
Matter of Isbell	27 B.R. 926 (Bankr. W.D.Wis. 1988)	Sale of business	Bar	WY	10
Matthal v. Proskowetz	537 S.W.2d 320 (Tex.Civ.App. 1976)	Salesperson	Hearing aids	NH	10
Matthews v. Barnes	155 Tenn. 110, 293 S.W.2d 993 (1927)	Counter person	Car rental	TN	2
Mattison v. Johnston	152 Ariz. 109, 730 P.2d 286 (1986)	Hair stylist	Beauty	AZ	3, 10
Maupin v. Stansbury	575 S.W.2d 695 (Ky.Ct.App. 1978)	No covenant	No covenant	KY	7
Max Garelick, Inc. v. Leonardo	105 R.I. 142, 250 A.2d 354 (1969)	Exclusive purchase contract	Grain	RI	4
May v. Young	125 Conn. 1, 2 A.2d 385 (1938)	Engineer	Industrial engineering	CT	2, 3, 3f, 3g, 11

McNease v. National Motor Club	238 Ga. 53, 231 S.E.2d 58 (1976)	Manager (district)	Insurance (automobile)	GA	4
McNeel Marble Co. v. Robinette	259 Ala. 66, 65 So.2d 221 (1953)	Manager, sales	Monuments and mausoleums	AL	3
McNeill Group v. Restivo	252 Ga. 112, 311 S.E.2d 831 (1984)	Occupation not specified	Not specified	GA	3
McRand, Inc. v. van Beelen	138 Ill.App.3d 1045, 93 Ill.Dec. 471, 486 N.E.2d 1306 (1st Dist. 1985)	Corporate officer (vice president)	Awards program planning	IL	2, 3, 3c, 3d, 3f, 3g, 4, 5, 6, 11, 14
McRand, Inc. v. van Beelen	138 Ill.App.3d 1045, 93 Ill.Dec. 471, 486 N.E.2d 1306 (1st Dist. 1985)	Corporate officer (vice president)	Incentive awards program planning	NY	3c
McRand, Inc. v. van Beelen	138 Ill.App.3d 1045, 93 Ill.Dec. 471, 486 N.E.2d 1306 (1985)	Corporate officer (director)	Incentive awards program planning	NY	3c
McRand, Inc. v. van Beelen	138 Ill.App.3d 1045, 93 Ill.Dec. 471, 486 N.E.2d 1306 (1st Dist. 1985)	Manager (senior accounts)	Awards program planning	IL	2, 3, 3c, 3d, 3f, 3g, 4, 5, 6, 11, 14
McRand, Inc. v. van Beelen	138 Ill.App.3d 1045, 93 Ill.Dec. 471, 486 N.E.2d 1306 (1985)	Manager (senior accounts)	Incentive awards program planning	NY	3c
McSlain v. Nursefinders of Mobile	598 So.2d 853 (Ala. 1992)	Recruiter	Employment agency (temporary, nurses)	AL	AT-57
Mead v. Anton	33 Wash.2d 741, 207 P.2d 227 (1949)	Sale of business	Restaurant	NH	10
Mead v. Anton	33 Wash.2d 741, 207 P.2d 227 (1949)	Sale of business	Restaurant	WA	10
Medical Specialists, Inc. v. Sleweon	652 N.E.2d 517, 10 IER Cases 1202 (Ind.App. 1995)	Physician	Health care	IN	3f, AT-75

Case	Citation	Role	Industry	State	Sections
Metal Lubricants Co. v. Engineered Lubricants Co.	411 F.2d 426 (8th Cir. 1969)	No covenant	No covenant	NJ	14
Metal & Salvage Ass'n, Inc. v. Siegel	121 A.D.2d 200, 503 N.Y.S.2d 26 (1st Dep't 1986)	No covenant	No covenant	NY	6, 14
Meteor Indus. v. Metalloy Indus.	149 A.D.2d 483, 539 N.Y.S.2d 972 (2d Dep't 1989)	Corporate officer (president)	Metal buying and selling (scrap, rod and mill products)	NY	3d, 5, 10
Meteor Indus. v. Metalloy Indus.	149 A.D.2d 483, 539 N.Y.S.2d 972 (2d Dep't 1989)	Sale of business	Metal buying and selling (scrap, rod and mill products)	NY	3d, 5, 10
Metro Traffic Control, Inc. v. Shadow Traffic Network	22 Cal.App.4th 853, 27 Cal.Rptr.2d 573 (Cal.App. 2 Dist. 1994)	Reporter (traffic)	Radio	CA	2, 3f, 7, 13
Metropolitan Ice Co. v. Ducas	291 Mass. 403, 196 N.E. 856 (1935)	Sale of business	Ice	MA	4, 14
Metropolitan Medical Group, P.C. v. Eaton	154 A.D.2d 252, 546 N.Y.S.2d 90 (1st Dep't 1989)	Psychologist	Health care (psychology)	NY	6
Metts v. Wenberg	158 S.C. 411, 155 S.E. 734 (1930)	Sale of business	Barber shop	SC	3f
Meyer v. Wineburgh	110 F.Supp. 957 (D.D.C. 1953)	Exterminator	Pest control	DC	3c, 3f
Meyer Ventures, Inc. v. Barnak	1990 WL 172648 (Del.Ch. No. 11502, November 2, 1990)	Recruiter	Employment agency (environmental, health, safety, and clinical health care industries)	DE	2, 5, 10
Miami Elecs. Center, Inc. v. Saporta	597 So.2d 903 (Fla. 3d Dist. Ct.App. 1992)	Shopping center management agreement	Shopping center	FL	6, AT-97
Michael I. Weintraub, M.D., P.C. v. Schwartz	131 A.D.2d 663, 516 N.Y.S.2d 946 (2d Dep't 1987)	Physician	Health care (Neurology)	NY	3f, 8

Microbiological Research Corp. v. Muna	625 P.2d 690 (Utah 1981)	Corporate officer (president)	Medical diagnostic kit manufacturing	UT	2
Microbiological Research Corp. v. Muna	625 P.2d 690 (Utah 1981)	Immunologist	Medical diagnostic kit manufacturing	UT	2
Microbiological Research Corp. v. Muna	625 P.2d 690 (Utah 1981)	Manager (general)	Medical diagnostic kit manufacturing	UT	2
Microbiological Research Corp. v. Muna	625 P.2d 690 (Utah 1981)	Microbiologist	Medical diagnostic kit manufacturing	UT	2
Microbiological Research Corp. v. Muna	625 P.2d 690 (Utah 1981)	Scientist	Medical diagnostic kit manufacturing	UT	2
Mid-States Paint & Chem. Co. v. Herr	746 S.W.2d 613 (Mo.App. 1988)	Salesperson	Paints	MO	2, 3d, 3f, 4, 7
Mid-West Presort Mailing Servs., Inc. v. Clark	No. 13215 (Ohio App. 9th Dist. 1988) (LEXIS States library, Ohio file)	Occupation not specified	Mail (pre-sort)	OH	AT-11
Middlesex Neurological Assocs. v. Cohen	3 Mass.App.Ct. 126, 324 N.E.2d 911 (1975)	Physician	Health care (Neurology)	MA	3, 9, 14
Midland-Ross Corp. v. Yokana	293 F.2d 411 (3d Cir. 1961)	No covenant	No covenant	MO	3d
Mike Bajalia, Inc., v. Pike	226 Ga. 131, 172 S.E.2d 676 (1970)	Realtor	Real estate	GA	2
Milkovich v. Sarri	295 Minn. 155, 203 N.W.2d 408 (1973)	No covenant	No covenant	MN	12
Millard Maintenance Serv. Co. v. Bernero	207 Ill.App.3d 736, 152 Ill.Dec. 692, 566 N.E.2d 379 (1st Dist. 1990)	Account executive (senior)	Building maintenance service	IL	2, 3c, 3f, 7, 14

Case	Citation	Occupation	Industry	State	
Miller v. Fairfield Bay, Inc.	247 Ark. 565, 446 S.W.2d 660 (1969)	Realtor	Real estate	AR	3f
Miller v. Fairfield Bay, Inc.	247 Ark. 565, 446 S.W.2d 660 (1969)	Salesperson	Real estate	AR	3f
Miller v. Foley	317 N.W.2d 710 (Minn. 1982)	No covenant	No covenant	MN	5
Miller v. Foulston, Siefkin, Powers & Eberhardt	246 Kan. 450, 790 P.2d 404 (1990)	Attorney (partner)	Law	KS	1
Miller v. Frankfort Bottle Gas	136 Ind.App. 456, 202 N.E.2d 395 (1964)	Delivery person	Gas (bulk)	IN	3f
Miller v. Kendall	541 P.2d 126 (Colo.App. 1975)	Instructor	Education (Music)	CO	3f, 9
Miller Constr. Co. v. First Indus. Technology Corp.	576 So.2d 748 (Fla. 3d Dist.Ct.App. 1991)	No covenant	No covenant	FL	14, AT-86
Miller Mechanical v. Ruth	300 So.2d 11 (Fla. 1974)	Occupation not specified	Not specified	FL	3, 3d, 4, 6
Miller Paper Co. v. Robert Paper Co.	901 S.W.2d 593 (Tex.Ct.App.—Amarillo 1995)	Salesperson	Chemical cleaners	TX	1, AT-4
Miller Paper Co. v. Robert Paper Co.	901 S.W.2d 593 (Tex.Ct.App.—Amarillo 1995)	Salesperson	Janitorial supplies, chemicals, and paper	TX	1, AT-4
Miller Paper Co. v. Robert Paper Co.	901 S.W.2d 593 (Tex.Ct.App.—Amarillo 1995)	Salesperson	Paper and janitorial supplies	TX	1, AT-4
Mills v. Murray	472 S.W.2d 6 (Mo.App. 1971)	Consultant	Finance (business and personal)	MO	3d, AT-68
Mills v. Murray	472 S.W.2d 6 (Mo.App. 1971)	Consultant	Management (medical and dental offices)	WY	3f, 10
Mills Constr. Co. v. Fairfield Sapphire Valley	86 N.C.App. 506, 358 S.E.2d 566 (1987)	No covenant	No covenant	NC	8

Milner Airco, Inc. of Charlotte, NC v. Morris	111 N.C.App. 866, 433 S.E.2d 811 (1993)	Installer	Air conditioning and heating equipment	NC	3, 3a, 3b, 3f, 5, 7
Milner Airco, Inc. of Charlotte, NC v. Morris	111 N.C.App. 866, 433 S.E.2d 811 (1993)	Installer's helper	Air conditioning and heating equipment	NC	3, 3a, 3b, 3f, 5, 7
Milward v. Gerstung Int'l Sport Educ.	268 Md. 483, 302 A.2d 14 (1973)	Instructor	Education (Physical)	MD	2, 3e, 3f, 14
Milwaukee Area Joint Apprenticeship Training Comm. for the Elec. Indus. v. Howell	67 F.3d 1333 (7th Cir. 1995)	No covenant	No covenant	WI	AT-17.1
Milwaukee Area Joint Apprenticeship Training Comm. for the Elec. Indus. v. Howell	67 F.3d 1333 (7th Cir. 1995)	Scholarship loan repayment agreement	Electrical trades	WI	AT-17.1
Minexa Ariz. v. Staubach	667 S.W.2d 563 (Tex.Ct.App.—Dallas 1984)	No covenant	No covenant	TX	5, 6
Minnesota Best Maid Cookie Co. v. Flour Pot Cookie Co.	412 N.W.2d 380 (Minn.Ct.App. 1987)	Settlement agreement	Cookie bakers	MN	9
Missouri Pac. R.R. v. Kansas Gas & Elec. Co.	862 F.2d 796 (10th Cir. 1988)	No covenant	No covenant	KS	12
Mo-Kan Cent. Recovery Co. v. Hedenkamp	671 S.W.2d 396 (Mo.App. 1984)	Repossessor (vehicle)	Repossession	MO	2, 3e
Modern Controls, Inc. v. Andreakis	578 F.2d 1264 (8th Cir. 1978)	Physicist	Computer equipment	MN	3c
Modern Laundry & Dry Cleaning Co. v. Farrer	536 A.2d 409 (Pa.Super. 1988)	Salesperson (route)	Laundry	PA	3a, 3b
Mohawk Maintenance Co. v. Kessler	52 N.Y.2d 276, 437 N.Y.S.2d 646, 419 N.E.2d 324 (1981)	Sale of business	Building maintenance services	NY	3d, 5, 14

Case	Citation	Position	Industry	State	Factors
Monogram Indus. v. SAR Indus.	64 Cal.App.3d 692, 134 Cal.Rptr. 714 (1976)	Sale of business	Portable toilet manufacturing	CA	1, 2, 3f, 7, 14
Moore v. Dover Veterinary Hosp.	116 N.H. 680, 367 A.2d 1044 (1976)	Veterinarian	Veterinary medicine	NH	3, 3a, 3d, 3e, 3f, 14
Moore Business Forms v. Foppiano	382 S.E.2d 499 (W.Va. 1989) (per curiam)	Salesperson	Forms (business)	WV	2, 3, 3f, 10, 14
Moorman & Givens v. Parkerson	127 La. 835, 54 So. 47 (1911)	Sale of business	Insurance agency	LA	4, 14
Morgan Lumber Sales Co. v. Toth	41 Ohio Misc. 17, 321 N.E.2d 907 (1974)	Salesperson	Lumber (wholesale)	OH	3c, 3f, 14
Morgan's Home Equip. v. Martucci	390 Pa. 618, 136 A.2d 838 (1957)	Salesperson	Medical equipment (home)	PA	2, 3, 3a, 4, 10
Morris v. Watsco, Inc.	385 Mass. 672, 433 N.E.2d 886 (1982)	No covenant	No covenant	MA	12
Morris v. Watsco, Inc.	385 Mass. 672, 433 N.E.2d 886 (1982)	No covenant	No covenant	MI	12
Morrison Metalweld Process Corp. v. Valent	97 Ill.App.3d 373, 52 Ill.Dec. 825, 422 N.E.2d 1034 (1st Dist. 1981)	Salesperson	Welding service	IL	3, 3e, 4, 6
Morse v. Municipal Court	13 Cal.3d 149, 118 Cal.Rptr. 14, 529 P.2d 46 (1974)	No covenant	No covenant	CA	1
Moshe Myerowitz, D.C., P.A. v. Howard	507 A.2d 578 (Me. 1986)	Chiropractor	Health care (Chiropractic)	ME	5, 7
Moss, Adams & Co. v. Shilling	179 Cal.App.3d 124, 224 Cal.Rptr. 456 (1986)	Accountant	Accounting	CA	2, 3a
Moss, Adams & Co. v. Shilling	179 Cal.App.3d 124, 224 Cal.Rptr. 456 (1986)	Manager	Accounting	CA	2, 3a

Case	Citation	Occupation	Industry	State	Notes
Mouldings, Inc. v. Potter	315 F.Supp. 704 (M.D.Ga. 1970)	Corporate officer (vice president)	Wood moulding manufacturing	GA	3c
Mouldings, Inc. v. Potter	315 F.Supp. 704 (M.D.Ga. 1970)	Manager (marketing)	Wood moulding manufacturing	GA	3c
Mouldings, Inc. v. Potter	315 F.Supp. 704 (M.D.Ga. 1970)	Manager (general, assistant)	Wood moulding manufacturing	GA	3c
Moz-Lew Builders v. Smith	174 Mont. 448, 571 P.2d 389 (1977)	No covenant	No covenant	MT	7
Muggill v. Reuben H. Donnelly Corp.	62 Cal.2d 239, 42 Cal.Rptr. 107, 398 P.2d 147 (1965)	Occupation not specified	Not specified	CA	1, 2, 12
Murphy v. Carron	536 S.W.2d 30 (Mo. 1976)	No covenant	No covenant	MO	7
Murphy v. Murphy	28 Ill.App.3d 475, 328 N.E.2d 642 (1975)	Sale of business	Insurance agency	IL	2
Murrco Agency v. Ryan	800 S.W.2d 600 (Tex.Ct.App.—Dallas 1990)	Salesperson	Insurance	TX	2, 3, 4, AT-72, AT-96
Mutual Loan Co. v. Pierce	245 Iowa 1051, 65 N.W.2d 405 (1954)	Manager (trainee)	Loan (small)	IA	2, 3f
My Laundry Co. v. Schmeling	129 Wis. 597, 109 N.W. 540 (1906)	Sale of business	Laundry	WI	3a
Nail Boutique v. Church	758 S.W.2d 206 (Mo.App. 1988)	Manicurist	Beauty	MO	3, 3a, 5
Nalco Chem. Co. v. Hall	237 F.Supp. 678 (E.D.La.), *aff'd*, 347 F.2d 90 (5th Cir. 1965)	Salesperson	Not specified	LA	2
Nalle Clinic Co. v. Parker	101 N.C.App. 341, 399 S.E.2d 363, 6 IER Cases 158 (1991)	Physician	Health care (Pediatric endocrinology)	NC	3, 3d, 3f, 5, 6, 7, 14
Nalle Clinic Co. v. Parker	101 N.C.App. 341, 399 S.E.2d 363, 6 IER Cases 158 (1991)	Physician	Health care (Endocrinology)	NC	3, 3d, 3f, 5, 6, 7, 14

Case	Citation		Industry	State	Sections
Napasco Int'l Western Div. v. Maxson	420 So.2d 1276 (La.App. 3d Cir. 1982)	Salesperson	Chemical products	LA	1
Nasco, Inc. v. Gimbert	239 Ga. 675, 238 S.E.2d 368 (1977)	Fund-raiser	Fund-raising	GA	12
Nashville Ry. & Light Co. v. Lawson	144 Tenn. 78, 227 S.W. 741 (1921)	No covenant	No covenant	TN	3
Nassau Sports v. Peters	352 F.Supp. 867 (E.D.N.Y. 1972)	No covenant	No covenant	NY	2
National Bank of Alaska v. J.B.L.&K. of Alaska	546 P.2d 579 (1976)	Sale of business	Insurance agency	AK	10
National Benefit Co. v. Union Hosp. Co.	45 Minn. 272, 47 N.W. 806 (1891)	Rivals' agreement	Hospital benefit certificate sales	MN	3f
National Chemsearch Corp. of N.Y. v. Hanker	309 F.Supp. 1278 (D.D.C. 1970)	Salesperson	Chemical products (commercial)	DC	3, 3d, 3f, 9, 10, 11, 12, 14
National Farmer's Union Serv. Corp. v. Edwards	220 Neb. 231, 369 N.W.2d 76 (1985)	Salesperson	Insurance	NE	3f
National Graphics Co. v. Dilley	681 P.2d 546 (Colo.App. 1984)	Occupation not specified	Graphics	CO	3, 4
National Hearing Aid Centers v. Avers	2 Mass.App.Ct. 285, 311 N.E.2d 573 (1974)	Salesperson	Hearing aids	MA	2, 14
National Micrographics v. OCE-Indus.	55 Md.App. 526, 465 A.2d 862 (1983)	Dealership agreement	Micrographics equipment	MD	10
National Motor Club of La. v. Conque	173 So.2d 238 (La.App. 3d Cir.), cert. denied, 170 So.2d 110 (1965)	Manager (district)	Automobile insurance club	LA	1, 2
National Motor Club of Mo. v. Noe	475 S.W.2d 16 (Mo. 1972)	Salesperson	Motor club	MO	3c

Case	Citation	Occupation	Industry	State	
National Oil Serv. of La. v. Brown	381 So.2d 1269 (La.App. 4th Cir. 1980)	Manager, sales	Waste oil collection	LA	1
National Oil Serv. of La. v. Brown	381 So.2d 1269 (La.App. 4th Cir. 1980)	Manager	Waste oil collection	LA	1
National Recruiters v. Cashman	323 N.W.2d 736 (Minn. 1982)	Recruiter	Employment agency	MN	3b, 3c
National Rejectors v. Trieman	409 S.W.2d 1 (Mo. 1966)	No covenant	No covenant	MO	2, 3d, 10
National School Studios v. Barrios	236 So.2d 309 (La.App. 4th Cir. 1970)	Salesperson	Photographic services (school pictures)	LA	4
National School Studios v. Superior School Photo Serv., Inc.	40 Wash.2d 263, 242 P.2d 756 (Sup.Ct. 1st Dep't 1952)	Salesperson	Photographic services (school pictures)	WA	3, 10
National Settlement Assocs. of Ga. v. Creel	256 Ga. 329, 349 S.E.2d 177 (1986)	Salesperson	Insurance	GA	3, 3d, 3f
National Starch & Chem. Corp. v. Newman	577 S.W.2d 99 (Mo.App. 1979)	Manager, sales (district)	Adhesives (industrial)	MO	12
National Survival Game of N.Y., Inc. v. NSG of LI Corp.	169 A.D.2d 760, 565 N.Y.S.2d 127 (2d Dep't 1991)	Occupation not specified	Not specified	NY	9, 10
National Teen-Ager Co. v. Scarborough	254 Ga. 467, 330 S.E.2d 117 (1985)	Corporate officer (director, state)	Beauty pageants	GA	3, 3d, 14
National Tile Bd. Corp. v. Panelboard Mfg. Co.	27 N.J. Super. 348, 99 A.2d 440 (Ch.Div. 1953)	No covenant	No covenant	NJ	14
Nationwide Advertising Serv., Inc. v. Kolar	14 Ill.App.3d 522, 302 N.E.2d 734 (1973)	Manager, sales (regional)	Advertising (personnel recruitment)	IL	2
Nationwide Mut. Ins. Co. v. Hart	73 Md.App. 406, 534 A.2d 999 (1988)	Salesperson	Insurance	MD	4, 5, 7, 14
Nazzaro v. Washington	81 N.Y.S.2d 769 (Sup.Ct. 1948)	Actor	Performing arts	NY	2
Nazzaro v. Washington	81 N.Y.S.2d 769 (Sup.Ct. 1948)	Performer (theatrical)	Performing arts	NY	2

Case	Citation	Occupation	Industry	State	
Nazzaro v. Washington	81 N.Y.S.2d 769 (Sup.Ct. 1948)	Theatrical performer (histrionics)	Performing arts	NY	2
NBZ, Inc. v. Pilarski	185 Wis.2d 827, 520 N.W.2d 93 (Wis.App. 1994)	Hair stylist	Beauty	WI	1, 2, 3, 3a, 3b, 3c, 3d, 3e, 3f, 7, 13
NCH Corp. v. Broyles	749 F.2d 247 (5th Cir. 1985)	Salesperson	Chemical cleaners	LA	1
NCN Co., Inc. v. Cavanaugh	627 N.Y.S.2d 446 (A.D. 2d Dep't 1995)	No covenant	No covenant	NY	5
Neal v. Superior Enters.	552 So.2d 1047 (La.App. 1st Cir. 1989)	Occupation not specified	Not specified	LA	8
Neeb-Kearney & Co. v. Rellstab	593 So.2d 741 (La.App. 4th Cir.), writ denied, 594 So.2d 1321 (La. 1992)	Corporate officer (vice president)	Coffee warehousing	LA	1, 2, 8, AT-84
Neff Athletic Lettering Co. v. Walters	524 F.Supp. 268 (S.D.Ohio 1981)	Salesperson	Clothing	OH	12
Nelms v. Morgan Portable Building Corp.	305 Ark. 284, 808 S.W.2d 314 (1991)	Manager (plant)	Portable building manufacturing	AR	12, AT-83
Nenow v. L.C. Cassidy & Son of Fla., Inc.	141 So.2d 636 (Fla. Dist.Ct.App. 1962)	Salesperson	Insulation	KS	14
Nesko Corp. v. Fontaine	19 Conn.Supp. 160, 110 A.2d 631 (1954)	Salesperson	Windows and doors (aluminum)	CT	3f
New England Canteen Serv. v. Ashley	372 Mass. 671, 363 N.E.2d 526 (1977)	Salesperson (route)	Food	MA	2
New England Eyecare of Waterbury, P.C. v. New England Eyecare, P.C	1991 WL 27919 (Conn. Super.Ct. No. 099465, Jan. 18, 1991)	Sale of business	Health care (Optometry practice)	CT	10

Case	Citation	Position	Industry	State	Notes
Norman Weil Textiles, Inc. v. Zaretsky	561 N.Y.S.2d 186 (App.Div. 1st Dep't 1990)	Corporate officer (president)	Textile	NY	5
North Am. Paper Co. v. Unterberger	172 Ill.App.3d 410, 122 Ill.Dec. 362, 526 N.E.2d 621, 3 IER Cases 1057 (1st Dist. 1988)	Manager (division)	Janitorial products	IL	3, 4
North Pac. Lumber Co. v. Oliver	286 Or. 639, 596 P.2d 931 (1979)	Lumber trader (hardwoods specialist)	Lumber wholesaling	OR	14
North Pac. Lumber Co. v. Moore	275 Or. 359, 551 P.2d 431 (1976)	Lumber trader (hardwoods specialist)	Lumber wholesaling	OR	2, 3f, 3g, 10, 14
Northern Telecom, Inc. v. Volt Information Sciences, Inc.	195 A.D.2d 1088, 601 N.Y.S.2d 38 (4th Dep't 1993)	Corporate officer (vice president)	Telecommunications	NY	5
Northern Va. Psychiatric Group, P.C. v. Halpern	19 Va.Cir. 279 (Fairfax County 1990)	Social worker (clinical, licensed)	Health care (social work)	VA	4
Novelty Bias Binding Co. v. Shevrin	342 Mass. 714, 175 N.E.2d 374 (1961)	Manager, sales and general	Plastic piece goods	MA	3, 3c, 3d
Novendstern v. Mt. Kisco Medical Group	177 A.D.2d 623, 576 N.Y.S.2d 329 (2d Dep't 1991)	Physician	Health care (Obstetrics and gynecology)	NY	2, 3f, 10
Numed, Inc. v. McNutt	724 S.W.2d 432 (Tex.Ct.App.—Fort Worth 1987)	No covenant	No covenant	TX	2
Nunn v. Orkin Exterminating Co.	256 Ga. 203, 350 S.E.2d 425 (1986)	Exterminator	Pest control	GA	3f, 3g
O'Brien v. Product Eng. Sales Co.	1988 WL 2436 (Ohio Ct.App. (Montgomery), No. 10417, Jan. 8, 1988) (unreported)	No covenant	No covenant	OH	3c
O'Hommell Co. v. Fink	115 W.Va. 686, 177 S.E. 619 (1934)	Salesperson	Chemicals (ceramic)	WV	3f

Case	Citation	Position	Industry	State	Issues
Olliver/Pilcher Ins. v. Daniels	148 Ariz. 530, 715 P.2d 1218 (1986)	Salesperson	Insurance	AZ	2, 3d, 3e, 3f, 4, 8, 14
Olson v. Swendiman	62 N.D. 649, 244 N.W. 870 (N.D. 1932)	Dentist	Health care (Dentistry)	ND	11, 14
Olsten Corp. v. Sommers	534 F.Supp. 395 (D. Ore. 1982)	Manager (branch)	Employment agency (temporary)	OR	3c
Olsten Corp. v. Sommers	534 F.Supp. 395 (D. Ore. 1982)	Salesperson	Employment agency (temporary)	OR	3c
Ondrasek v. Tenneson	158 Wis. 690, 462 N.W.2d 915 (Wis.Ct.App. 1990)	No covenant	No covenant	WI	12
Orange County v. Webster	503 So.2d 988 (Fla. 5th Dist.Ct.App. 1982)	No covenant	No covenant	FL	7
Orchard Container Corp. v. Orchard	601 S.W.2d 299 (Mo.App. 1980)	Corporate officer (president)	Corrugated box manufacturing	MO	3d, 3f, 4, 10
Orchid Software v. Prentice-Hall, Inc.	804 S.W.2d 208 (Tex.Ct.App.—Austin 1991)	No covenant	No covenant	TX	10
Oregon Steam Navigation Co. v. Windsor	87 U.S. (20 Wall.) 64, 22 L.Ed. 315 (1873)	Sale of steamboat	Transportation	CT	3
Original Vincent & Joseph, Inc. v. Schiavone	36 Del.Ch. 548, 134 A.2d 843 (1957)	Hair stylist	Beauty	DE	2, 3f
Orion Broadcasting, Inc. v. Forsythe	477 F.Supp. 198 (W.D. Ky. 1979)	Broadcaster	Broadcasting (Television)	KY	9
Orkin Exterminating Co. v. Broussard	346 So.2d 1274 (La.App. 3d Cir.), writ denied, 350 So.2d 902 (La. 1977)	Exterminator	Pest control	LA	1, 2

Case	Citation	Type	Industry	State	Sections
Orkin Exterminating Co. of Raleigh v. Griffin	258 N.C. 179, 128 S.E.2d 139 (1962)	Exterminator	Pest control	NC	3
Orthotic & Prosthetic Lab, Inc. v. Pott	851 S.W.2d 633 (Mo.App. 1993)	Sale of business	Orthotic and prosthetic lab	MO	13, AT-10
Osage Glass, Inc. v. Donovan	693 S.W.2d 71 (Mo. 1985)	Manager (operations)	Glass (automobile) installation	MO	2, 3, 3f, 5, 6, 9, 14, AT-21
Osta v. Moran	208 Ga.App. 544, 430 S.E.2d 837 (1993)	Physician	Health care (Oncology)	GA	2, 3f, 4, AT-23
Oudenhoven v. Nishioka	52 Wis.2d 503, 190 N.W.2d 920 (1971)	Physician	Health care (Neurosurgery)	WI	3
Overholt Crop Ins. Serv. Co. v. Bredeson	437 N.W.2d 698 (Minn.Ct.App. 1989)	Salesperson	Insurance	MN	3a, 3e, 3f, 3g, 5, 7
OVRS Acquisition Corp. v. Community Health Servs., Inc.	657 N.E.2d 117 (Ind.App. 1995) (applying Indiana procedural law and choice of law rules)	Management agreement	Health care (Respiratory therapy)	IN	7, 12
OVRS Acquisition Corp. v. Community Health Servs., Inc.	657 N.E.2d 117 (Ind.App. 1995) (applying Kentucky substantive law)	Management agreement	Health care (Respiratory therapy)	KY	3a, 3b, 3d, 3f, 10
Owens v. Penn Mut. Life Ins. Co.	851 F.2d 1053, 3 IER Cases 1144 (8th Cir. 1988)	Salesperson	Insurance	AR	2, 3, 3f
Owens v. RMA Sales	183 Ga.App. 340, 358 S.E.2d 857 (1990)	Distributorship agreement	Paint remover	GA	3
Oxman v. Sherman	239 S.C. 218, 122 S.E.2d 559 (1961)	Salesperson	Insurance	SC	2, 3f, 4, 9

Case	Citation	Position	Industry	State	Ref
Parker v. EBSCO Indus.	282 Ala. 98, 209 So.2d 383 (1968)	Corporate officer (vice president)	Advertising	AL	1
Parker v. EBSCO Indus.	282 Ala. 98, 209 So.2d 383 (1968)	Manager, sales	Advertising	AL	1
Parker v. EBSCO Indus.	282 Ala. 98, 209 So.2d 383 (1968)	Sales trainer	Advertising	AL	1
Parker Tampa Two v. Somerset Dev. Corp.	544 So.2d 1018 (Fla. 1989)	No covenant	No covenant	FL	10, AT-67
Parsons Supply v. Smith	22 Wash.App. 520, 591 P.2d 821 (1979)	Manager (business)	Supplies	WA	8
Parsons Supply v. Smith	22 Wash.App. 520, 591 P.2d 821 (1979)	Salesperson	Supplies	WA	8
Parsons Supply v. Smith	22 Wash.App. 520, 591 P.2d 821 (1979)	Secretary (officer)	Supplies	WA	8
Parsons Supply v. Smith	22 Wash.App. 520, 591 P.2d 821 (1979)	Treasurer	Supplies	WA	8
Pasant v. Jackson Nat'l Life Ins. Co.	52 F.3d 94 (5th Cir. 1995) (applying Texas law)	Corporate officer (vice president)	Insurance	TX	3b
Pasek, In re	983 F.2d 1524 (10th Cir. 1993)	Accountant	Accounting	WY	AT-15
Patterson Int'l Corp. v. Herrin	25 Ohio Misc. 79, 264 N.E.2d 361 (1970)	Salesperson	Games (coin-operated soccer)	OH	8
Paul Robinson, Inc. v. Haege	218 Ga.App. 578, 462 S.E.2d 396 (1995)	Salesperson	Artwork	GA	3g, AT-42
PCx Corp. v. Ross	168 Ill.App.3d 1047, 119 Ill.Dec. 474, 522 N.E.2d 1333 (1st Dist. 1988)	Salesperson	Computers	IL	2, 3, 3d, 3f, 3g, 5, 7, 10
Peat Marwick Main & Co. v. Haas	818 S.W.2d 381 (Tex. 1991)	Accountant (partner)	Accounting	TX	1, 3d, 3f, 3g, 4, 10, 11

Case	Citation	Position	Industry	State	No.
Perez v. Riviero	534 So.2d 914 (Fla. Dist.Ct.App. 1988)	No covenant	No covenant	FL	2
Perlmuter Printing Co. v. Strome, Inc.	436 F.Supp. 409 (N.D.Ohio 1976)	No covenant	No covenant	OH	12
Perman v. ArcVentures, Inc.	554 N.E.2d 982, 5 IER Cases 338 (Ill.App. 1st Dist. 1990)	Corporate officer (director, bioservices)	Pharmacy service	IL	3
Perman v. ArcVentures, Inc.	554 N.E.2d 982, 5 IER Cases 338 (Ill.App. 1st Dist. 1990)	Salesperson	Physician billing service	IL	3
Perry v. Moran	109 Wash.2d 691, 748 P.2d 224 (1987), *aff'd as modified,* 111 Wash.2d 885, 766 P.2d 1096 (en banc), *cert. denied,* 109 S.Ct. 328 (1989)	Accountant	Accounting	WA	2, 3, 3d, 3g, 10, 13, 14
Pestel Milk Co. v. Model Dairy Prods. Co.	39 Ohio Law Abs. 197, 52 N.E.2d 651 (Ohio App. 1943)	Salesperson (route)	Dairy	OH	AT-11
Peters v. Davidson, Inc.	172 Ind.App. 39, 359 N.E.2d 556 (1977)	Salesperson	Not specified	IN	6
Peterson v. Don Peterson & Assocs.	234 Neb. 651, 452 N.W.2d 517 (1990)	Salesperson	Insurance	NE	3d
Peterson-Jorwic Group v. Pecora	224 Ill.App.3d 460, 166 Ill.Dec. 718, 586 N.E.2d 676 (1st Dist. 1991)	Manufacturer's representative	Appliances	IL	5
Philip G. Johnson & Co. v. Salmen	211 Neb. 123, 317 N.W.2d 900 (1982)	Accountant	Accounting	NE	3, 3f, 4, 14
Philip G. Johnson & Co. v. Salmen	211 Neb. 123, 317 N.W.2d 900 (1982)	Accountant	Accounting	WY	3d

Case	Citation	Position	Business	State	Codes
Ponders, Inc. v. Norman	246 Ga. 647, 272 S.E.2d 345 (1980)	Salesperson	Office supplies	GA	3
Porter Indus. v. Higgins	680 P.2d 1339 (Colo.App. 1984)	Manager	Janitorial service	CO	1, 2, 3, 3g, 5, 7, AT-59
Portland Gasoline Co. v. Superior Mtg. Co.	150 Tex. 533, 243 S.W.2d 823 (1951)	No covenant	No covenant	TX	AT-21
Posey v. Monier Resources	768 S.W.2d 915 (Tex.Ct.App.—San Antonio 1989)	Manager, sales (regional)	Admixtures (concrete drying and setting additives)	TX	3f
Post v. Merrill, Lynch, Pierce, Fenner & Smith	48 N.Y.2d 84, 421 N.Y.S.2d 847, 397 N.E.2d 358 (1979)	Stock broker	Securities	NY	8, 14
Power Distribution, Inc. v. Emergency Power Eng'g Inc.	569 F.Supp. 54, 1 IER Cases 239 (E.D. Va. 1983)	Salesperson	Computer power supply equipment design, manufacture, and marketing	VA	3f, AT-2, AT-21
Pratt v. Prodata, Inc.	885 P.2d 786 (Utah 1994)	Computer programmer	Computer programming services	UT	AT-90
Preferred Meal Sys. v. Guse	199 Ill.App.3d 710, 145 Ill.Dec. 736, 557 N.E.2d 506 (1st Dist. 1990)	Corporate officer	Meal (preportioned) service	IL	2
Premier Indus. Corp. v. Marlow	292 Ala. 407, 295 So.2d 396, cert. denied, 419 U.S. 1033 (1974)	Salesperson	Maintenance supplies (industrial)	AL	3f
Premix, Inc. v. Zappitelli	561 F.Supp. 269 (N.D. Ohio 1983)	Chemist	Plastic molding compounds manufacturing	OH	3a, 3g, 9, 10, 14

Case	Citation	Supervisor (department)	Business	State	§§
Premix, Inc. v. Zappitelli	561 F.Supp. 269 (N.D. Ohio 1983)	Supervisor (department)	Plastic molding compounds manufacturing	OH	3a, 3g, 9, 10, 14
Presto-X-Co. v. Ewing	442 N.W.2d 85 (Iowa 1989)	Exterminator	Pest control	IA	3f, 5, 9, 11
Price v. State, Dep't of Public Saf., Lic., Con. & D.I. Div.	325 So.2d 759 (La.App. 1st Cir. 1976)	No covenant	No covenant	LA	5
Primo Enter. v. Bachner	148 A.D.2d 350, 539 N.Y.S.2d 320 (1st Dep't 1989)	Salesperson	Clothing (custom-printed, promotional)	NY	2, 3
Prinz Office Equip. Co. v. Pesko	1990 WL 7996 (Ohio Ct. App. (Summit), No. CA-14155, Jan. 31, 1990) (unreported)	Salesperson	Office equipment	OH	3c
Production Finishing Corp. v. Shields	158 Mich.App. 479, 405 N.W.2d 171 (1987)	Corporate officer (director)	Steel polishing	MI	1
Production Finishing Corp. v. Shields	158 Mich.App. 479, 405 N.W.2d 171 (1987)	Corporate officer	Steel polishing	MI	1
Professional Business Servs. v. Gustafson	285 Or. 307, 590 P.2d 729 (1979)	Bookkeeper	Medical services	OR	9
Professional Business Servs. v. Gustafson	285 Or. 307, 590 P.2d 729 (1979)	Secretary	Medical services	OR	9
Professional Investigations & Consulting Agency v. Kingsland	69 Ohio App.3d 753, 591 N.E.2d 1265 (Ohio App. 10th Dist. 1990)	Detective	Private investigation	OH	3d, 3f, 3g, 4, 5, AT-35, AT-36, AT-54, AT-86

Case	Citation	Occupation	Service/Business	State	References
Property Tax Assocs. v. Staffeldt	800 S.W.2d 349 (Tex.Ct.App.—El Paso 1990)	Attorney	Ad valorem property tax lowering service	TX	1, 3d, 3f, 4, 9, AT-1, AT-33
Property Tax Representatives, Inc. v. Chatham	891 S.W.2d 153 (Mo.App. 1995)	Appraiser	Ad valorem property tax lowering service	MO	3f, 8, 9, 10, 11, AT-19, AT-66, AT-90
Prudential Ins. Co. of Am. v. Semperean	171 Ill.App.3d 810, 121 Ill.Dec. 709, 525 N.E.2d 1016 (1st Dist. 1988)	Salesperson	Insurance	IL	3, 4
Public Sys. v. Towry	587 So.2d 829, 6 IER Cases 1076 (Ala. 1991)	Consultant	Grant application preparation	AL	2
Public Sys. v. Towry	587 S.2d 829, 6 IER Cases 1076 (Ala. 1991)	Corporate officer (vice president)	Grant application preparation	AL	2
Puga v. Suave Shoe Corp.	374 So.2d 552 (Fla. 3d Dist.Ct.App. 1979)	Occupation not specified	Shoe	FL	6
Purchasing Assocs., Inc. v. Weitz	13 N.Y.2d 267, 246 N.Y.S.2d 600, 196 N.E.2d 245 (1963)	Occupation not specified	Data processing	NY	2, 3f, 4, 14
Puritan-Bennett Corp. v. Richter	8 Kan.App.2d 311, 657 P.2d 589 (1983)	Corporate officer (director, operations)	Oxygen equipment (aircraft, emergency)	KS	3, 3a, 3c, 4, 9, 14
Puritan-Bennett Corp. v. Richter	235 Kan. 251, 679 P.2d 206 (1984)	Corporate officer (director, operations)	Oxygen equipment (aircraft, emergency)	KS	2, 3c, 14
Puritan/Churchill Chem. Co. v. Eubank	245 Ga. 334, 265 S.E.2d 16 (1980)	Salesperson	Janitorial supplies	GA	3, 3f
Quad-States, Inc. v. Vande Mheen	220 Neb. 161, 368 N.W.2d 795 (1985)	Sale of business	Used trucks, parts, scrap	NE	3e, 10

Ranch Hands Foods v. Polar Pak Foods	690 S.W.2d 437 (Mo.App. 1985)	Corporate officer	Food	MO	3c, 9, 12
Ranch Hands Foods v. Polar Pak Foods	690 S.W.2d 437 (Mo.App. 1985)	Corporate officer (president)	Food	MO	3c, 9, 12
Rao v. Rao	718 F.2d 219, 1 IER Cases 267 (7th Cir. 1983)	Physician	Health care (Cardiovascular and thoracic surgery)	IL	8
Rapp Ins. Agency v. Baldree	231 Ill.App.3d 1038, 173 Ill.Dec. 962, 597 N.E.2d 936 (5th Dist. 1992)	Salesperson	Insurance	IL	2, 14
Rash v. Toccoa Clinic Medical Ass'n	253 Ga. 322, 320 S.E.2d 170 (1984)	Physician (partner)	Health care	GA	3d, 3f, AT-22, AT-65
Raven v. A. Klein & Co.	195 N.J. Super. 209, 478 A.2d 1208 (App.Div. 1984)	Occupation not specified	Box manufacturing	NJ	2, 3, 4, 9, 10, 12
Raymundo v. Hammond Clinic Ass'n	449 N.E.2d 276 (Ind.App. 1983)	Physician	Health care	IN	3f, 10, 14
Reading Aviation Serv. v. Bertolet	454 Pa. 488, 311 A.2d 628 (1973)	Corporate officer (chairman)	Aviation service	PA	3f, 4
Reading Aviation Serv. v. Bertolet	454 Pa. 488, 311 A.2d 628 (1973)	Corporate officer (president)	Aviation service	PA	3f, 4
Rebsamen Ins. Co. v. Milton	269 Ark. 737, 600 S.W.2d 441 (App. 1980)	Salesperson	Insurance	AR	3
Recon Exploration, Inc. v. Hodges	798 S.W.2d 848 (Tex.Ct.App.—Dallas 1990)	Microwave spectrometer operator	Oil exploration	TX	3
Recon Exploration, Inc. v. Hodges	798 S.W.2d 848 (Tex.Ct.App.—Dallas 1990)	Pilot (helicopter)	Oil exploration	TX	3

Case	Citation	Transaction	Industry	State	Ref.
Reeves v. Sargent	200 S.C. 494, 21 S.E.2d 184 (1942)	Sale of business	Photography	SC	12
Refrigeration Indus., Inc. v. Nemmers	880 S.W.2d 912 (Mo.App. S.D. 1994)	Salesperson	Refrigeration equipment	MO	2, 5, 10
Regional Sales Agency v. Reichert	784 P.2d 1210 (Utah Ct. App. 1989)	Salesperson	Manufacturer's representative	UT	10
Rego Displays v. Fournier	119 R.I. 469, 379 A.2d 1098 (1977)	No covenant	No covenant	RI	2, 14
Rehabilitation Specialists v. Koering	404 N.W.2d 301 (Minn.Ct.App. 1987)	Therapist	Health care (Occupational therapy)	MN	2
Reid v. Johnson	851 S.W.2d 120 (Mo.App. 1993)	Physician	Health care	MO	AT-74
Reidman Agency, Inc. v. Musnicki	79 A.D.2d 1094, 435 N.Y.S.2d 837 (1981)	Salesperson	Insurance	NY	3f
Reiman Const. Co. v. Jerry	709 P.2d 1271 (Wyo. 1985)	No covenant	No covenant	WY	10
Reinhardt Printing Co. v. Feld	142 Ill.App.3d 9, 96 Ill.Dec. 97, 490 N.E.2d 1302 (1st Dist. 1986)	Salesperson	Printing (commercial)	IL	2, 7
Rem Metals Corp. v. Logan	278 Or. 715, 565 P.2d 1080 (1977)	Repair wedger	Metal industry	OR	2, 3e, 14
Rensema v. Nichols	83 Or.App. 322, 731 P.2d 1048 (1986) (per curiam)	Rivals' agreement	Towing services	OR	3d, 3f
Rental Uniform Serv. of Florence v. Dudley	278 S.C. 274, 301 S.E.2d 142 (1983)	Salesperson (route)	Laundry	SC	3, 3b, 3f, 7, 10, AT-82
Renwood Food Prods. v. Schaefer	240 Mo.App. 939, 223 S.W.2d 144 (1949)	Salesperson	Food (frozen)	MO	3a
Research & Trading Corp. v. Pfuhl	1992 WL 345465 (Del.Ch., No. 12527, Nov. 18, 1992)	Salesperson	Fall-protection equipment	DE	2, 3, 3c, 3f, 3g, 5, 8, 9, 10, AT-12, AT-38

Case	Citation	Occupation	Industry	State	References
Research & Trading Corp. v. Powell	468 A.2d 1301 (Del.Ch. No. 12527, Nov. 18, 1983)	Salesperson	Fall-protection equipment	DE	3c, 3f, 14
Retina Servs. v. Garson	182 Ill.App.3d 851, 131 Ill.Dec. 276, 538 N.E.2d 651 (1st Dist. 1989)	Physician	Health care (Ophthalmology)	IL	2, 3d, 3f, 7, 14
Rich Prods. Corp. v. Parucki	178 A.D.2d 1024, 578 N.Y.S.2d 345 (4th Dep't 1991)	Occupation not specified	Not specified	NY	2, 3f
Richardson v. Paxton	203 Va. 790, 127 S.E.2d 113 (1962)	Salesperson	Marine and industrial supplies (chemical)	VA	3, 3b, 3e, 3f, 4, 14, AT-23
Richmond Bros., Inc. v. Westinghouse Bdcst. Co.	357 Mass. 106, 256 N.E.2d 304 (Mass. 1970)	Broadcaster	Broadcasting (Radio)	MA	3, 14
Riddick v. Suncoast Beauty College, Inc.	579 So.2d 855 (Fla. 2d Dist.Ct.App. 1991)	Sale of business	Hair stylist	FL	AT-21
Ridge Community Investors, Inc. v. Berry	293 N.C. 688, 239 S.E.2d 566 (1977)	No covenant	No covenant	NC	5
Ridgefield Park Transp. v. Uhl	803 F.Supp. 1467 (S.D. Ind. 1992)	Sale of business	Trucking company	IN	14
Ridley v. Krout	63 Wyo. 252, 180 P.2d 124 (1947)	Mechanic	Repair shop	WY	2, 3, 3b, 3c, 3d, 3f, 3g, 4, 14
Riedman Corp. v. Jarosh	290 S.C. 252, 349 S.E.2d 404 (1986)	Salesperson	Insurance	SC	3a
Rimes v. Club Corp. of Am.	542 S.W.2d 909 (Tex.Civ.App.— Dallas 1976)	Occupation not specified	Country club management	TX	5, 7
Ring Computer Sys. v. Paradata Computer Networks	1990 WL 132615 (Minn.Ct.App. 1990) (unpublished)	No covenant	No covenant	MN	2, 3f

Rio Grande Oil Co. v. State	539 S.W.2d 917 (Tex.Civ.App.—Houston [1st Dist.] 1976)	No covenant	No covenant	TX	3
Rippe v. Doran	4 Wash.App. 952, 486 P.2d 107 (1971)	Sale of business	Car wash	WA	3d
Rita Personnel Servs. v. Kot	229 Ga. 314, 191 S.E.2d 79 (1972)	Franchise	Employment agency	GA	4
Ritz v. Music, Inc.	189 Pa.Super. 106, 150 A.2d 160 (1959)	Salesperson	Music supplier (telephonic)	PA	8
Riverview Florist v. Watkins	51 Wash.App. 658, 754 P.2d 1055 (1988)	Sale of business	Nursery (floral, baby's breath)	WA	5, 6, 7, 10, 11
Roane-Barker v. Southeastern Hosp. Supply Corp.	99 N.C.App. 30, 392 S.E.2d 663 (1970)	No covenant	No covenant	NC	10
Roanoke Eng'g Sales Co. v. Rosenbaum	223 Va. 548, 290 S.E.2d 822 (1982)	Corporate officer	Building supplies	VA	2, 3d, 3f, 5, 9, 14, AT-42
Roanoke Eng'g Sales Co. v. Rosenbaum	223 Va. 548, 290 S.E.2d 822 (1982)	Salesperson	Building supplies	VA	2, 3d, 3f, 5, 9, 14, AT-42
Robbins v. Finlay	645 P.2d 623 (Utah 1982)	Salesperson	Hearing aids	UT	2, 3, 3e, 5, 10, 14
Robert B. Vance & Assocs., Inc. v. Baronet Corp.	487 F.Supp. 790 (N.D.Ga. 1979)	No covenant	No covenant	GA	10
Robert Clifton Assocs. v. O'Connor	338 Pa.Super. 246, 487 A.2d 947 (1985)	Recruiter	Employment agency	PA	3d, 3f
Robert S. Weiss & Assocs. v. Wiederlight	208 Conn. 525, 546 A.2d 216 (1988)	Salesperson	Insurance	CT	1, 3, 3d, 3f, 3g, 8, 10
Roberts v. Pfefer	13 Cal.App.3d 93, 91 Cal.Rptr. 308 (1970)	Physician (partner)	Health care	CA	3f, 4

Roberts v. Tifton Medical Clinic	206 Ga.App. 612, 426 S.E.2d 188 (1992)	Physician	Health care	GA	3, AT-22
Robins & Weil v. Mason	70 N.C.App. 537, 320 S.E.2d 693, disc. rev. denied, 312 N.C. 495, 322 S.E.2d 559 (1984)	Salesperson	Insurance	NC	3a, 5, 7
Robinson v. Computer Servicenters	346 So.2d 940 (Ala. 1977)	Corporate officer (chief executive officer)	Data processing	AL	8, 14
Robinson v. Computer Servicenters	346 So.2d 940 (Ala. 1977)	Corporate officer (president)	Data processing	AL	8, 14
Rochester v. Rochester Corp.	316 F.Supp. 139 (E.D.Va. 1970)	Manager, sales	Not specified	VA	3f, 3g, 12
Rocky Mountain Turbines, Inc. v. 660 Syndicate, Inc.	623 P.2d 758 (Wyo. 1981)	No covenant	No covenant	WY	7
Roessler v. Burwell	119 Conn. 289, 176 A. 126 (1934)	Salesperson	Delicatessen products	CT	3c, 3f
Roessler v. Burwell	119 Conn. 289, 176 A. 126 (1934)	Salesperson	Delicatessen products	SC	3c
Roger Zitrin, M.D. P.A. v. Glaser	621So.2d 748 (Fla. 4th Dist.Ct.App. 1993)	No covenant	No covenant	FL	AT-58
Rogers v. Runfola & Assocs.	57 Ohio St.3d 5, 565 N.E.2d 540, 6 IER Cases 160 (1991)	Court reporter	Public stenography	OH	3b, 3b, 3c, 3d, 3f, 4, 9, AT-10
Rollins v. American State Bank	487 N.E.2d 842 (Ind.App. 1986)	Salesperson	Insurance	IN	3c
Rollins Burdick Hunter of Wis. v. Hamilton	101 Wis.2d 460, 304 N.W.2d 752 (1981)	Salesperson	Insurance	WI	2, 3, 3d, 3f, 3g, 3g, 14
Rollins Protective Servs. Co. v. Palermo	249 Ga. 138, 287 S.E.2d 546 (1982)	Manager trainee	Alarms (fire and burglar)	GA	3d, 3f, 4, 14, AT-55
Rollins Protective Servs. Co. v. Palermo	249 Ga. 138, 287 S.E.2d 546 (1982)	Salesperson	Alarms (fire and burglar)	GA	3d, 3f, 4, 14, AT-55

Case	Citation	Occupation	Industry	State	References
Rollins Protective Servs. v. Shaffer Co.	383 Pa.Super. 598, 557 A.2d 413, 4 IER Cases 485 (1989)	Occupation not specified	Security service	PA	3f, 5, 6
Rosewood Mortgage Corp. v. Hefty	383 N.W.2d 456 (Minn.Ct.App. 1986)	Salesperson	Mortgages (secondary)	MN	6, 14
Ross v. Champion Computer Corp.	582 So.2d 152, 16 Fla. L. Weekly D1893 (Fla. 4th Dist.Ct.App. 1991)	Occupation not specified	Not specified	FL	7, 10, AT-67
Roth v. Gamble-Skogmo, Inc.	532 F.Supp. 1029 (D.Minn. 1982)	Corporate officer (chief executive officer)	Grocery	AK	3
Roth v. Gamble-Skogmo, Inc.	532 F.Supp. 1029 (D.Minn. 1982)	Corporate officer (chief executive officer)	Grocery chain	MN	4, 10
Roto-Die, Inc. v. Lesser	899 F.Supp. 1515 (W.D. Va. 1995)	Corporate officer (secretary)	Rotary tooling manufacturing	VA	3, 3e, 3f, 4, AT-2, AT-21, AT-23, AT-39, AT-54.1, AT-86A, AT-96
Roto-Die, Inc. v. Lesser	899 F.Supp. 1515 (W.D.Va. 1995)	Corporate officer (director, marketing and sales)	Rotary tooling manufacturing	VA	3, 3e, 3f, 4, AT-2, AT-21, AT-23, AT-39, AT-54.1, AT-85.2, AT-96
Roto-Die, Inc. v. Lesser	899 F.Supp. 1515 (W.D. Va. 1995)	Marketing director	Rotary tooling manufacturing	VA	3, 3e, 3f, 4, AT-2, AT-21, AT-23, AT-39, AT-54.1, AT-85.2, AT-96

Case	Citation	Role	Industry	State	Codes
Rush v. Mewson Exterminators, Inc.	261 Ala. 610, 75 So.2d 112 (1954)	Exterminator	Pest control	AL	3
Russell v. Birmingham Oxygen Service, Inc.	408 So.2d 90 (Ala. 1981)	Sale of business	Respiratory therapy (home)	AL	AT-85A, AT-89A
Russell v. Mullis	479 So.2d 727 (Ala. 1985)	Sale of business	Convenience store	AL	AT-43
S. Hammond Story Agency v. Baer	202 Ga.App. 281, 414 S.E.2d 287 (1991), reconsideration denied (Dec. 19, 1991), cert. denied (Feb. 4, 1992)	Occupation not specified	Not specified	GA	AT-23
S&S Chopper Serv. v. Scripter	59 Ohio App.2d 311, 394 N.E.2d 1011 (1977)	Pilot (helicopter)	Agricultural spraying (aerial)	OH	12
Sabetay v. Sterling Drug	69 N.Y.2d 329, 514 N.Y.S.2d 209, 506 N.E.2d 919, 2 IER Cases 150 (1987)	No covenant	No covenant	NY	3c
Sabina v. Dahlia Corp.	650 So.2d 96 (Fla. 2d Dist.Ct.App. 1995)	Salesperson	Insurance	FL	5, 7
Safeguard Business Sys. v. Schaeffer	822 S.W.2d 640 (Tex.Ct.App.—Dallas 1991)	Salesperson	Not specified	TX	2, 3f, 3g, 4, 5, 7
Safelite Glass Corp. v. Fuller	15 Kan.App.2d 531, 807 P.2d 677, 6 IER Cases 417 (Kan.App. 1991)	Manager (district)	Automobile glass	KS	14, AT-10
Safety Equip. Sales & Serv. v. Williams	22 N.C.App. 410, 206 S.E.2d 745 (1974)	Recharger	Fire fighting equipment	NC	3a, 3f
Safier's, Inc. v. Bialer	59 Ohio Law Abs. 292, 42 Ohio Op. 209, 93 N.E.2d 734 (Ohio C.P. 1950)	Salesperson	Candy, cigarettes, and tobacco	OH	AT-11
Sakowitz v. Steck	669 S.W.2d 105 (Tex. 1984)	Buyer (assistant)	Gifts and stationery	TX	13, AT-90

Case	Citation			CT	AT-80
Sassone v. Lepore	226 Conn. 773, 629 A.2d 357 (1993)	Sale of business	Home inspection	CT	AT-80
Satellite Indus., Inc. v. Keeling	396 N.W.2d 635 (Minn.Ct.App. 1986)	Salesperson	Portable restrooms	MN	3c, 4, 6, 10
Satellite Indus., Inc. v. Stutz	437 So.2d 222 (Fla. 4th Dist.Ct.App. 1988)	Salesperson	Satellite equipment	FL	1, 6
Saul v. Thalis	156 F.Supp. 408 (D.D.C. 1957)	Salesperson	Barber/beauty shop equipment	DC	2, 3a, 3b, 8
Sawyer-Adecor Int'l Inc. v. Anglin	198 Mont. 440, 646 P.2d 1194 (1982)	No covenant	No covenant	MT	7
Schaeffer v. Frey	403 Pa.Super. 560, 589 A.2d 752 (1991)	No covenant	No covenant	PA	5, 7
Schlytter v. Baker	580 F.2d 848 (5th Cir. 1978)	No covenant	No covenant	AR	AT-89
Schneller v. Hayes	176 Wash. 115, 28 P.2d 273 (1934)	Optician	Health care (Optical)	WA	3c
Schnucks Twenty-Five, Inc. v. Bettendorf	595 S.W.2d 279 (Mo.App. 1979)	Sale of business	Grocery	MO	3d, AT-10
Schott v. Beussink	817 S.W.2d 540 (Mo.App. 1991)	Accountant	Accounting	MO	10
Schulenburg v. Signatrol, Inc.	33 Ill.2d 379, 212 N.E.2d 865 (1965)	No covenant	No covenant	MO	3d
Schulhalter v. Salerno	279 N.J.Super. 504, 653 A.2d 596 (App.Div. 1995)	Accountant (partner)	Accounting	NJ	3, AT-82
Schulhalter v. Salerno	279 N.J.Super. 504, 653 A.2d 596 (App.Div. 1995)	Accountant	Accounting	NJ	3, AT-82
Schultz & Assocs. of the Se. v. Ingram	38 N.C.App. 422, 248 S.E.2d 345 (1978)	Auditor (accounts payable)	Not specified	NC	3f, 4

Case	Citation	Role	Industry	State	§
Service Sys. Corp. v. Harris	41 A.D.2d 20, 341 N.Y.S.2d 702 (1973)	Corporate officer (director, regional)	Building maintenance	NY	3
Service Sys. Corp. v. Van Bortel	174 Ill.App.3d 412, 528 N.E.2d 378 (1st Dist. 1988)	Corporate officer (vice president)	Food service management	IL	3
Service Sys. Corp. v. Van Bortel	174 Ill.App.3d 412, 528 N.E.2d 378 (1st Dist. 1988)	Corporate officer (chief executive officer)	Food service management	IL	3
Service Sys. Corp. v. Van Bortel	174 Ill.App.3d 412, 528 N.E.2d 378 (1st Dist. 1988)	Corporate officer (president)	Food service management	IL	3
Service Centers of Chicago v. Minogue	180 Ill.App.3d 447, 129 Ill.Dec. 367, 535 N.E.2d 1132 (1st Dist. 1989)	Salesperson	Records storage and retrieval (medical)	IL	2
Sewall v. Feller	288 Mich. 107, 284 N.W. 662 (1939)	Sale of business	Store	MI	AT-73A
Seymour v. Buckley	628 So.2d 554 (Ala. 1993) (applying Indiana law)	License agreement	Paintless car-dent removal	IN	3, 5
Seymour v. Buckley	628 So.2d 554 (Ala. 1993)	Occupation not specified	Paintless car-dent-removal	AL	5
Shandor v. Wells Nat'l Serv. Corp.	478 F.Supp. 12 (N.D.Ga. 1979)	Manager, sales	Television installations (hospital sites)	GA	11
Shankman v. Coastal Psychiatric Assocs.	258 Ga. 294, 368 S.E.2d 753 (1988)	Physician	Health care (Psychiatry)	GA	AT-65
Shapiro v. Regent Printing Co.	192 Ill.App.3d 1005, 140 Ill.Dec. 142, 549 N.E.2d 793 (1st Dist. 1989)	Salesperson	Printing (commercial)	IL	2, 3c, 5
Shattuck v. Kinetic Concepts, Inc.	49 F.3d 1106 (5th Cir. 1995)	Sales director	Medical products	TX	AT-1.1

Case	Citation	Role	Industry	State	Sections
Shreveport Laundries v. Teagle	139 So.2d 563, dismissed as moot, 144 So.2d 183 (La.App. 2d Cir. 1932)	Salesperson (route)	Laundry	LA	3a
Shubert Theatrical Co. v. Gallagher	206 A.D. 514, 201 N.Y.S. 577 (1923)	Actor	Performing arts	NY	14
Shubert Theatrical Co. v. Gallagher	206 A.D. 514, 201 N.Y.S. 577 (1923)	Performer	Performing arts (Vaudeville)	NY	14
Sidco Paper Co. v. Aaron	465 Pa. 586, 351 A.2d 250 (1976)	Salesperson	Paper (printing, low-grade, odd lots of)	PA	3, 3f, 4, 7, 14
Silver v. Goldberger	231 Md. 1, 188 A.2d 155 (1963)	Recruiter	Employment agency	MD	2, 3e
Silvers v. Dis-Com Secs.	403 So.2d 1133 (Fla. 4th Dist.Ct.App. 1981)	Stock broker (discount)	Securities	FL	3e, 3f, 6, 14
Simko, Inc. v. Graymar	55 Md. 561, 464 A.2d 1104 (1983)	Salesperson	Office equipment	MD	3c
Singer v. Habif, Arogeti & Wynne, P.C.	250 Ga. 376, 297 S.E.2d 473 (1982)	Accountant	Accounting	GA	3f, 3g
Skinner v. Elrod	417 S.E.2d 599 (S.C. 1992)	Sale of business	Photography	SC	AT-7
Skyland Broadcasting Corp. v. Hamby	75 Ohio Laws Abs. 585, 141 N.E.2d 783 (1957)	Broadcaster	Broadcasting (Radio)	OH	3f
Skyland Broadcasting Corp. v. Hamby	75 Ohio Laws Abs. 585, 141 N.E.2d 783 (1957)	Disc jockey	Broadcasting (Radio (hillbilly entertainment))	OH	3f
Slisz v. Munzenreider Corp.	411 N.E.2d 700 (Ind.App. 1980)	Manager (store, partner)	Not specified	IN	2
Sloane, Inc. v. House & Assocs.	311 Md. 36, 532 A.2d 694 (1987)	No covenant	No covenant	MD	10
Small v. Springs Indus.	292 S.C. 481, 357 S.E.2d 452, 2 IER Cases 266 (1987)	No covenant	No covenant	SC	3a

Case	Citation	Position	Industry	State	Ref.
Smith & English, Partners v. Board of Educ. of City of Liberal	115 Kan. 155, 222 P. 101 (1924)	No covenant	No covenant	KS	14
Smith-Scharff Paper Co. v. Blum	813 S.W.2d 27, 6 IER Cases 867 (Mo.App. 1991)	Salesperson	Paper and janitoral supplies	MO	7, 8, 14, AT-38
Smith Walters, Kuehn, Burnett & Hughes v. Burnett	192 Ill.App.3d 693, 139 Ill.Dec. 617, 548 N.E.2d 1331 (3d Dist. 1989)	Attorney (partner)	Law	IL	5, 7
Smithereen Co. v. Renfroe	325 Ill. App. 229, 59 N.E.2d 545 (1st Dist. 1945)	Manager	Pest control	IL	3c
Snelling & Snelling v. Dupay Enters.	125 Ariz. 362, 609 P.2d 1062 (App. 1980)	Franchise	Employment agency	AZ	2
Socia v. Trovato	197 A.D.2d 916, 602 N.Y.S.2d 270 (4th Dep't 1993)	Sale of business	Not specified	NY	AT-96
Solari Indus., Inc. v. Malady	55 N.J. 571, 264 A.2d 53 (1970)	Corporate officer (chief executive officer)	Teleindicator manufacturing	NJ	2, 3, 3b, 3d, 3g, 4, 12, 14
Solari Indus., Inc. v. Malady	55 N.J. 571, 264 A.2d 53 (1970)	Corporate officer (director)	Teleindicator manufacturing	NJ	2, 3, 3b, 3d, 3g, 4, 12, 14
Solari Indus., Inc. v. Malady	55 N.J. 571, 264 A.2d 53 (1970)	Corporate officer (president)	Teleindicator manufacturing	NJ	2, 3, 3b, 3d, 3g, 4, 12, 14
Solari Indus., Inc. v. Malady	55 N.J. 571, 264 A.2d 53 (1970)	Corporate officer (chief executive officer)	Teleindicator manufacturing	RI	4
Solari Indus., Inc. v. Malady	55 N.J. 571, 264 A.2d 53 (1970)	Corporate officer (director)	Teleindicator manufacturing	RI	4
Solari Indus., Inc. v. Malady	55 N.J. 571, 264 A.2d 53 (1970)	Corporate officer (president)	Teleindicator manufacturing	RI	4

Case	Citation	Position	Industry	State	Section
Solari Indus., Inc. v. Malady	55 N.J. 571, 264, A.2d 53 (1970)	Corporate officer (chief executive officer)	Teleindicator manufacturing	WY	4
Solari Indus., Inc. v. Malady	55 N.J. 571, 264, A.2d 53 (1970)	Corporate officer (director)	Teleindicator manufacturing	WY	4
Solari Indus., Inc. v. Malady	55 N.J. 571, 264, A.2d 53 (1970)	Corporate officer (president)	Teleindicator manufacturing	WY	4
Solomon v. Flowarr Mgmt.	1989 Tenn.App. LEXIS 446 (Tenn. App. Jun. 16, 1989)	No covenant	No covenant	TN	12
Somerset v. Reyner	233 S.C. 324, 104 S.E.2d 344 (1958)	Sale of business	Silversmith spinner	SC	3, 3d, 3f, 4, 14
Source Servs. Corp. v. Bogdan	1995 U.S.App. LEXIS 335N (4th Cir., No. 94-1791, Feb. 21, 1995)	Manager (branch)	Employment agency (data processing personnel)	MD	2
South Bay Radiology Medical Assocs. v. W.M. Asher, M.D., Inc.	220 Cal.App.3d 1074, 269 Cal. Rptr. 15 (1990)	Physician (partner)	Health care (Radiology)	CA	1
South Bend Consumers Club v. United Consumers Club	572 F.Supp. 209 (N.D.Ind. 1983)	Franchise	Consumer buying club	IN	4
South Carolina Fin. Corp. of Anderson v. West Side Fin. Co.	236 S.C. 109, 113 S.E.2d 329 (1960)	Corporate officer (vice president)	Bank	SC	3f
South St. Pump & Mach. Co. v. Forslund	25 Mo.App. 262, 29 S.W.2d 165 (1930)	No covenant	No covenant	MO	9
Southeastern Beverage Co. v. Dillard	233 Ga. 346, 211 S.E.2d 299 (1974)	Occupation not specified	Beverage	GA	3d
Southern Ill. Medical Business Assocs. v. Camillo	190 Ill.App.3d 664, 138 Ill.Dec. 4, 546 N.E.2d 1059 (5th Dist. 1989)	Phlebotomist	Medical lab	IL	2, 3b, 5, 6, 7, 14

Southworth v. Davison	106 Minn. 119, 118 N.W. 363 (1908)	Sale of business	Laundry	MN	3f
Space Aero Prods. Co. v. R.E. Darling Co.	238 Md. 93, 208 A.2d 74, reargument denied, 238 Md. 93, 208 A.2d 699, cert. denied, 382 U.S. 843 (1965)	No covenant	No covenant	MD	2
Spartan Leasing v. Pollar	101 N.C.App. 450, 400 S.E.2d 476 (1991)	No covenant	No covenant	NC	2, AT-92, AT-94
Special Prods. Mfg., Inc. v. Douglass	169 A.D.2d 891, 564 N.Y.S.2d 615 (3d Dep't 1991)	Salesperson	Metal-hardness testing equipment	NY	10
Special Prods. Mfg., Inc. v. Douglass	553 N.Y.S.2d 506, 5 IER Cases 335 (App.Div. 3d Dep't 1990)	Service person	Hardness-testing equipment	NY	3c
Special Prods. Mfg., Inc. v. Douglass	169 A.D.2d 891, 564 N.Y.S.2d 615 (3d Dep't 1991)	Service person	Metal-hardness testing equipment	NY	10
Special Prods. Mfg., Inc. v. Douglass	159 App.Div.2d 847, 553 N.Y.S.2d 506 (1990)	Service technician	Hardness-testing equipment	KS	14
Specialized Alarm Servs. v. Kauska	189 Ga.App. 863, 377 S.E.2d 703 (1989), reh'g denied (Jan. 19, 1989)	Occupation not specified	Alarms	GA	3g
Spectrum Emergency Care v. St. Joseph's Hosp. & Health Center	479 N.W.2d 848 (N.D. 1992)	Physician (independent contractor)	Health care (Emergency room)	ND	1, 11, 14
Spheeris Sporting Goods v. Spheeris on Capitol	459 N.W.2d 581 (Wis.Ct.App. 1990)	Lease	Building	WI	7
Spiegel v. Thomas, Mann & Smith, P.C.	811 S.W.2d 528 (Tenn. 1991)	Attorney (partner)	Law	NJ	AT-49, AT-95

			Law	Attorney (partner)	
Spiegel v. Thomas, Mann & Smith, P.C.	811 S.W.2d 528 (Tenn. 1991)	TN			1, 3, 14, AT-2, AT-30
Spielvogel v. Zitofsky	175 A.D.2d 830, 573 N.Y.S.2d 198 (2d Dep't 1991)	NY	Vertical blinds manufacturing	Occupation not specified	10
Spitz, Sullivan, Wachtell & Falcetta v. Murphy	No. CV 86 0322422, 1991 WL 112718 (Conn.Super.Ct. June 13, 1991)	CT	Accounting	Accountant (partner)	2, 3, 3f, 3g, 10
Sprague's Aetna Trailer Sales v. Hruz	172 Colo. 469, 474 P.2d 216 (1970)	CO	Trailers	Salesperson	3e
Spring Steels, Inc. v. Molloy	400 Pa. 354, 162 A.2d 370 (1960)	PA	No covenant	No covenant	2
Springfield Rare Coin Galleries Inc. v. Mileham	250 Ill.App.3d 922, 189 Ill.Dec. 511, 620 N.E.2d 479 (4th Dist. 1993)	IL	Coin dealership	Middleman	2, 3f, AT-23
St. Paul Fire & Marine Ins. Co. v. Cumiskey	204 Mont. 350, 665 P.2d 223 (1983)	MT	No covenant	No covenant	14
St. Paul Surplus Lines Ins. Co. v. International Playtex Inc.	245 Kan. 258, 777 P.2d 1259 (1989), *cert. denied*, 107 L.Ed. 774 (1990)	KS	No covenant	No covenant	12
Sta-Home Health Agency v. Umphers	562 So.2d 1258 (Miss. 1990)	MS	Health care (Nursing service (home))	Nurse	3, 7
Stamatakis Indus., Inc. v. King	165 Ill.App.3d 879, 117 Ill. Dec. 419, 520 N.E.2d 770 (1987)	IL	Graphic arts	Sale of business	4
Standard Brands, Inc. v. Zumpe	264 F.Supp. 254 (E.D.La. 1967)	LA	Coffee/tea processing	Manager (plant)	1
Standard Chautauqua Sys. v. Gift	120 Kan. 101, 242 P. 145 (1926)	KS	No covenant	No covenant	14
Standard Hydraulics v. Kerns	387 S.E.2d 130 (W.Va. 1989) (per curiam)	WV	Hydraulics	Corporate officer (vice president)	9, 10

Case	Citation	Position	Forms (business) and equipment	State	Factors
Standard Register Co. v. Kerrigan	238 S.C. 54, 119 S.E.2d 533 (1961)	Salesperson	Forms (business) and equipment	SC	2, 3, 3b, 3c, 3d, 3f, 6, 12, 14
Standard-Crescent City Surgical Supplies, Inc. v. Mouton	535 So.2d 1301 (La.App. 5th Cir. 1988)	Salesperson	Medical equipment (surgical supplies)	LA	1
Stanley Tulchin Assocs., Inc. v. Vignola	186 A.D.2d 183, 587 N.Y.S.2d 761 (2d Dep't 1992)	Debt collector	Collection agency	NY	3f, 6
State v. Maine State Employees Ass'n	482 A.2d 461 (Me. 1984)	No covenant	No covenant	ME	7
State Chem. Mfg. Co. v. Lopez	642 So.2d 1127 (Fla.App. 3 Dist. 1994)	Manager, sales	Chemicals	FL	3f, 5, 6
State Farm Mut. Auto Ins. Co. v. Dempster	174 Cal.App.2d 418, 344 P.2d 821 (1959)	Salesperson	Insurance	CA	2, 3f
State Medical Oxygen & Supply v. American Medical Oxygen Co.	240 Mont. 70, 782 P.2d 1272 (1989)	Salesperson	Medical equipment (oxygen/allied health care supply)	MT	1, 3, 3d, 3e, 14
Statesville Medical Group, P.A. v. Dickey	106 N.C.App. 669, 418 S.E.2d 256, 7 IER Cases 1095 (1992)	Physician	Health care (Endocrinology)	NC	3, 3d, 3f, 7
Steamatic of Kan. City v. Rhea	763 S.W.2d 190, 4 IER Cases 53 (Mo.App. 1988)	Salesperson	Cleaning service	MO	2, 3e
Steggles v. National Discount Corp.	326 Mich. 44, 39 N.W.2d 237 (1949)	No covenant	No covenant	MI	9
Stein Steel & Supply Co. v. Tucker	219 Ga. 844, 136 S.E.2d 355 (1964)	Night watchman	Security	GA	3
Stein Steel & Supply Co. v. Tucker	219 Ga. 844, 136 S.E.2d 355 (1964)	Truck driver	Transportation	GA	3

Case	Citation	Role	Industry	State	Sections
Steinke v. Boeing Co.	525 F.Supp. 234 (D. Mont. 1981)	No covenant	No covenant	MT	12
Sterner v. Marathon Oil Co.	767 S.W.2d 686, 4 IER Cases 592 (Tex. 1989)	No covenant	No covenant	TX	3c
Stevenson v. Parsons	96 N.C.App. 93, 384 S.E.2d 291 (1989)	Veterinarian	Veterinary medicine	NC	3, 3a, 3b, 7
Stevenson v. Parsons	96 N.C.App 93, 384 S.E.2d 291 (1989)	Veterinarian	Veterinary medicine	WY	3b
Stipp v. Wallace Plating, Inc.	96 Idaho 5, 523 P.2d 822 (1974)	Corporate officer (vice president)	Bumper rechroming	ID	2
Stocks v. Banner Am. Corp.	599 S.W.2d 665 (Tex.Ct.App.—Texarkana 1980)	Corporate officer (vice president)	Cassette tape manufacturing	TX	3g
Stokes v. Enmark Collaborative	634 S.W.2d 571 (Mo.App. 1982)	No covenant	No covenant	MO	8
Stokes v. Moore	262 Ala. 59, 77 So.2d 331 (1955)	Manager	Finance	AL	3f
Stone v. Grasselli Chem. Co.	65 N.J. Eq. 776, 55 A. 736 (E.&A. 1903)	Salesperson	Depilatories (animal skins)	NJ	10
Stone & Webster Eng'g Corp. v. Brunswick Pulp & Paper Co.	209 A.2d 890 (Del. Super. Ct. 1965)	No covenant	No covenant	DE	12
Stoner v. South Peninsula Zoning Comm'n	75 So.2d 831 (Fla. 1954)	No covenant	No covenant	FL	5
Storer v. Brock	351 Ill. 643, 184 N.E. 868 (1933)	Physician	Health care	IL	3d, 3f
Storz Broadcasting Co. v. Courtney	178 So.2d 40 (Fla. 3d Dist.Ct.App. 1965), *cert. denied*, 188 So.2d 315 (Fla. 1966)	Broadcaster	Broadcasting (Radio)	FL	14, AT-42
Stover v. Spielman	1 Pa.Super. 526 (1896)	Sale of business	Bakery, candy, and ice cream shop	PA	10, 14

Case	Citation	Occupation	Business	State	
Streiff v. American Family Mut. Ins. Co.	118 Wis.2d 602, 348 N.W.2d 505 (1984)	Salesperson	Insurance	WI	4
Stringer v. Herron	424 S.E.2d 547, 8 IER Cases 87 (S.C.Ct.App. 1992)	Veterinarian	Veterinary medicine	SC	3, 3f, 14, AT-82
Stroud v. Northwestern Nat'l Ins. Co.	360 So.2d 528 (La.App. 2d Cir. 1978)	No covenant	No covenant	LA	4, 14
Struck v. Plymouth Mortgage Co.	414 Mass. 118, 605 N.E.2d 296 (1993)	No covenant	No covenant	MA	AT-52
Suave Shoe Corp. v. Fernandez	390 So.2d 799 (Fla. 3d Dist.Ct.App. 1980) (per curiam)	Occupation not specified	Not specified	FL	3
Sub Station II v. Banasiak	(Tenn.Ct.App. June 15, 1984) (LEXIS, Employ library, Tenn. file)	License agreement	Sandwich shop	TN	10
Suburban Coat, Apron & Linen Supply Co. v. LeBlanc	300 Mass. 509, 15 N.E.2d 828 (1938)	Salesperson (route)	Linen service	MA	5
Suburban Gas of Grand Junction v. Bockelman	157 Colo. 78, 401 P.2d 268 (1965)	Salesperson	Propane gas	CO	3f
Suggs v. Glenn	1989 Tenn.App. LEXIS, Employ library, Tenn. file)	Corporate officer (president)	Hardware retailing	TN	3f
Suggs v. Glenn	1989 Tenn.App., No. 837, Jan. 20, 1989	Manager (store)	Hardware retailing	TN	3f
Suitter v. Holiday Inn Southwest	864 S.W.2d 436 (Mo.App. 1993) (per curiam)	Occupation not specified	Hotel	MO	7
Sulmonetti v. Hayes	347 Mass. 390, 198 N.E.2d 297 (1964)	Sale of business	Fuel oil retailer	MA	5

Case	Citation	Occupation	Industry	State	Sections
Sun Elastic Corp. v. O.B. Indus.	603 So.2d 516 (Fla. 3d Dist.Ct.App. 1992)	Occupation not specified	Not specified	FL	5, 6, 9, 11
Sun Oil Co. v. Whitaker	424 S.W.2d 505 (Tex. 1982)	No covenant	No covenant	TX	5
Sunstates Refrigerated Servs., Inc. v. Griffin	216 Ga.App. 61, 449 S.E.2d 858 (1994)	Corporate officer (chief executive officer)	Warehouse services (cold storage for peanut industry; frozen storage for local food processors)	GA	2, 3, 3f, 4, AT-29, AT-86A
Super-Maid Cook-Ware Corp. v. Hamil	50 F.2d 830 (5th Cir. 1931)	Salesperson	Cookware (aluminum)	NC	3c
Superior Gearbox Corp. v. Edwards	869 S.W.2d 239 (Mo.App. 1993)	Corporate officer (president)	Gearbox manufacturing	MO	2, 3, 3d, 3f, 4, 8, 9, 11, 14, AT-7, AT-68
Superior Gearbox Corp. v. Edwards	869 S.W.2d 239 (Mo.App. 1993)	Corporate officer (chief executive officer)	Gearbox manufacturing	MO	2, 3, 3d, 3f, 4, 8, 9, 11, AT-7,AT-68
Supplies for Industry v. Christensen	135 Ariz. 107, 659 P.2d 660 (1983)	Corporate officer (president)	Mining and construction industry equipment manufacturing	AZ	9
Support Systems Assocs., Inc. v. Tavolacci	135 A.D.2d 704, 522 N.Y.S.2d 604 (2d Dep't 1987)	Engineer	Electrical engineering	NY	10
Surgidev Corp. v. Eye Technology, Inc.	648 F.Supp. 661 (D.Minn. 1986), aff'd, 828 F.2d 452 (8th Cir. 1987)	Corporate officer (president)	Intraocular lens manufacturing	MN	12
Surgidev Corp. v. Eye Technology, Inc.	648 F.Supp. 661 (D.Minn. 1986), aff'd, 828 F.2d 452 (8th Cir. 1987)	Corporate officer (director, sales support)	Intraocular lens manufacturing	MN	12

Case	Citation	Occupation	Industry	State	References
Surgidev Corp. v. Eye Technology, Inc.	648 F.Supp. 661 (D.Minn. 1986), *aff'd*, 828 F.2d 452 (8th Cir. 1987)	Manager, sales	Intraocular lens manufacturing	MN	12
Swenson v. File	3 Cal.3d 389, 90 Cal.Rptr. 580, 475 P.2d 852 (1970)	Accountant (partner)	Accounting	CA	1, 3d
System Concepts, Inc. v. Dixon	669 P.2d 421 (Utah 1983)	Manager, sales	Cable television equipment	UT	3, 3b, 3c, 3d, 3f, 5, 6, 7, 10
Systems Concepts, Inc. v. Dixon	669 P.2d 421 (Utah 1983)	Manager, sales	Cable television equipment	WY	3f
T.K. Communications, Inc. v. Herman	505 So.2d 484 (Fla. 4th Dist.Ct.App.), *rev. denied*, 513 So.2d 1061 (Fla. 1987)	Disc jockey (mobile)	Entertainment	FL	1, 6, AT-84
Taff v. Brayman	518 P.2d 298 (Colo.App. 1974)	Occupation not specified	Insurance adjustment and appraisal	CO	3f
Take-A-Break Coffee Serv., Inc. v. Grose	(Del.Ch. C.A. No. 11217, May 14, 1990)	Salesperson (route)	Coffee	DE	3
Talarico v. United Furniture Workers Pension Fund A	479 F.Supp. 1072 (D.Neb. 1979)	No covenant	No covenant	NE	5
Tannenbaum v. Biscayne Osteopathic Hosp., Inc.	190 So.2d 777 (Fla. 1966)	Physician	Health care (Radiology, osteopathic)	FL	14, AT-86
Tannenbaum v. Biscayne Osteopathic Hosp., Inc.	190 So.2d 777 (Fla. 1966)	Physician	Health care (Osteopathic radiology)	FL	14, AT-86
Tannenbaum v. Biscayne Osteopathic Hosp., Inc.	190 So.2d 777 (Fla. 1966)	Physician	Health care	FL	14, AT-86
Taquino v. Teledyne Monarch Rubber	893 F.2d 1488 (5th Cir. 1990)	No covenant	No covenant	LA	4, 14

Case	Citation	Capacity	Business	State	Sections
Thames v. Davis & Goulet Ins.	420 So.2d 1041 (Miss. 1982)	Salesperson	Insurance	MS	3e
Theatre Time Clock v. Stewart	276 F.Supp. 593 (E.D.La. 1967)	Salesperson	Advertising (movie-theater intermission)	LA	2
Thermo-Guard, Inc. v. Cochran	596 A.2d 188 (Pa.Super. 1991)	Salesperson	Windows (replacement)	PA	2, 3, 3f, 4, 5, 7
Thermorama, Inc. v. Buckwold	267 Minn. 551, 125 N.W.2d 844 (1964)	Salesperson	Clothing (wholesale)	MN	6
Thomas v. Best Mfg. Corp.	234 Ga. 787, 218 S.E.2d 68 (1975)	Electrician	Manufacturing	GA	3f
Thomas v. Coastal Indus. Servs.	214 Ga. 832, 108 S.E.2d 328 (1959)	Driver	Uniform rentals	GA	3c, 3f
Thomas v. Coastal Indus. Servs.	214 Ga. 832, 108 S.E.2d 328 (1959)	Salesperson	Uniform rentals	GA	3c, 3f
Thomas v. Coastal Indus. Servs.	214 Ga. 832, 108 S.E.2d 328 (1959)	Supervisor	Uniform rentals	GA	3c, 3f
Thomas v. Gavin	15 N.M. 660, 110 P.2d 841 (1910)	Sale of business	Lumber business	NM	11
Thompson v. Wiik, Reimer & Sweet	391 So.2d 1016 (Ala. 1980)	Accountant	Accounting	AL	1, 14
Thompson, Breeding, Dunn, Cresswell & Sparks v. Bowlin	765 S.W.2d 743 (Tenn.Ct.App. 1987)	Accountant	Accounting	TN	2, 3f, 3g, 10, 11
Thompson Recruiting Advertising, Inc. v. Wedes	651 F.Supp. 107 (E.D.La 1986)	Manager, sales	Advertising	MI	1
Threlkeld v. Steward	24 Okla. 403, 103 P. 630 (1909)	Sale of business	Pharmaceutical business	OK	3d
Thur v. IPCO Corp.	173 A.D.2d 344, 569 N.Y.S.2d 713 (1st Dep't 1991)	Sale of business	Hospital supply company	NY	AT-86, AT-90
Tidwell Flying Serv. v. Smith Corp.	1992 WL 70302 (Ark.App. No. CA-91-429, Apr. 1, 1992)	Pilot	Flying service	AR	AT-3, AT-29

Tiffany Indus. v. Commercial Grain Bin Co.	714 F.2d 799 (8th Cir. 1989)	No covenant	No covenant	AR	12
Tiffany Sands, Inc. v. Mezhibovsky	463 So.2d 349 (Fla. 3d Dist.Ct.App. 1985)	Hair stylist	Beauty	FL	3f
Time Assocs., Inc. v. Blake Realty, Inc.	212 A.D.2d 879, 622 N.Y.S.2d 816 (3d Dep't 1995)	Sale of business	Real estate brokerage	NY	10, AT-25A, AT-36
Timenterial, Inc. v. Dagata	29 Conn.Supp. 180, 277 A.2d 512 (Super. Ct. Hartford Cty. 1971)	Salesperson	Mobile homes and offices	CT	3c, 3f, 4
Titus v. Superior Court, Maricopa County	91 Ariz. 18, 368 P.2d 874 (1962)	Broadcaster	Broadcasting (Radio)	AZ	3f, 9
Titus v. Superior Court, Maricopa County	91 Ariz. 18, 368 P.2d 874 (1962)	Disc jockey	Broadcasting (Radio)	AZ	3f, 9
Titus & Donnelly, Inc. v. Poto	205 A.D.2d 475, 614 N.Y.S.2d 10 (1st Dep't 1994)	Sale of business	Securities brokerage (municipal bonds)	NY	5
Toch v. Eric Schuster Corp.	490 S.W.2d 618 (Tex.Civ.App.—Dallas 1972)	Salesperson	Picture frames and molding (wholesale)	TX	3g
Tolman Laundry Co. v. Walker	171 Md. 7, 187 A. 836 (1936)	Salesperson (route)	Laundry	MD	3a, 3f
Tom James Co. v. Mendrop	819 S.W.2d 251 (Tex.Ct.App.—Fort Worth 1991)	Salesperson	Clothing (men's, custom)	TX	2, 5, 6, 7
Tomasello, Inc. v. de Los Santos	394 So.2d 1069 (Fla. 4th Dist.Ct.App. 1981)	Exterminator	Pest control	FL	2, 3d, 3e, 3f
Tomei v. Tomei	235 Ill.App.3d 166, 176 Ill.Dec. 716, 602 N.E.2d 23 (1st Dist. 1992)	Salesperson	Insurance	IL	3f, 11, 14
Torbett v. Wheeling Dollar Sav. & Trust Co.	314 S.E.2d 166 (W.Va 1983)	Trust officer	Bank	WV	1, 3, 3f, 7

Case	Citation	Occupation	Industry	State	Code
Torrence v. Hewitt Assocs.	143 Ill.App.3d 520, 97 Ill.Dec. 592, 493 N.E.2d 74 (1986)	Attorney	Employee benefits consulting	IL	2, AT-6
Torrence v. Hewitt Assocs.	143 Ill.App.3d 520, 97 Ill.Dec. 592, 493 N.E.2d 74 (1986)	Attorney (partner)	Law	WY	3f
Torrence v. Hewitt Assocs.	143 Ill.App.3d 520, 97 Ill.Dec. 592, 493 N.E.2d 74 (1986)	Consultant	Employee benefits	IL	2, AT-6
Torrence v. Hewitt Assocs.	143 Ill.App.3d 520, 97 Ill.Dec. 592, 493 N.E.2d 74 (1986)	Consultant	Employee benefits	WY	3f
Torrington Creamery, Inc. v. Davenport	126 Conn. 515, 12 A.2d 780 (1940)	Manager	Dairy	CT	3, 3b, 3f
Total Health Physicians, S.C. v. Barrientos	151 Ill.App.3d 726, 104 Ill.Dec. 580, 502 N.E.2d 1240 (1986)	Physician	Health care	IL	2, 4
Toulmin v. Becker	69 Ohio Laws Abs. 109, 124 N.E.2d 778 (Ohio Ct.App. 1954)	Attorney	Law (Patent)	OH	3f
Tower Oil & Technology Co. v. Buckley	99 Ill.App.3d 637, 425 N.E.2d 1060 (1st Dist. 1981)	Salesperson	Lubricants (industrial)	IL	10
Town & Country House & Homes Serv., Inc. v. Evans	189 A.2d 390 (Conn. 1963)	No covenant	No covenant	CT	2
Town Line Repairs, Inc. v. Anderson	90 A.D.2d 517, 455 N.Y.S.2d 28 (1982)	Sale of business	Automobile body and repair	NY	3d
Townsend v. Collord	575 S.W.2d 422 (Tex.Civ.App., Fort Worth 1978)	Occupation not specified	Title insurance	DE	AT-12
Transport Co. of Texas v. Robertson Transports, Inc.	152 Tex. 551, 261 S.W.2d 549 (1953)	No covenant	No covenant	TX	5

Case	Citation	Role	Industry	State	Ref
Travel Masters v. Sar Tours	742 S.W.2d 837 (Tex.Civ.App.—Dallas 1987)	Travel agent	Travel	TX	2, 3, 3a, 3c, 3f, 4, 13, AT-90
Treasure Chem. v. Team Laboratory Chem. Corp.	609 P.2d 285 (1980)	Salesperson	Chemicals (industrial)	MT	4
Triangle Leasing v. McMahon	385 S.E.2d 360 (N.C.App. 1989), aff'd in part and rev'd in part, 327 N.C. 224, 393 S.E.2d 854 (1990)	Rental agent	Vehicle leasing	NC	3, 3e, 3f, 4, 5
Triangle Sheet Metal Works v. Silver	154 Conn. 116, 222 A.2d 220 (1966)	No covenant	No covenant	CT	3f
Tricon Metals & Serv. v. Topp	537 So.2d 1331 (Miss. 1989)	Manager, sales	Metal	MS	10
Troup v. Heacock	367 So.2d 691 (Fla. 1st Dist.Ct.App. 1979)	Salesperson	Insurance	FL	8
Truly Nolen Exterminating v. Blackwell	125 Ariz. 481, 610 P.2d 483 (1980)	Exterminator	Pest control	AZ	3f
Tull v. Turek	37 Del.Ch. 190, 139 A.2d 368 (1958)	Sale of business	Nursing home	DE	10
Turner v. Robinson	214 Ga. 729, 107 S.E.2d 648 (1959)	Bidding agent	Tunnel drilling	AL	3d
Tuttle v. Riggs-Warfield-Roloson, Inc.	251 Md. 45, 246 A.2d 588 (1968)	Salesperson	Insurance	CT	3g
Tuttle v. Riggs-Warfield-Roloson, Inc.	251 Md. 45, 246 A.2d 588 (1968)	Salesperson	Insurance	MD	3c, 3d, 3f, 3g, 9, 10
Twenty Four Collection v. Keller	389 So.2d 1062 (Fla. 3d Dist.Ct.App. 1980), review denied, 419 So.2d 1048 (Fla. 1982)	Buyer	Clothing (women's retail)	FL	1, 4, 5, 9, 14

Case	Citation	Role	Industry	State	
Twin City Line Co. v. Harding Glass Co.	283 U.S. 353 (1931)	No covenant	No covenant	CT	14
Tyler v. Eufala Tribune Publishing Co.	500 So.2d 1005 (Ala. 1986)	Bookkeeper	Publishing (shoppers' guide)	AL	3, 3f, 9, 14
Tyler v. Eufala Tribune Publishing Co.	500 So.2d 1005 (Ala. 1986)	Photographer	Publishing (shoppers' guide)	AL	3, 3f, 9, 14
Tyler Enters. of Elwood v. Shafer	214 Ill.App.3d 145, 158 Ill.Dec. 50, 573 N.E.2d 863 (3d Dist. 1991)	Manager, sales	Lawn care products	IL	2, 3, 3f, 5
Tyler Enters. of Elwood v. Shafer	214 Ill.App.3d 145, 158 Ill.Dec. 50, 573 N.E.2d 863 (3d Dist. 1991)	Salesperson	Lawn care products	IL	2, 3, 3f, 5
U Shop Rite v. Richard's Paint Mfg. Co.	369 So.2d 1033 (Fla. 4th Dist.Ct.App. 1979)	Rivals' agreement	Not specified	FL	3d
U.S. v. U.S. Gypsum Co.	333 U.S. 364 (1946)	No covenant	No covenant	WY	7
U.S. v. Richberg	398 F.2d 523 (5th Cir. 1968)	No covenant	No covenant	WY	7
U3S Corp. of Am. v. Parker	202 Ga.App. 374, 414 S.E.2d 513, reconsideration denied (December 20, 1991), cert. denied (March 20, 1992)	Consultant	Computer service	GA	3f, 4
Uarco, Inc. v. Eastland	584 F.Supp. 1259 (D.Kan. 1984)	Salesperson	Forms (business)	KS	2, 3b, 5, 6
UNC Teton Exploration Drilling, Inc. v. Peyton	774 P.2d 584 (Wyo. 1989)	No covenant	No covenant	WY	10
Uni-Worth Enters. v. Wilson	244 Ga. 636, 261 S.E.2d 572 (1979)	Corporate officer	Automobile glass replacement service	GA	3f, 3g, 4
Uniform Rental Div., Inc. v. Moreno	83 A.D.2d 629, 441 N.Y.S.2d 538 (2d Dep't 1981)	Salesperson	Uniform rentals	CT	3g

Case	Citation	Position	Industry	State	Ref
Vacco Indus. v. Van Den Berg	5 Cal.App.4th 34, 6 Cal.Rptr. 2d 602 (1992)	Engineer	Military and aerospace petrochemical and nuclear power industry products manufacturing	CA	1, 8
Valco Cincinnati, Inc. v. N&D Machining Serv.	24 Ohio St.2d 41, 24 Ohio B. 83, 492 N.E.2d 814, 59 A.L.R.4th 629 (1986)	Manager (production)	Glue applicator equipment manufacturing	OH	2
Vascular & Gen. Surgical Assocs. v. Loiterman	234 Ill.App.3d 1, 175 Ill.Dec. 232, 599 N.E.2d 1246 (1st Dist. 1992)	Physician	Health care (Vascular surgery)	IL	2, 3, 3f, 14, AT-44
Vermont Elec. Supply Co. v. Andrus	132 Vt. 195, 315 A.2d 456 (1974)	Designer	Kitchens (appliances)	VT	2, 3, 3b, 3e, 3f, 5, 7, 8, 10
Vermont Elec. Supply Co. v. Andrus	132 Vt. 195, 315 A.2d 456 (1974)	Salesperson	Design (kitchens (appliances))	VT	2, 3, 3b, 3e, 3f, 5, 7, 8, 10
Village Key & Saw Shop, Inc. v. Gupton	639 So.2d 102 (Fla. 5th Dist.Ct.App. 1994)	Installer	Alarms	FL	1, 5, 14, AT-84
Vlasin v. Len Johnson & Co.	235 Nev. 450, 455 N.W.2d 772, 5 IER Cases 748 (1990)	Manager	Insurance	NE	2, 3, 3d, 3f, 4
Voices, Inc. v. Metal Tone Mfg. Co.	19 N.J. Eq. 324, 182 A. 880 (Ch.Div.), aff'd, 120 N.J. Eq. 618, 187 A. 370 (E.&A. 1936), cert. denied, 300 U.S. 656 (1937)	License agreement	Doll voice devices	NJ	14
Von Bremen v. MacMonnies	200 N.Y. 41, 93 N.E. 186 (1910)	Sale of business	Grocery (fancy) importing	NY	14
Voorhees v. Guyan Machinery Co.	191 W.Va. 450, 446 S.E.2d 672 (1994)	Salesperson	Coal industry equipment and supplies	WV	2, 3e, 3f, AT-90

Walter Implement, Inc. v. Focht	107 Wash.2d 553, 730 P.2d 1340 (1987)	No covenant	No covenant	WA	10
Ward v. Process Control Corp.	247 Ga. 583, 277 S.E.2d 671 (1981)	Exterminator	Pest control	GA	3f, 4
Ware v. Money-Plan Int'l	467 So.2d 1072 (Fla. 2d Dist.Ct.App. 1985)	Salesperson (independent contractor)	Insurance	FL	1
Water Processing Technologies, Inc. v. Ridgeway	618 So.2d 533 (La.App. 4th Cir. 1993)	Distributorship agreement	Water processing equipment	LA	1, 3f, 4
Water Servs. v. Tesco Chems.	410 F.2d 163 (5th Cir. 1969)	Engineer (field)	Water purifier manufacturing	GA	4
Water Servs. v. Tesco Chems.	410 F.2d 163 (5th Cir. 1969)	Salesperson	Water purifier manufacturing	GA	4
Waterfall Farm Sys. Inc. v. Craig	1995 U.S. App. LEXIS 17181 (D. Md., No. H-94-1247, Sept. 23, 1995)	Occupation not specified	Farming (hydroponic)	MD	3c
Waterfield Mortgage Co. v. O'Connor	172 Ind.App. 673, 361 N.E.2d 924 (1977)	Occupation not specified	Mortgage	IN	3, 3f
Watkins v. Avnet, Inc.	122 Ga.App. 474, 177 S.E.2d 582 (1970)	Manager (branch)	Motor products	GA	3
Watlow Elec. Mfg. Co. v. Wrob	899 S.W.2d 585 (Mo.App. 1995)	Settlement agreement	Thermocouple manufacturing and sales	MO	3f, AT-12
Watmet, Inc. v. Robinson	116 A.D.2d 998, 498 N.Y.S.2d 619 (4th Dep't 1986)	Salesperson	Manufacturer's representative	NY	7
Watson v. Waffle House	253 Ga. 671, 324 S.E.2d 175 (1985)	Lease	Restaurant	GA	3, 4, 14

Case	Citation	Position	Industry	State	Notes
Welcome Wagon v. Haschert	125 Ind.App. 503, 127 N.E.2d 103 (1955)	Hostess	Advertising	IN	2, 3f, 4, 9, 14
Welcome Wagon v. Morris	224 F.2d 693 (4th Cir. 1974)	Hostess	Advertising	VA	4, AT-85.2
Welcome Wagon Int'l v. Hostesses, Inc.	199 Neb. 27, 255 N.W.2d 865 (1977)	Hostess	Advertising	NE	3f, 4
Welcome Wagon Int'l v. Pender	255 N.C. 244, 120 S.E.2d 739 (1961)	Hostess	Advertising	NC	3f, 4
Wellendorf v. Local Union 377	1988 WL 59811 (Ohio Ct.App. (Mahoning), No. 87 C.A. 37, Jun. 7, 1988) (unreported)	No covenant	No covenant	OH	3c
Wells v. Auberry	429 N.E.2d 679 (Ind.App. 1982)	No covenant	No covenant	IN	5
Welles v. O'Connell	23 Conn.Supp. 335, 183 A.2d 287 (1962)	Salesperson	Real estate	CT	3f, 5, 6, 9
Wells v. Wells	9 Mass. App. Ct. 321, 400 N.E.2d 1317 (1980)	Owner (divorce)	Health care (Nursing service)	MA	2, 14
Wells v. Wells	9 Mass.App.Ct. 321, 400 N.E.2d 1317 (1980)	Owner (divorce)	Nursing (home) service	MA	2, 4, 5
Wells v. Wells	9 Mass. App. Ct. 321, 400 N.E.2d 1317 (1980)	Sale of business	Health care (Nursing service; divorce)	MA	2, 14
Wells v. Wells	9 Mass. App. Ct. 321, 400 N.E.2d 1317 (1980)	Sale of business	Health care (Home nursing service; divorce)	MA	2, 14
Wells v. Wells	9 Mass. App. Ct. 321, 400 N.E.2d 1317 (1980)	Sale of business	Home nursing service (Divorce)	MA	2, 14
Wells v. Wells	9 Mass. App. Ct. 321, 400 N.E.2d 1317 (1980)	Sale of business	Nursing service (Divorce)	MA	2, 14

				DE	10
White v. Metropolitan Merchandise Mart	107 A.2d 892 (Del.Super. 1954)	No covenant	No covenant		
White v. Sullivan	667 S.W.2d 305 (Ky.Ct.App. 1983)	Accountant	Accounting	KY	3f, 10
White Dairy Co. v. Davidson	283 Ala. 63, 214 So.2d 416 (1968)	Manager, sales	Dairy	AL	3f
Whiteco Indus., Inc. v. Nickolick	549 N.E.2d 396 (Ind.App. 1990)	No covenant	No covenant	IN	7
Whitefoot v. Hanover Ins. Co.	561 P.2d 717 (Wyo. 1977)	No covenant	No covenant	WY	7
Whiteside v. Griffis & Griffis, P.C.	902 S.W.2d 739 (Tex.Ct.App.—Austin 1995)	Attorney (shareholder)	Law	TX	3f, AT-6.1, AT-29, AT-30, AT-85
Whiteside v. Griffis & Griffis, P.C.	902 S.W.2d 739 (Tex.Ct.App.—Austin 1995)	Attorney	Law	TX	3f, AT-6.1, AT-29, AT-30, AT-85
Whitmyer Bros., Inc. v. Doyle	58 N.J. 25, 274 A.2d 577 (1971)	Corporate officer	Highway guard rail, sign, and fence erection	NJ	2, 5, 6, 14
Whitmyer Bros., Inc. v. Doyle	58 N.J. 25, 274 A.2d 577 (1971)	Corporate officer (director)	Highway guard rail, sign, and fence erector business	NJ	2, 5, 6, 14
Whittaker Gen. Medical Corp. v. Daniel	324 N.C. 523, 379 S.E.2d 824, reh'g denied, 325 N.C. 231, 381 S.E.2d 792, reh'g denied, 325 N.C. 277, 384 S.E.2d 531 (1989)	Salesperson	Medical equipment	NC	2, 3, 3b, 3e, 3g, 4, 10, AT-71
Whittenberg v. Williams	110 Colo. 418, 135 P.2d 228 (1943)	Exterminator	Pest control	CO	3f, 4
Whittinsville Plaza v. Kotseas	378 Mass. 85, 390 N.E.2d 243 (1979)	Shopping center covenant	Shopping center	MA	5

Wichita Wire, Inc. v. Lenox	11 Kan.App.2d 459, 726 P.2d 287 (1986)	No covenant	No covenant	KS	6
Widowsky v. Dudek	30 Conn.Supp. 288, 310 A.2d 766 (1972)	No covenant	No covenant	CT	3f
Wiley v. Royal Cup	258 Ga. 357, 370 S.E.2d 744 (1988)	Manager, sales	Coffee supply	GA	2, 3, 3c, 3d, 4
William B. Tanner Co. v. Taylor	530 S.W.2d 517 (Tenn.Ct.App. 1974)	Manager, sales	Media firm	TN	2, 3f, 5
Williams v. Hobbs	9 Ohio App.3d 331, 460 N.E.2d 287 (1983)	Osteopath	Health care (Osteopathic)	OH	3f, 7, 14
Williams v. Hobbs	9 Ohio App.3d 331, 460 N.E.2d 287 (1983)	Physician	Health care (Osteopathic)	OH	3f, 7, 14
Williams v. Vista Vestra, Inc.	178 Conn. 323, 422 A.2d 274 (1979)	No covenant	No covenant	CT	14
Williams & Montgomery v. Stellato	195 Ill.App.3d 544, 142 Ill.Dec. 359, 552 N.E.2d 1100 (1st Dist. 1980)	Attorney	Law (Insurance defense)	IL	2, 5, 6
Williamson v. Palzer	199 Ga.App. 35, 404 S.E.2d 131 (1991)	Sale of business	Florist	GA	10
Willis v. Dictograph Sales Corp.	222 Ind. 523, 54 N.E.2d 774 (1944)	Dealership agreement	Hearing aids	IN	3f
Willman v. Beheler	499 S.W.2d 770 (Mo. 1973)	Physician	Health care	MO	8, 9, 11
Wilmar, Inc. v. Corsillo	24 N.C.App. 271, 210 S.E.2d 427 (1974), cert. denied, 286 N.C. 421, 211 S.E.2d 802 (1975)	Salesperson	Janitorial supplies	NC	3

Case	Citation	Position	Industry	State	Sections
Wilmar, Inc. v. Liles	13 N.C.App. 71, 185 S.E.2d (1971), cert. denied, 280 N.C. 305, 186 S.E.2d 178 (1972)	Salesperson	Automotive and janitorial supplies	NC	3, 3b, 3c
Wilmington Trust Co. v. Consistent Asset Mgmt.	1987 WL 8459 (Del.Ch. March 25, 1987)	Corporate officer	Securities	DE	5, 14
Wilmington Trust Co. v. Consistent Asset Mgmt.	1987 WL 8459 (Del.Ch., No. 8667, Mar. 25, 1987)	Money manager	Securities	DE	5, 14
Wilmot H. Simonson Co. v. Green Textile Assocs.	755 F.2d 217 (1st Cir. 1985)	Sale of business	Beverage	NH	AT-21
Wilson v. Chemco Chem. Co.	711 S.W.2d 265 (Tex.Ct.App.—Dallas 1986)	Salesperson (independent contractor)	Chemicals	TX	3d, 3f, 9
Wilson v. Clarke	470 F.2d 1218 (1st Cir. 1972) (applying Massachusetts law)	Psychologist	Consulting (employment)	MA	1
Wilson v. Gamble	180 Miss. 499, 177 So. 363 (1937)	Physician	Health care	MS	3, 3d, 3f
Windsor-Douglas Assocs. v. Patterson	179 Ga.App. 674, 347 S.E.2d 362 (1986)	Recruiter	Employment agency	GA	3g
Wineburgh v. Meyer	95 U.S.App. D.C. 262, 221 F.2d 543 (1955) (per curiam)	Exterminator	Pest control	DC	3c, 3f
Winston v. Bourgeois, Bennett Thokey & Hickey	432 So.2d 936 (La.App. 4th Cir. 1983)	Accountant (partner)	Accounting	LA	1
Wirum & Cash, Architects v. Cash	837 P.2d 692 (Alaska 1992)	Architect	Architecture	AK	3, 3f, 3g, 4, 10, AT-45
Wisconsin Ice & Coal Co. v. Lueth	213 Wis. 42, 250 N.W. 819 (1933)	Delivery person	Ice	WA	3a
Wolf v. Colonial Life & Accident Ins. Co.	420 S.E.2d 217 (S.C. 1992)	Salesperson	Insurance	SC	2, 3, 3b, 3d, 3f, 3g, 10

Case	Citation	Party	Industry	State	Sections
Wood v. May	73 Wash.2d 307, 438 P.2d 587 (1968)	Horseshoer	Horseshoeing	RI	4
Wood v. May	73 Wash.2d 307, 438 P.2d 587 (1968)	Horseshoer	Horseshoeing	WA	2, 3, 3b, 3c, 3f, 4
Wood v. May	73 Wash.2d 307, 438 P.2d 587 (1968)	Horseshoer	Horseshoeing	WY	4
Woodward Ins v. White	437 N.E.2d 59 (Ind.App. 1981)	Sale of business	Insurance agency	IN	3
World Wide Health Studios v. Desmond	222 So.2d 517 (La.App. 1969)	Manager	Health spa	LA	10
Worldwide Auditing Servs. v. Richter	587 A.2d 772 (Pa.Super. 1991)	Corporate officer (executive)	Medical cost-containment service	PA	2, 3, 3f, 3g, 4, 5, 7, 8, 9, 11, AT-1, AT-32, AT-42
Worrie v. Boze	191 Va. 916, 62 S.E.2d 876 (1951)	Instructor	Education (Dance)	VA	2, 3f, 3g, 5, 6, 7, 8, 11
Worth Chem. Corp. v. Freeman	261 N.C.App. 780, 136 S.E.2d 118 (1964)	Salesperson	Chemicals	NC	3b
Wretham Co. v. Cann	345 Mass. 737, 189 N.E.2d 559 (1963)	Salesperson	Manufacturer's representative (heating and plumbing supplies, electrical appliances)	MA	12
Wright & Seaton v. Prescott	420 So.2d 623 (Fla. 4th Dist.Ct.App. 1982) *reh'g denied,* (Nov. 1, 1982)	Salesperson	Insurance	FL	3a, 3c
Wunderlich v. Fortas	776 S.W.2d 953 (Tenn. App. 1989)	No covenant	No covenant	TN	10

Case	Citation	Role	Industry	State	Factors
Wyatt v. Dishong	127 Ill.App.3d 716, 469 N.E.2d 608 (5th Dist. 1984)	Chiropractor	Health care (Chiropractic)	IL	4, 8
Wyatt Safety Supply v. Industrial Safety Prods.	566 So.2d 728 (Ala. 1990)	Sale of business	Safety equipment sales	AL	1, 14, AT-88
Wyckoff v. Painter	145 W.Va. 310, 115 S.E.2d 80 (1960)	Salesperson	Insurance	WV	3f, 3g, 14
Wyoming Bancorp. v. Bonham	563 P.2d 1382 (Wyo. 1977)	No covenant	No covenant	WY	10
Xerographics, Inc. v. Thomas	537 So.2d 140 (Fla. 2d Dist.Ct.App. 1988)	Manager (field)	Photocopier	FL	1, 3, 3f, 4, 6, 9, 14
Xerographics, Inc. v. Thomas	537 So.2d 140 (Fla. 2d Dist.Ct.App. 1988)	Service technician	Photocopiers	FL	1, 3, 3f, 4, 6, 9, 14
Yakus v. United States	321 U.S. 414, 64 S.Ct. 660, 88 L.Ed. 834 (1944)	No covenant	No covenant	IN	5
Young v. Altenhaus	472 So.2d 1152 (Fla. 1985)	No covenant	No covenant	FL	1, 6, AT-84
Young v. Mastrom, Inc.	99 N.C. 120, 392 S.E.2d 446, 5 IER Cases 814 (N.C.App.), *disc. review denied*, 327 N.C. 488, 397 S.E.2d 239 (1990)	Bookkeeper	Not specified	NC	2, 3, 3a, 3b, 3c, 7
Zeff, Farrington & Assocs. v. Farrington	168 Colo. 48, 449 P.2d 813 (1969)	Engineer	Civil (soil and foundation) engineering	CO	3d
Zellner v. Stephen D. Conrad, M.D. P.C.	183 A.D.2d 250, 589 N.Y.S.2d 903, 8 IER Cases 4 (2d Dep't 1992)	Physician	Health care (Ophthalmology)	NY	3, 3c, 3f, 11, 14
Zep Mfg. Co. v. Hartcock	824 S.W.2d 654 (Tex.Ct.App.—Dallas 1992)	Chemist	Chemical (industrial) manufacturing	TX	2, 3a, 4, 10, AT-90

		Sale of business	Health care (Medical practice (anesthesiology))		
Zickler v. Schultz	603 So.2d 916 (Ala. 1992)			AL	AT-48
Zinn v. Walker	87 N.C.App. 325, 361 S.E.2d 314 (1987), *disc. rev. denied*, 321 N.C. 747, 366 S.E.2d 871 (1988)	No covenant	No covenant	NC	AT-71
Zmotny v. Phillips	529 S.W.2d 760 (Tex. 1975)	No covenant	No covenant	TX	7
Zoecon Indus. v. American Stockman Tag Co.	713 F.2d 1174 (5th Cir. 1983)	No covenant	No covenant	AL	2
Zoning Bd. of Adjustment of Sparta Township v. Service Elec. Cable Television of N.J.	198 N.J.Super. 370, 487 A.2d 331 (App.Div. 1985)	No covenant	No covenant	NJ	5
Zurich Depository Corp. v. Gilenson	121 A.D.2d 443, 503 N.Y.S.2d 415 (Dep't 1986)	No covenant	No covenant	NY	2
Zurich Ins. Co. v. Allen	436 So.2d 1094 (Fla. 3d Dist.Ct.App. 1983)	No covenant	No covenant	FL	12

Indexes

Index of Employment Covenant Cases Specifying Occupation

For the "State" column, see the list of state abbreviations on page xviii in this volume if necessary.

For the "Question Nos." column:

- *See the "List of General Questions" beginning at page xvi of this volume for the meaning of question numbers, and page numbers for particular states.*
- *An "AT-" followed by a number (e.g., AT-1) indicates information is contained in a discussion of an Additional Topic; see the "Finding List of Additional Topics" beginning at page xxx of this volume to identify the topic concerned if necessary, and for the page numbers for particular states.*

For the "Citation" column, where the state is noted and it varies from that listed in the "State" column, this indicates a discussion of a case decided in another state. Cases not listed here are included in other indexes as follows:

- *Cases in which no occupation was mentioned in the court decision are listed by industry in the "Index of Employment Covenant Cases Not Specifying Occupation."*
- *Cases which involved a sale of business rather than an occupation are listed by industry in the "Index of Sale-of-Business Covenant Cases."*
- *Cases involving covenants relating to other types of transactions are listed by transaction/relationship in the "Index of Covenant Cases Not Involving Employment or Sale of Business."*
- *Cases not involving covenants are listed by state in the "Index of Cases Not Involving Covenants"*

Cases listed either in this index or in the "Index of Employment Covenant Cases Not Specifying Occupation" may be searched together by industry, using the "Index of Employment Covenant Cases by Industry." In that index, the term "Not specified" in the "Occupation" column is a signal to consult the "Index of Employment Covenant Cases Not Specifying Occupation," rather than the index below for additional information.

Editors Note: Cases decided by the Texas Court of Appeals before September 1, 1981, are cited as "Tex. Civ. App." After that date, cases are cited as "Tex. Ct. App." The change in the court's name and the rules for proper citation in documents submitted to Texas courts are explained in the Texas Rules of Form.

Occupation	Industry	State	Question Nos.	Case Name	Citation
Account executive	Advertising	MN	7	*Creative Communications Consultants v. Gaylord*	403 N.W.2d 654 (Minn.Ct.App. 1987)
Account executive	Meeting planning	IL	2	*Creative Entertainment Inc. v. Lorenz*	265 Ill.App.3d 343, 202 Ill.Dec. 571, 638 N.E.2d 217 (1994)
Account executive	Public relations	NY	3, 3a, 3e, 3f, 3g, 9, 10	*Mallory Factor, Inc. v. Schwartz*	146 A.D.2d 465, 536 N.Y.S.2d 752 (1st Dep't 1989)
Account executive (assistant)	Commercial property	LA	1, 3g	*Alexander & Alexander v. Simpson*	370 So.2d 670 (La.App. 4th Cir.) *writ denied*, 371 So.2d 836 (La. 1979)
Account executive (senior)	Building maintenance service	IL	2, 3c, 3f, 7, 14	*Millard Maintenance Serv. Co. v. Bernero*	207 Ill.App.3d 736, 152 Ill.Dec. 692, 566 N.E.2d 379 (1st Dist. 1990)
Account executive (senior)	Investments	NY	3, 3f	*Investor Access Corp. v. Doremus & Co.*	588 N.Y.S.2d 842 (App.Div. 2d Dep't 1992)
Account manager	Employment agency (temporary)	OK	4	*Key Temporary Personnel, Inc. v. Cox*	884 P.2d 1213 (Okla. 1994)
Accountant	Accounting	AL	1	*Burkett v. Adams*	361 So.2d 1 (Ala. 1978)
Accountant	Accounting	AL	1, 3f, 12, 14, AT-49, AT-87, AT-90	*Cherry, Bekaert & Holland v. Brown*	582 So.2d 502 (Ala. 1991)
Accountant	Accounting	AL	1, 14	*Gant v. Warr*	286 Ala. 387, 240 So.2d 383 (1970)
Accountant	Accounting	AL	1, 14	*Thompson v. Wiik, Reimer & Sweet*	391 So.2d 1016 (Ala. 1980)
Accountant	Accounting	CA	2, 3a	*Moss, Adams & Co. v. Shilling*	179 Cal.App.3d 124, 224 Cal.Rptr. 456 (1986)
Accountant	Accounting	DE	2, 3, 3b, 3c, 3f, 14	*Faw, Casson & Co. v. Cranston*	375 A.2d 463 (Del.Ch. 1977)
Accountant	Accounting	FL	3f	*Cherry, Bekaert & Holland v. LaSalle*	413 So.2d 436 (Fla. 3d Dist.Ct.App. 1982)

Accountant	Accounting	GA	2, 3f, 3g	Dougherty, McKinnon & Luby, P.C. v. Greenwald, Denzik & Davis, P.C.	213 Ga.App. 891, 447 S.E.2d 94 (1994)
Accountant	Accounting	GA	3, 3g	Fuller v. Kolb	238 Ga. 602, 234 S.E.2d 517 (1977)
Accountant	Accounting	GA	3f, 3g	Singer v. Habif, Arogeti & Wynne, P.C.	250 Ga. 376, 297 S.E.2d 473 (1982)
Accountant	Accounting	IN	3d, 3g	Ebbeskotte v. Tyler	127 Ind.App. 433, 142 N.E.2d 905 (1957)
Accountant	Accounting	IN	2, 3e, 3g, 4, 10, 11, 14	Seach v. Richards, Dieterle & Co.	439 N.E.2d 208 (Ind.App. 2d Dist. 1982)
Accountant	Accounting	KY	3f, 10	White v. Sullivan	667 S.W.2d 305 (Ky.Ct.App. 1983)
Accountant	Accounting	ME	3c	Smith, Batchelder & Rugg v. Foster	119 N.H. 679, 406 A.2d 1310 (1979)
Accountant	Accounting	MD	2, 3f, 4, 10, 11, 14	Holloway v. Faw, Casson & Co.	319 Md. 324, 572 A.2d 510 (1990)
Accountant	Accounting	MD	2, 3g, 4, 10, 11, 14	Holloway v. Faw, Casson & Co.	78 Md.App. 205, 552 A.2d 1311 (1989) (Holloway I), cert. granted, 559 A.2d 375, aff'd in part and rev'd in part, 319 Md. 324, 572 A.2d 510 (Md. 1990)
Accountant	Accounting	MO	10	Schott v. Beussink	817 S.W.2d 540 (Mo.App. 1991)
Accountant	Accounting	MT	1, 2, 3, 3a, 3d, 3e, 3f, 3g, 14	Dobbins, DeGuire & Tucker v. Rutherford, McDonald & Olson	218 Mont. 392, 708 P.2d 577 (1985)
Accountant	Accounting	ND	14	Biever, Drees, Nordell v. Coutts	305 N.W.2d 33 (N.D. 1981)
Accountant	Accounting	NE	3b, 3f, 7, 14	Dana F. Cole & Co. v. Byerly	211 Neb. 903, 320 N.W.2d 916 (1982)

Accountant	Accounting	WY	3d	Philip G. Johnson & Co. v. Salmen	211 Neb. 123, 317 N.W.2d 900 (1982)
Accountant	Accounting	WY	10	Weinrauch v. Kashkin	64 A.D.2d 897, 407 N.Y.S.2d 885 (1978)
Accountant	Accounting (tax)	FL	3b, 3c	Criss v. Davis, Presser & LaFaye	494 So.2d 525, *review denied*, 501 So.2d 1281 (Fla. 1st Dist.Ct.App. 1986)
Accountant	Accounting (tax)	NH	3	Seach v. Richards, Dieterle & Co.	439 N.E.2d 208 (Ind.Ct.App. 1982)
Accountant	Insurance	MI	3g	Follmer, Rudzewicz & Co. v. Kosko	420 Mich. 394, 362 N.W.2d 676 (1984)
Accountant (partner)	Accounting	CA	1, 3d	Swenson v. File	3 Cal.3d 389, 90 Cal.Rptr. 580, 475 P.2d 852 (1970)
Accountant (partner)	Accounting	CT	2, 3, 3f, 3g, 10	Spitz, Sullivan, Wachell & Falcetta v. Murphy	No. CV 86 0322422, 1991 WL 112718 (Conn.Super.Ct. June 13, 1991)
Accountant (partner)	Accounting	IL	3f, 13, AT-23	Decker, Berta & Co. v. Berta	225 Ill.App.3d 24, 167 Ill.Dec. 190, 587 N.E.2d 72 (4th Dist. 1992)
Accountant (partner)	Accounting	LA	1	Winston v. Bourgeois, Bennett Thokey & Hickey	432 So.2d 936 (La.App. 4th Cir. 1983)
Accountant (partner)	Accounting	MD	14, AT-49	Faw, Casson & Co. v. Everngman	99 Md.App. 129, 616 A.2d 426 (1992)
Accountant (partner)	Accounting	NV	11, 12	Engel v. Ernst	102 Nev. 392, 724 P.2d 215 (1986) (applying Colorado law)
Accountant (partner)	Accounting	NJ	3, AT-82	Schulhalter v. Salerno	279 N.J.Super. 504, 653 A.2d 596 (App.Div. 1995)
Accountant (partner)	Accounting	NY	2, 3, 6	Arthur Young & Co. v. Black	97 A.D.2d 369, 466 N.Y.S.2d 10 (1st Dep't 1983)

Occupation	Specified	State	Sections	Case	Citation
Accountant (partner)	Accounting	NY	2, 3, 3c	Arthur Young & Co. v. Galasso	142 Misc.2d 738, 538 N.Y.S.2d 424 (Sup.Ct. 1989)
Accountant (partner)	Accounting	NY	7	Deloitte & Touche L.L.P. v. Chiampou and Travis	636 N.Y.S.2d 679 (App.Div. 4th Dep't 1995)
Accountant (partner)	Accounting	SC	8	Derrick, Stubbs & Stith v. Rogers	256 S.C. 395, 182 S.E.2d 724 (1971)
Accountant (partner)	Accounting	SC	3a, AT-49	J.W. Hunt & Co. v. Davis	437 S.E.2d 557 (S.C. 1993)
Accountant (partner)	Accounting	TX	1, 3d, 3f, 3g, 4, 10, 11	Peat Marwick Main & Co. v. Haas	818 S.W.2d 381 (Tex. 1991)
Accountant (partner)	Accounting	VA	3e, 3f, 3g, 10, 14	Foti v. Cook	220 Va. 800, 263 S.E.2d 430 (1980)
Actor	Performing arts	NY	2	Nazzaro v. Washington	81 N.Y.S.2d 769 (Sup.Ct. 1948)
Actor	Performing arts	NY	14	Shubert Theatrical Co. v. Gallagher	206 A.D. 514, 201 N.Y.S. 577 (1923)
Actuary	Actuarial services	NC	2, 3, 3d, 3e, 3f, 4, 9, AT-23, AT-42	Hartman v. W.H. Odell & Assocs., Inc.	450 S.E.2d 912 (N.C.App. 1994)
Adjuster	Insurance	DE	2, 3f	John Roane, Inc. v. Tweed	33 Del.Ch. 4, 89 A.2d 548 (1952)
Adjuster	Insurance	KY	2, 3, 3a, 3b, 3c, 3d	Central Adjustment Bureau v. Ingram Assocs.	622 S.W.2d 681 (Ky.Ct.App. 1981)
Adjuster	Insurance	KY	2, 3, 3d, 3e, 3f, 4	Hammons v. Big Sandy Claims Serv.	567 S.W.2d 313 (Ky.Ct.App. 1978)
Adjuster	Insurance	MS	3f	Bagwell v. H.B. Wellborn & Co.	247 Miss. 564, 156 So.2d 739 (1963)
Adjuster	Insurance	NC	3, 3b, 3c	James C. Greene Co. v. Kelley	261 N.C. 166, 134 S.E.2d 166 (1964)

Administrator	Printing	IL	8	Wessel Co. v. Busa	28 Ill.App.3d 686, 329 N.E.2d 414 (1st Dist. 1975)
Advertising executive	Advertising	MN	3f, 10	Harris v. Bolin	310 Minn. 391, 247 N.W.2d 600 (Minn. 1980)
Agent (booking)	Entertainment (musical)	WI	3, 3e, 3f, 14	Gary Van Zeeland Talent, Inc. v. Sandas	84 Wis.2d 202, 267 N.W.2d 242 (1978)
Agent (booking)	Entertainment (theatrical)	NY	2	Frederick Bros. Artists Corp. v. Yates	271 App.Div. 69, 62 N.Y.S.2S 714 (1946), aff'd, 296 N.Y. 820, 72 N.E.2d 13 (1947) (per curiam)
Appraiser	Ad valorem property tax lowering service	MO	3f, 8, 9, 10, 11, AT-19, AT-66, AT-90	Property Tax Representatives, Inc. v. Chatham	891 S.W.2d 153 (Mo.App. 1995)
Architect	Architecture	AK	3, 3f, 3g, 4, 10, AT-45	Wirum & Cash, Architects v. Cash	837 P.2d 692 (Alaska 1992)
Art supervisor	Heat-applied graphics (transfers)	OH	2, 3, 4, 5, 6, 7	Levine v. Beckman	48 Ohio App.3d 24, 548 N.E.2d 267 (1988)
Asbestos-abatement technician	Asbestos abatement	NC	3f, 6, 7, 8, 14	Masterclean of N.C. v. Guy	82 N.C.App. 45, 345 S.E.2d 692 (1986)
Attorney	Ad valorem property tax lowering service	TX	1, 3d, 3f, 4, 9, AT-1, AT-33	Property Tax Assocs. v. Staffeldt	800 S.W.2d 349 (Tex.Ct.App.—El Paso 1990)
Attorney	Employee benefits consulting	IL	2, AT-6	Torrence v. Hewitt Assocs.	143 Ill.App.3d 520, 97 Ill.Dec. 592, 493 N.E.2d 74 (1986)
Attorney	Law	IN	AT-5A	Blackburn v. Sweeney	53 F.3d 825 (7th Cir. 1995)
Attorney	Law	MO	14, AT-79, AT-85	White v. Medical Review Consultants	831 S.W.2d 662 (Mo.App. 1992)
Attorney	Law	NY	AT-49, AT-79	Bigda v. Fischbach Corp.	898 F.Supp. 1004 (S.D.N.Y. 1995)
Attorney	Law	TX	3f, AT-6.1, AT-29, AT-30, AT-85	Whiteside v. Griffis & Griffis, P.C.	902 S.W.2d 739 (Tex.Ct.App.—Austin 1995)

Attorney (partner)	Law	IN	AT-85	*Kelly v. Smith*	588 N.E.2d 1306 (Ind.App. 4th Dist. 1992) *vacated on other grounds*, 611 N.E.2d 118 (Ind. 1993)
Attorney (partner)	Law	KS	1	*Miller v. Foulston, Siefkin, Powers & Eberhardt*	246 Kan. 450, 790 P.2d 404 (1990)
Attorney (partner)	Law	MA	1	*Meehan v. Shaughnessy*	404 Mass. 419, 535 N.E.2d 1255 (1989)
Attorney (partner)	Law	NJ	AT-49, AT-95	*Cohen v. Lord, Day & Lord*	75 N.Y.2d 85, 551 N.Y.S.2d 157, 550 N.E.2d 410 (1989)
Attorney (partner)	Law	NJ	AT-49, AT-95	*Denburg v. Parker Chapin, Flattau & Klimpl*	184 A.D.2d 343, 586 N.Y.S.2d 107 (1992), *modified and aff'd*, 82 N.Y.2d 375, 604 N.Y.S.2d 900, 624 N.E.2d 995 (1993)
Attorney (partner)	Law	NJ	3, 14	*Dwyer v. Jung*	133 N.J. Super. 343, 336 A.2d 498 (Ch.Div.) *aff'd o.b.*, 137 N.J.Super 135, 348 A.2d 208 (App.Div. 1975)
Attorney (partner)	Law	NJ	AT-49, AT-95	*Gray v. Martin*	63 Or.App. 173, 663 P.2d 1285, *review denied*, 295 Or. 541, 668 P.2d 384 (1983)
Attorney (partner)	Law	NJ	AT-49, AT-95	*Hagen v. O'Connell, Goyak & Ball, P.C.*	68 Or.App. 700, 683 P.2d 563 (1984)
Attorney (partner)	Law	NJ	AT-49, AT-95	*Howard v. Babcock*	7 Cal.Rptr.2d 687 (Ct.App. 1992), *aff'd in part and rev'd in part*, 6 Cal.4th 409, 25 Cal.Rptr. 80, 863 P.2d 150 (1993)
Attorney (partner)	Law	NJ	AT-49, AT-95	*Jacob v. Norris, McLaughlin & Marcus*	128 N.J. 10, 607 A.2d 142 (1992)

Role	Industry	State	Paragraph	Case	Citation
Auditor (accounts payable)	Not specified	NC	3f, 4	Schultz & Assocs. of the Se. v. Ingram	38 N.C.App. 422, 248 S.E.2d 345 (1978)
Baker	Bagels	VT	7	In re Burlington Bakery	549 A.2d 1044 (Vt. 1988)
Baker	Bakery	WY	3, 3f, 4, 8, 14, AT-93	Dutch Maid Bakeries v. Schleicher	58 Wyo. 374, 131 P.2d 630 (1942)
Bank officer (loan)	Bank	FL	3f	Flammer v. Patton	245 So.2d 854 (Fla. 1971)
Bartender	Bar	LA	1, 3	Daiquiri's III on Bourbon, Ltd. v. Wandfluh	608 So.2d 222 (La.App. 5th Cir. 1992), writ denied, 610 So.2d 801 (La. 1993)
Bidding agent	Tunnel drilling	AL	3d	Turner v. Robinson	214 Ga. 729, 107 S.E.2d 648 (1959)
Booking agent	Theatrical	NY	2	Frederick Bros. Artists Corp. v. Yates	271 A.D. 69, 62 N.Y.S.2S 714 (1946), aff'd, 296 N.Y. 820, 72 N.E.2d 13 (1947) (per curiam)
Bookkeeper	Medical services	OR	9	Professional Business Servs. v. Gustafson	285 Or. 307, 590 P.2d 729 (1979)
Bookkeeper	Not specified	NC	2, 3, 3a, 3b, 3c, 7	Young v. Mastrom, Inc.	99 N.C. 120, 392 S.E.2d 446, 5 IER Cases 814 (N.C.App.), disc. review denied, 327 N.C. 488, 397 S.E.2d 239 (1990)
Bookkeeper	Publishing (shoppers' guide)	AL	3, 3f, 9, 14	Tyler v. Eufala Tribune Publishing Co.	500 So.2d 1005 (Ala. 1986)
Bookkeeper	Service station	OR	3c	Bouska v. Wright	49 Or.App. 763, 621 P.2d 69 (1980)
Bookseller (partner)	Book retailing	MA	5	Old Corner Bookstore v. Upham	194 Mass. 101, 80 N.E.2d 228 (1907)
Broadcaster	Broadcasting (Radio)	AL	2, 3f, 5, 10, 11	Cullman Broadcasting Co. v. Bosley	373 So.2d 830 (Ala. 1979)
Broadcaster	Broadcasting (Radio)	AZ	3f, 9	Titus v. Superior Court, Maricopa County	91 Ariz. 18, 368 P.2d 874 (1962)

Position	Industry	State	Clauses	Case	Citation
Buyer	Clothing (women's retail)	FL	1, 4, 5, 9, 14	Twenty Four Collection v. Keller	389 So.2d 1062 (Fla. 3d Dist.Ct.App. 1980), review denied, 419 So.2d 1048 (Fla. 1982)
Buyer (assistant)	Gifts and stationery	TX	13, AT-90	Sakowitz v. Steck	669 S.W.2d 105 (Tex. 1984)
Cashier	Loan company	MD	3, 3f	Tawney v. Mutual Sys.	186 Md. 508, 47 A.2d 372 (1946)
Chemist	Chemical (industrial) manufacturing	TX	2, 3a, 4, 10, AT-90	Zep Mfg. Co. v. Hartcock	824 S.W.2d 654 (Tex.Civ.App., Dallas 1992)
Chemist	Plastic molding compounds manufacturing	OH	3a, 3g, 9, 10, 14	Premix, Inc. v. Zappitelli	561 F.Supp. 269 (N.D. Ohio 1983)
Chief operating officer	Debt collection	IL	5	McCormick v. Empire Accounts Serv.	49 Ill.App.3d 415, 364 N.E.2d 420 (1st Dist. 1977)
Chief operating officer	Hotel	NV	2, 3f, 14	Hotel Riviera v. Torres	97 Nev. 399, 632 P.2d 1155 (1981)
Chief operating officer	Meat (mail order)	IL	5	Armour & Co. v. United Am. Food Processers	37 Ill.App.3d 132, 345 N.E.2d 795 (1976)
Chiropractor	Health care (Chiropractic)	GA	3d, 3f	Carroll v. Harris	243 Ga. 34, 252 S.E.2d 461 (1979)
Chiropractor	Health care (Chiropractic)	ID	3	Frantz v. Parke	111 Idaho 1005, 729 P.2d 1068 (Ct.App. 1986)
Chiropractor	Health care (Chiropractic)	IL	4, 8	Wyatt v. Dishong	127 Ill.App.3d 716, 469 N.E.2d 608 (5th Dist. 1984)
Chiropractor	Health care (Chiropractic)	ME	5, 7	Moshe Myerowitz, D.C., P.A. v. Howard	507 A.2d 578 (Me. 1986)
Chiropractor	Health care (Chiropractic)	MN	3c	Kari Family Clinic of Chiropractic P.A. v. Bohnen	349 N.W.2d 868 (Minn.Ct.App. 1984)
Chiropractor	Health care (Chiropractic)	PA	5, 6, AT-54.1	Dice v. Clinicorp.	887 F.Supp. 803 (W.D. Pa. 1995)

Consultant	Law (Labor)	CA	2	John F. Matull & Assocs. v. Cloutier	194 Cal.App.3d 1049, 240 Cal.Rptr. 211, 2 IER Cases 1731 (1987)
Consultant	Lighting products (outdoor)	IL	2	Quality Lighting v. Benjamin	227 Ill.App.3d 880, 169 Ill.Dec. 890, 592 N.E.2d 377 (1st Dist. 1992)
Consultant	Management	NJ	2, 3a, 14	A.T. Hudson & Co. v. Donovan	216 N.J. Super. 426, 524 A.2d 412 (App.Div. 1987)
Consultant	Management	PA	3f, 8, AT-38.1, AT-54.1 AT-89.1	DeMuth v. Miller	652 A.2d 891 (Pa.Super. 1995)
Consultant	Management (medical and dental offices)	WY	3f, 10	Mills v. Murray	472 S.W.2d 6 (Mo.App. 1971)
Consultant	Management consulting	NY	10	Scientific Mgt. Inst., Inc. v. Mirrer	29 A.D.2d 962, 289 N.Y.S.2d 336 (2d Dep't 1968)
Consultant	Medical/dental office business services	IA	2, 3d, 4	Baker v. Starkey	259 Iowa 480, 144 N.W.2d 889 (1966)
Consultant	Service station	OR	3c	Bouska v. Wright	49 Or.App. 763, 621 P.2d 69 (1980)
Consultant	Tax/accounting	MN	4, 10	Dean Van Horn Consulting Assocs. v. Wold	395 N.W.2d 405, 1 IER Cases 1696 (Minn.Ct.App. 1986)
Consultant	Unemployment insurance advice	MO	3a	Reed, Roberts Assocs. v. Bailenson	537 S.W.2d 238 (Mo.App. 1976)
Consultant (acquisitions)	Publisher (microfiche)	NY	2, 3	Diaz v. Indian Head, Inc.	402 F.Supp. 111 (N.D. Ill.), aff'd, 525 F.2d 694 (7th Cir. 1975)
Consultant (crop and soil)	Agricultural consulting	SD	2, 3b, 3f, 5, 10	Centrol, Inc. v. Morrow	489 N.W.2d 890 (S.D. 1992)
Consultant (partnership)	Management (medical and dental practices)	TX	3	Henshaw v. Kroecke	656 S.W.2d 416 (Tex. 1983)
Corporate officer	Automobile glass replacement service	GA	3f, 3g, 4	Uni-Worth Enters. v. Wilson	244 Ga. 636, 261 S.E.2d 572 (1979)

Position	Industry	State	Clauses	Case	Citation
Corporate officer	Steel polishing	MI	1	Production Finishing Corp. v. Shields	158 Mich.App. 479, 405 N.W.2d 171 (1987)
Corporate officer (chairman)	Aviation service	PA	3f, 4	Reading Aviation Serv. v. Bertolet	454 Pa. 488, 311 A.2d 628 (1973)
Corporate officer (chairman)	Newspaper	AL	5, 7, 8	Harkness v. Scottsboro Newspapers	529 So.2d 100 (Ala. 1988)
Corporate officer (chief executive officer)	Check cashing	MO	3b, 8, AT-37	Panther v. Mr. Good-Rents, Inc.	817 S.W.2d 1 (Mo.App. 1991)
Corporate officer (chief executive officer)	Data processing	AL	8, 14	Robinson v. Computer Servicenters	346 So.2d 940 (Ala. 1977)
Corporate officer (chief executive officer)	Food service management	IL	3	Service Sys. Corp. v. Van Bortel	174 Ill.App.3d 412, 528 N.E.2d 378 (1st Dist. 1988)
Corporate officer (chief executive officer)	Gearbox manufacturing	MO	2, 3, 3d, 3f, 4, 8, 9, 11, AT-7, AT-68	Superior Gearbox Corp. v. Edwards	869 S.W.2d 239 (Mo.App. 1993)
Corporate officer (chief executive officer)	Grocery	AK	3	Roth v. Gamble-Skogmo, Inc.	532 F.Supp. 1029 (D.Minn. 1982)
Corporate officer (chief executive officer)	Grocery chain	MN	4, 10	Roth v. Gamble-Skogmo, Inc.	532 F.Supp. 1029 (D.Minn. 1982)
Corporate officer (chief executive officer)	Laundry, uniform rental	IN	2	In re Uniservices	517 F.2d 492 (7th Cir. 1975)

Occupation	Industry	State	Sections	Case	Citation
Corporate officer (chief executive officer)	Product packaging	NY	3f, 5, 8, 10	*Borne Chem. Co. v. Dictrow*	85 A.D.2d 646, 445 N.Y.S.2d 406 (2d Dep't 1981)
Corporate officer (chief executive officer)	Teleindicator manufacturing	NJ	2, 3, 3b, 3d, 3g, 4, 12, 14	*Solari Indus., Inc. v. Malady*	55 N.J. 571, 264 A.2d 53 (1970)
Corporate officer (chief executive officer)	Teleindicator manufacturing	RI	4	*Solari Indus., Inc. v. Malady*	55 N.J. 571, 264 A.2d 53 (1970)
Corporate officer (chief executive officer)	Teleindicator manufacturing	WY	4	*Solari Indus., Inc. v. Malady*	55 N.J. 571, 264, A.2d 53 (1970)
Corporate officer (chief executive officer)	Textile	NY	5	*Norman Weil Textiles, Inc. v. Zaretsky*	561 N.Y.S.2d 186 (App.Div. 1st Dep't 1990)
Corporate officer (chief executive officer)	Warehouse services (cold storage warehouse services for peanut industry and frozen storage warehouse services for local food processors)	GA	2, 3, 3f, 4, AT-29, AT-86A	*Sunstates Refrigerated Servs., Inc. v. Griffin*	216 Ga.App. 61, 449 S.E.2d 858 (1994)
Corporate officer (controller)	Meat processing	AK	3	*Gagliardi Bros., Inc. v. Caputo*	538 F.Supp. 525 (E.D.Pa. 1982)
Corporate officer (director)	Automobile dealership	TN	AT-29	*Dobbs v. Guenther*	846 S.W.2d 270 (Tenn.App. 1992)
Corporate officer (director)	Building products manufacturing	FL	AT-21	*Bolen Int'l, Inc. v. Meadow*	191 So.2d 51 (Fla. 3d Dist.Ct.App. 1966), *cert. denied*, 200 So.2d 808 (Fla. 1967)

Position	Business	State	Sections	Case	Citation
Corporate officer (director)	Building supply	PA	3, 3f, 9, AT-16, AT-42	*Krauss v. M. L. Klaster & Sons*	434 Pa. 403, 254 A.2d 1 (1969)
Corporate officer (director)	Freight forwarding	LA	1	*Marine Forwarding & Shipping Co. v. Barone*	154 So.2d 528 (La.App. 1963)
Corporate officer (director)	Hardware business	NC	3f	*Keith v. Day*	81 N.C.App. 185, 343 S.E.2d 562 (1986)
Corporate officer (director)	Highway guard rail, sign, and fence erector business	NJ	2, 5, 6, 14	*Whitmyer Bros., Inc. v. Doyle*	58 N.J. 25, 274 A.2d 577 (1971)
Corporate officer (director)	Hospital	IL	2, 3, 3f, 5, 11	*Sarah Bush Lincoln Health Center v. Perket*	238 Ill.App.3d 958, 178 Ill.Dec. 819, 605 N.E.2d 613 (4th Dist. 1992)
Corporate officer (director)	Incentive awards program planning	NY	3c	*McRand, Inc. v. van Beelen*	138 Ill.App.3d 1045, 93 Ill.Dec. 471, 486 N.E.2d 1306 (1985)
Corporate officer (director)	Insurance	IL	2, AT-6	*Frank B. Hall & Co. v. Payseur*	78 Ill.App.3d 230, 33 Ill.Dec. 522, 396 N.E.2d 1246 (1979)
Corporate officer (director)	Manufacturing	CA	1	*Radiant Indus. v. Skirving*	33 Cal.App.3d 401, 109 Cal.Rptr. 96 (1973)
Corporate officer (director)	Steel polishing	MI	1	*Production Finishing Corp. v. Shields*	158 Mich.App. 479, 405 N.W.2d 171 (1987)
Corporate officer (director)	Teleindicator manufacturing	NJ	2, 3, 3b, 3d, 3g, 4, 12, 14	*Solari Indus., Inc. v. Malady*	55 N.J. 571, 264 A.2d 53 (1970)
Corporate officer (director)	Teleindicator manufacturing	RI	4	*Solari Indus., Inc. v. Malady*	55 N.J. 571, 264 A.2d 53 (1970)
Corporate officer (director)	Teleindicator manufacturing	WY	4	*Solari Indus., Inc. v. Malady*	55 N.J. 571, 264, A.2d 53 (1970)
Corporate officer (director)	Water/sewer supplies wholesaling	IL	AT-23	*Central Water Works Supply, Inc. v. Fisher*	240 Ill.App.3d 952, 181 Ill.Dec. 545, 608 N.E.2d 618 (4th Dist. 1993)

Position	Business type	State	Provisions	Case	Citation
Corporate officer (executive)	Building supply	PA	3, 3f, 9, AT-16, AT-42	Krauss v. M. L. Klaster & Sons	434 Pa. 403, 254 A.2d 1 (1969)
Corporate officer (executive)	Developer (office park)	GA	3d, 4, AT-55	Koger Properties v. Adams-Cates Co.	247 Ga. 68, 274 S.E.2d 329 (1981)
Corporate officer (executive)	Medical cost-containment service	PA	2, 3, 3f, 3g, 4, 5, 7, 8, 9, 11, AT-1, AT-32, AT-42	Worldwide Auditing Servs. v. Richter	587 A.2d 772 (Pa.Super. 1991)
Corporate officer (executive)	Typography	PA	3, 3f, 10, AT-19, AT-41	Boyce v. Franklin Printing Co.	580 A.2d 1382 (Pa.Super. 1990), appeal denied, 593 A.2d 413 (Pa. 1991)
Corporate officer (executive)	Typography	PA	10	Boyce v. Smith-Edwards-Dunlap Co.	580 A.2d 1382 (Pa. 1990)
Corporate officer (president)	Aviation service	PA	3f, 4	Reading Aviation Serv. v. Bertolet	454 Pa. 488, 311 A.2d 628 (1973)
Corporate officer (president)	Business forms	IL	3c, 5, 6	Office Elecs. v. Grafik Forms	56 Ill.App.3d 395, 14 Ill.Dec. 320, 372 N.E.2d 125 (2d Dist. 1978)
Corporate officer (president)	Corrugated box manufacturing	MO	3d, 3f, 4, 10	Orchard Container Corp. v. Orchard	601 S.W.2d 299 (Mo.App. 1980)
Corporate officer (president)	Data processing	AL	8, 14	Robinson v. Computer Servicenters	346 So.2d 940 (Ala. 1977)
Corporate officer (president)	Debt collection	IL	5	McCormick v. Empire Accounts Serv.	49 Ill.App.3d 415, 364 N.E.2d 420 (1st Dist. 1977)
Corporate officer (president)	Electronics manufacturing	CA	2, 3d, 14	Loral Corp. v. Moyes	174 Cal.App.3d 268, 219 Cal.Rptr. 836 (1985)
Corporate officer (president)	Food	MO	3c, 9, 12	Ranch Hands Foods v. Polar Pak Foods	690 S.W.2d 437 (Mo.App. 1985)
Corporate officer (president)	Food service management	IL	3	Service Sys. Corp. v. Van Bortel	174 Ill.App.3d 412, 528 N.E.2d 378 (1st Dist. 1988)

Position	Industry	State	Clause	Case	Citation
Corporate officer (president)	Product packaging	NY	3f, 5, 8, 10	Borne Chem. Co. v. Dictrow	85 A.D.2d 646, 445 N.Y.S.2d 406 (2d Dep't 1981)
Corporate officer (president)	Security service	WI	3e	Matter of Cent. Watch	22 B.R. 561, 9 Bankr.Ct.Dec. 523 (1982)
Corporate officer (president)	Teleindicator manufacturing	NJ	2, 3, 3b, 3d, 3g, 4, 12, 14	Solari Indus., Inc. v. Malady	55 N.J. 571, 264 A.2d 53 (1970)
Corporate officer (president)	Teleindicator manufacturing	RI	4	Solari Indus., Inc. v. Malady	55 N.J. 57i; 264 A.2d 53 (1970)
Corporate officer (president)	Teleindicator manufacturing	WY	4	Solari Indus., Inc. v. Malady	55 N.J. 571, 264, A.2d 53 (1970)
Corporate officer (president)	Textile	NY	5	Norman Weil Textiles, Inc. v. Zaretsky	561 N.Y.S.2d 186 (App.Div. 1st Dep't 1990)
Corporate officer (president)	Travel	PA	3b, 3c	Wainwright's Travel Serv. v. Schmolk	347 Pa.Super. 199, 500 A.2d 476 (1985)
Corporate officer (secretary)	Electrical contracting	NY	AT-49, AT-79	Bigda v. Fischbach Corp.	898 F.Supp. 1004 (S.D.N.Y. 1995)
Corporate officer (secretary)	Rotary tooling manufacturing	VA	3, 3e, 3f, 4, AT-2, AT-21, AT-23, AT-39, AT-54.1, AT-86A, AT-96	Roto-Die, Inc. v. Lesser	899 F.Supp. 1515 (W.D. Va. 1995)
Corporate officer (vice president)	Advertising	AL	1	Parker v. EBSCO Indus.	282 Ala. 98, 209 So.2d 383 (1968)
Corporate officer (vice president)	Advertising	GA	4, AT-23	White v. Fletcher-Mayo Assocs.	251 Ga. 203, 303 S.E.2d 746, 1 IER Cases 218 (1983)
Corporate officer (vice president)	Automobile dealership	GA	4, AT-23, AT-53A	Redmond v. Royal Ford	244 Ga. 711, 261 S.E.2d 585 (1979)
Corporate officer (vice president)	Awards program planning	IL	2, 3, 3c, 3d, 3f, 3g, 4, 5, 6, 11, 14	McRand, Inc. v. van Beelen	138 Ill.App.3d 1045, 93 Ill.Dec. 471, 486 N.E.2d 1306 (1st Dist. 1985)

Position	Business	State	Provisions	Case	Citation
Corporate officer (vice president)	Direct marketing (mailing lists)	NY	7	Perez v. Computer Directions Group, Inc.	177 A.D.2d 359, 576 N.Y.S.2d 114 (1st Dep't 1991)
Corporate officer (vice president)	Food service management	IL	3	Service Sys. Corp. v. Van Bortel	174 Ill.App.3d 412, 528 N.E.2d 378 (1st Dist. 1988)
Corporate officer (vice president)	Foreign currency exchange and precious metal firms	DC	2	Ruesch v. Ruesch Int'l Monetary Servs.	479 A.2d 295 (D.C.App. 1984)
Corporate officer (vice president)	Fund-raising (police groups)	IN	3g, 5, 9, 14	JAK Productions, Inc. v. Wiza	986 F.2d 1080 (7th Cir. 1993)
Corporate officer (vice president)	Grant application preparation	AL	2	Public Sys. v. Towry	587 S.2d 829, 6 IER Cases 1076 (Ala. 1991)
Corporate officer (vice president)	Grocery and discount pharmacy chain retailing	MA	1, 2, 3f, 4, 14	Kroger v. Stop & Shop Cos.	13 Mass.App. 310, 432 N.E.2d 566, further appellate review denied (1982)
Corporate officer (vice president)	Hydraulics	WV	9, 10	Standard Hydraulics v. Kerns	387 S.E.2d 130 (W.Va. 1989) (per curiam)
Corporate officer (vice president)	Incentive awards program planning	NY	3c	McRand, Inc. v. van Beelen	138 Ill.App.3d 1045, 93 Ill.Dec. 471, 486 N.E.2d 1306 (1st Dist. 1985)
Corporate officer (vice president)	Insurance	IL	2, AT-6	Frank B. Hall & Co. v. Payseur	78 Ill.App.3d 230, 33 Ill.Dec. 522, 396 N.E.2d 1246 (1979)
Corporate officer (vice president)	Insurance	MO	AT-6, AT-21	Universal Underwriters Ins. Co. v. Lyon	896 S.W.2d 762 (Mo.App. 1995)
Corporate officer (vice president)	Insurance	TX	3b	Pasant v. Jackson Nat'l Life Ins. Co.	52 F.3d 94 (5th Cir. 1995) (applying Texas law)
Corporate officer (vice president)	Insurance	WY	3f	Commercial Bankers Life Ins. Co. of Am. v. Smith	516 N.E.2d 110 (Ind.App. 3d Dist. 1987)
Corporate officer (vice president)	Maintenance product manufacturing	AL	1	C&C Prod. v. Fidelity & Deposit Co.	512 F.2d 1375 (5th Cir. 1975)

Corporate officer (vice president)	Unemployment law, tax, and employee benefits consulting	NY	2, 3, 3d, 3f, 5, 14	*Reed, Roberts Assocs. v. Strauman*	40 N.Y.2d 303, 386 N.Y.S.2d 677, 353 N.E.2d 590 *rearg. denied*, 40 N.Y.2d 918, 389 N.Y.S.2d 1027, 357 N.E.2d 1033 (1976)
Corporate officer (vice president)	Wood moulding manufacturing	GA	3c	*Mouldings, Inc. v. Potter*	315 F.Supp. 704 (M.D.Ga. 1970)
Corporate officer (vice president)	Wood veneer manufacturing	IN	3d	*Ackerman v. Kimball Int'l, Inc.*	634 N.E.2d 778 (Ind.App. 1994), *aff'd as modified*, 652 N.E.2d 507 (Ind. 1995)
Corporate officer (vice president, assistant)	Bank	AK	3	*DeCristofaro v. Security Nat'l Bank*	664 P.2d 167 (Alaska 1983)
Cosmetologist	Beauty	TX	3a	*Carl Coiffure, Inc. v. Mourlot*	410 S.W.2d 209 (Tex.Civ.App. 1967)
Counsellor	Financial management	NC	3b	*Mastrom, Inc. v. Warren*	18 N.C.App. 199, 196 S.E.2d 528 (1973)
Counter person	Car rental	TN	2	*Matthews v. Barnes*	155 Tenn. 110, 293 S.W.2d 993 (1927)
Counter person	Car rental	WI	3a, 3c, 3f, 14	*Behnke v. Hertz Corp.*	70 Wis.2d 818, 235 N.W.2d 690 (1975)
Courier	Automobile tag and title	MD	2, 3, 3f	*Becker v. Bailey*	268 Md. 93, 299 A.2d 835 (1973)
Court reporter	Court reporting	MA	6	*Edgecomb v. Edmonston*	257 Mass. 12, 153 N.E. 99 (1926)
Court reporter	Court reporting	SC	3f, 10, 14	*Depositions And . . . Inc. v. Campbell*	406 S.E.2d 390, 6 IER Cases 999 (S.C.Ct.App. 1991)
Court reporter	Public stenography	OH	3b, 3b, 3c, 3d, 3f, 4, 9, AT-10	*Rogers v. Runfola & Assocs.*	57 Ohio St.3d 5, 565 N.E.2d 540, 6 IER Cases 160 (1991)

Occupation	State	Provisions	Case	Citation
Dentist	MI	1, 4, 14	Compton v. Lepak, D.D.S., P.C.	154 Mich.App. 360, 397 N.W.2d 311 (1986), leave denied, 428 Mich. 862 (1987)
Dentist	MN	2, 5, 7	Saliterman v. Finney	361 N.W.2d 175 (Minn.Ct.App. 1985)
Dentist	ND	11, 14	Olson v. Swendiman	62 N.D. 649, 244 N.W. 870 (N.D. 1932)
Dentist	IL	14	People v. Spounias	20 Ill.App.2d 184, 155 N.E.2d 326 (1959)
Dentist	NV	3	Karpinski v. Ingrasci	28 N.Y.2d 45, 320 N.Y.S.2d 1, 268 N.E.2d 751 (1971)
Dentist	NY	2, 3, 3f, 5, 11	Karpinski v. Ingrasci	28 N.Y.2d 45, 320 N.Y.2d 1 268 N.E.2d 751 (1971)
Dentist (independent contractor)	CO	1	Smith v. Sellers	747 P.2d 15 (Colo.App. 1987)
Dentist (independent contractor)	KS	14	Saliterman v. Finney	361 N.W.2d 175 (Minn.App. 1985)
Designer	MO	AT-68	Contour Chair Lounge Co. v. Aljean Furniture Mfg. Co.	403 S.W.2d 922 (Mo.App. 1966)
Designer	VT	2, 3, 3b, 3e, 3f, 5, 7, 8, 10	Vermont Elec. Supply Co. v. Andrus	132 Vt. 195, 315 A.2d 456 (1974)
Designer	DE	3, 5, 14	McCann Surveyors v. Evans	611 A.2d 1 (Del.Ch. 1987)
Detective	OH	3d, 3f, 3g, 4, 5, AT-35, AT-36, AT-54, AT-86	Professional Investigations & Consulting Agency v. Kingsland	69 Ohio App.3d 753, 591 N.E.2d 1265 (Ohio App. 10th Dist. 1990)

Profession	Specialty	State	Sections	Case	Citation
Electrologist	Beauty	IL	2, 5, 8	Booth v. Greber	48 Ill.App.3d 213, 6 Ill.Dec. 477, 363 N.E.2d 6 (1977)
Electrologist	Beauty	NY	3a, 3d, 3f, 10	Curtis v. Amela-Bouyea	137 A.D.2d 944, 525 N.Y.S.2d 69 (3d Dep't 1988)
Engineer	Aeronautical engineering	FL	3g, 14, AT-41, AT-86	Sanz v. R.T. Aerospace Corp.	650 So.2d 1057 (Fla. 3d Dist.Ct.App. 1995)
Engineer	Audio engineering (recording studio)	IL	2, 3f, 5, 7, 14	Audio Properties, Inc. v. Kovach	275 Ill. App. 3d 145, 211 Ill. Dec. 651, 655 N.E.2d 1034 (1st Dist. 1995)
Engineer	Automated system design	IL	2, 14	Capsonic Group v. Swick	181 Ill.App.3d 988, 537 N.E.2d 1378 (2d Dist. 1989)
Engineer	Chemical engineering	DE	5	E.I. duPont de Nemours & Co. v. American Potash & Chem. Co.	200 A.2d 428 (Del.Ch. 1964)
Engineer	Civil (concrete aggregates testing) engineering	MD	3f	E.L. Conwell & Co. v. Gutberlet	429 F.2d 527 (4th Cir. 1970)
Engineer	Civil (soil and foundation) engineering	CO	3d	Zeff, Farrington & Assocs. v. Farrington	168 Colo. 48, 449 P.2d 813 (1969)
Engineer	Civil engineering	MN	2, 4, 5, 7, 9	Cherne Indus. v. Grounds & Assocs.	278 N.W.2d 81 (Minn. 1979)
Engineer	Civil engineering	MT	1, 3, 3d, 3e, 3f, 7, 14	Daniels v. Thomas, Dean & Hoskins	804 P.2d 359 (Mont. 1990)
Engineer	Computer assisted design (class rings)	MN	2	Jostens v. National Computer Sys.	318 N.W.2d 691 (Minn. 1982)
Engineer	Computer systems engineering	TX	2, 5, 7	Electronic Data Sys. Corp. v. Powell	524 S.W.2d 343 (Tex.Civ.App.—Dallas 1975, writ ref'd n.r.e.)

Occupation	Industry	State	Section	Case	Citation
Engineer	Mechanical (ceramics, tobacco and other industries; designing and manufacturing machines for) engineering	NC	3d	Engineering Assocs., Inc. v. Pankow	258 N.C. 137, 150 S.E.2d 56 (1966)
Engineer	Military and aerospace petrochemical and nuclear power industry products manufacturing	CA	1, 8	Vacco Indus. v. Van Den Berg	5 Cal.App.4th 34, 6 Cal.Rptr. 2d 602 (1992)
Engineer	Mud (oil well drilling service) engineering	CO	12	Dresser Indus. v. Sandrick	732 F.2d 783 (10th Cir. 1984)
Engineer	Plastic container	CT	5, 12	Continental Group v. Kinsley	422 F.Supp. 838 (D.Conn. 1976)
Engineer	Recording studio (audio)	IL	2, 3f, 5, 7, 14	Audio Properties, Inc. v. Kovach	275 Ill.App.3d 145, 211 Ill.Dec. 651, 655 N.E.2d 1034 (1st Dist. 1995)
Engineer	Telecommunications testing (remote access)	MD	3, 3f	Hekimian Laboratories v. Domain Sys.	664 F.Supp. 493, 2 IER Cases 928 (S.D. Fla. 1987)
Engineer (field)	Water purifier manufacturing	GA	4	Water Servs. v. Tesco Chems.	410 F.2d 163 (5th Cir. 1969)
Esthetician	Beauty (facial spa salon)	SC	2, 3, 3f, 4	Faces Boutique, Ltd. v. Gibbs	455 S.E.2d 707 (S.C.App. 1995)
Estimator	Fire detection and extinguishing equipment	IN	AT-18	Holman v. Korsen Protection Servs.	580 N.E.2d 984 (Ind.App.2d Dist. 1991)
Estimator	Insurance clean-up and reconstruction	IN	2, 3f	Captain & Co. v. Towne	404 N.E.2d 1159 (Ind.App. 1980)

Exterminator	Pest control	FL	2, 3d, 3e, 3f	Tomasello, Inc. v. de Los Santos	394 So.2d 1069 (Fla. 4th Dist.Ct.App. 1981)
Exterminator	Pest control	GA	3f, 3g	Nunn v. Orkin Exterminating Co.	256 Ga. 203, 350 S.E.2d 425 (1986)
Exterminator	Pest control	GA	3g	Orkin Exterminating Co. v. Pelfrey	237 Ga. 284, 227 S.E.2d 251 (1976)
Exterminator	Pest control	GA	3, 3d, 3g	Orkin Exterminating Co. v. Walker	251 Ga. 536, 307 S.E.2d 914 (1984)
Exterminator	Pest control	GA	3f, 4	Ward v. Process Control Corp.	247 Ga. 583, 277 S.E.2d 671 (1981)
Exterminator	Pest control	IA	3, 3f, 9, 10, 14	Orkin Exterminating Co. v. Burnett	259 Iowa 1218, 146 N.W.2d 320 (1966)
Exterminator	Pest control	IA	3f, 5, 9, 11	Presto-X-Co. v. Ewing	442 N.W.2d 85 (Iowa 1989)
Exterminator	Pest control	KS	14	Abalene Pest Control Serv., Inc. v. Powell	8 A.D.2d 734, 187 N.Y.S.2d 381 (1959)
Exterminator	Pest control	LA	AT-32	Allied Bruce Terminix Co. v. Guillory	649 So.2d 652 (La.App. 3d Cir. 1994)
Exterminator	Pest control	LA	1, 2	"Bugs" Burger Bugs Killer v. Keiser	463 So.2d 45 (La.App. 5th Cir. 1985)
Exterminator	Pest control	LA	1	Hirsch v. Miller	187 So.2d 709 (La. 1966)
Exterminator	Pest control	LA	1, 2	Orkin Exterminating Co. v. Broussard	346 So.2d 1274 (La.App. 3d Cir.), writ denied, 350 So.2d 902 (La. 1977)
Exterminator	Pest control	MS	3, 3d, 3f, 4	Redd Pest Control Co. v. Heatherly	248 Miss. 34, 157 So.2d 133 (1963)
Exterminator	Pest control	NC	3	Orkin Exterminating Co. of Raleigh v. Griffin	258 N.C. 179, 128 S.E.2d 139 (1962)

Occupation	Industry	State	Sections	Case	Citation
Hair stylist	Beauty	FL	3f	*Tiffany Sands, Inc. v. Mezhibovsky*	463 So.2d 349 (Fla. 3d Dist.Ct.App. 1985)
Hair stylist	Beauty	GA	3d, 3f	*Fleury v. AFAB, Inc.*	205 Ga. 642, 423 S.E.2d 49 (Ga.App. 1992)
Hair stylist	Beauty	GA	3d	*Johnson v. Lee*	243 Ga. 642, 423 S.E.2d 49 (Ga.App. 1992)
Hair stylist	Beauty	IL	2, 3, 5, 14	*LSBZ Inc. v. Brokis*	237 Ill.App.3d 415, 177 Ill.Dec. 866, 603 N.E.2d 1240 (2d Dist. 1992)
Hair stylist	Beauty	LA	1, 3g	*John Jay Esthetic Salon v. Woods*	377 So.2d 1363 (La.App. 4th Cir. 1979)
Hair stylist	Beauty	MA	2, 3, 3a, 3f, 5	*Avallone v. Elizabeth Arden Sales Corp.*	344 Mass. 556, 183 N.E.2d 496 (1962)
Hair stylist	Beauty	NY	3, 5, 14	*Family Affair Haircutters, Inc. v. Detling*	110 A.D.2d 745, 488 N.Y.S.2d 204 (2d Dep't 1985)
Hair stylist	Beauty	TX	3a	*Carl Coiffure, Inc. v. Mourlot*	410 S.W.2d 209 (Tex.Civ.App. 1967)
Hair stylist	Beauty	WI	1, 2, 3, 3a, 3b, 3c, 3d, 3e, 3f, 7, 13	*NBZ, Inc. v. Pilarski*	185 Wis.2d 827, 520 N.W.2d 93 (Wis.App. 1994)
Horseshoer	Horseshoeing	RI	4	*Wood v. May*	73 Wash.2d 307, 438 P.2d 587 (1968)
Horseshoer	Horseshoeing	WA	2, 3, 3b, 3c, 3f, 4	*Wood v. May*	73 Wash.2d 307, 438 P.2d 587 (1968)
Horseshoer	Horseshoeing	WY	4	*Wood v. May*	73 Wash.2d 307, 438 P.2d 587 (1968)
Horticulturist	Nursery	FL	5	*Lovell Farms, Inc. v. Levy*	641 So.2d 103, 9 IER Cases 435 (Fla. 3d Dist.Ct.App. 1994)
Host (show)	Broadcasting (Television)	OH	3f, 7, 14	*Clooney v. Scripps-Howard Broadcasting Co. WCPO Television Div.*	35 Ohio App.2d 124, 300 N.E.2d 256 (1973)
Hostess	Advertising	IA	6, 10	*Briggs v. Boston*	15 F.Supp. 763 (N.D. Iowa 1936)

Hostess	Advertising	IN	2, 3f, 4, 9, 14	Welcome Wagon v. Haschert	125 Ind.App. 503, 127 N.E.2d 103 (1955)
Hostess	Advertising	NC	3f, 4	Welcome Wagon Int'l v. Pender	255 N.C. 244, 120 S.E.2d 739 (1961)
Hostess	Advertising	NE	3f, 4	Welcome Wagon Int'l v. Hostesses, Inc.	199 Neb. 27, 255 N.W.2d 865 (1977)
Hostess	Advertising	OH	2, 3, 3a, 14	Briggs v. Butler	140 Ohio St. 499, 45 N.E.2d 757 (1942)
Hostess	Advertising	VA	4, AT-85.2	Welcome Wagon v. Morris	224 F.2d 693 (4th Cir. 1974)
Hygienist (industrial)	Industrial hygiene consulting	CO	1, AT-89, AT-90	Occusafe, Inc. v. EG&G Rocky Flats, Inc.	54 F.2d 618 (10th Cir. 1995)
Immunologist	Medical diagnostic kit manufacturing	UT	2	Microbiological Research Corp. v. Muna	625 P.2d 690 (Utah 1981)
Income tax preparer	Income tax preparation	AL	3f	Clayton & Assocs. v. McNaughton	279 Ala. 159, 182 So.2d 890 (1966)
Income tax preparer	Income tax preparation	NY	2, AT-30A	HBD, Inc. v. Ryan	203 A.D.2d 326, 610 N.Y.S.2d 300 (App.Div. 2d Dep't 1994)
Industrial hygienist	Industrial hygiene consulting	CO	1, AT-89, AT-90	Occusafe, Inc. v. EG&G Rocky Flats, Inc.	54 F.2d 618 (10th Cir. 1995)
Inspector	Pipe	LA	1	Lamb v. Quality Inspection Servs.	398 So.2d 643 (La.App. 3d Cir. 1981)
Inspector (home)	Home inspection	CT	6	Gardocki v. Goldring Home Inspections, Inc.	6 C.S.C.R. 988 (November 18, 1991)
Installer	Air conditioning and heating equipment	NC	3, 3a, 3b, 3f, 5, 7	Milner Airco, Inc. of Charlotte, NC v. Morris	111 N.C.App. 866, 433 S.E.2d 811 (1993)
Installer	Alarms	FL	1, 5, 14, AT-84	Gupton v. Village Key & Saw Shop, Inc.	656 So.2d 475, 10 IER Cases 1224 (Fla. 1995)

Installer	Alarms	FL	1, 5, 14, AT-84	Village Key & Saw Shop, Inc. v. Gupton	639 So.2d 102 (Fla. 5th Dist.Ct.App. 1994)
Installer	Alarms	GA	1, 2, 3, 3f, AT-20	Vortex Protective Serv., Inc. v. Dempsey	218 Ga.App. 763, 463 S.E.2d 67 (1995)
Installer	Automobile air conditioners	FL	1, 2, 3, 3e, 4, 5, 6, 14, AT-84	Hapney v. Central Garage	579 So.2d 127, 6 IER Cases 353, 16 Fla. L. Weekly D359 (Fla. 2d Dist.Ct.App.), review denied, 591 So.2d 180 (Fla. 1991)
Installer	Automobile roof	AL	2, 3, 14	DeVoe v. Cheatham	413 So.2d 1141 (Ala. 1982)
Installer (equipment, factory)	Textiles	SC	7	Lowndes Prods. v. Brower	259 S.C. 322, 191 S.E.2d 761 (1972)
Installer's helper	Air conditioning and heating equipment	NC	3, 3a, 3b, 3f, 5, 7	Milner Airco, Inc. of Charlotte, NC v. Morris	111 N.C.App. 866, 433 S.E.2d 811 (1993)
Instructor	Education (Dance)	AL	3, 3f	Hill v. Rice	259 Ala. 587, 67 So.2d 789 (1953)
Instructor	Education (Dance)	NC	3f	Amdar, Inc. v. Satterwhite	37 N.C.App. 410, 246 S.E.2d 165 (1978)
Instructor	Education (Dance)	OH	2, 3, 3d, 3e, 3f, 4, 5, 6, 13, 14	Arthur Murray Dance Studios of Cleveland v. Witter	62 Ohio Laws Abs. 17, 105 N.E.2d 685 (C.P. 1952)
Instructor	Education (Dance)	TX	10	Arabesque Studios v. Academy of Fine Arts Int'l	529 S.W.2d 564 (Tex.Civ.App.—Dallas 1975)
Instructor	Education (Dance)	VA	2, 3f, 3g, 5, 6, 7, 8, 11	Worrie v. Boze	191 Va. 916, 62 S.E.2d 876 (1951)
Instructor	Education (Driving (truck))	LA	1, 2, 7	Diesel Driving Academy v. Ferrier	563 So.2d 898 (La.App. 2d Cir. 1990)
Instructor	Education (Music)	CO	3f, 9	Miller v. Kendall	541 P.2d 126 (Colo.App. 1975)
Instructor	Education (Physical)	MD	2, 3e, 3f, 14	Milward v. Gerstung Int'l Sport Educ.	268 Md. 483, 302 A.2d 14 (1973)

Manager	Accounting	CA	2, 3a	Moss, Adams & Co. v. Shilling	179 Cal.App.3d 124, 224 Cal.Rptr. 456 (1986)
Manager	Automobile glass installation	IA	2, 3b, 3c, 3d, 3e, 3f, 4, 5	Iowa Glass Depot, Inc. v. Jindrich	338 N.W.2d 376 (Iowa 1983)
Manager	Bakery	DE	3a, 3f	Capital Bakers, Inc. v. Leahy	20 Del.Ch. 407, 178 A. 648 (1935)
Manager	Brush excavation	AR	3f	McLeod v. Meyer	237 Ark. 173, 372 S.W.2d 220 (1963)
Manager	Chemical	GA	4	Kem Mfg. Corp. v. Sant	182 Ga.App. 135, 355 S.E.2d 437 (1987)
Manager	Chemical processing equipment manufacturing	VA	8, 14	Grant v. Carotek, Inc.	737 F.2d 410 (4th Cir. 1984)
Manager	Dairy	CT	3, 3b, 3f	Torrington Creamery, Inc. v. Davenport	126 Conn. 515, 12 A.2d 780 (1940)
Manager	Debt collection	AR	3c, 3f, 4, 12	Credit Bureau Management Co. v. Huie	254 F.Supp. 547 (E.D. Ark. 1966) (applying Texas law)
Manager	Debt collection	ID	2, 5	Drong v. Coulthard	87 Idaho 486, 394 P.2d 283 (1964)
Manager	Electrical contracting	CO	1, 3, 3d, 3e, 3f, 6, 14 AT-59	Harrison v. Albright	40 Colo.App. 227, 577 P.2d 302 (1977)
Manager	Employment agency (data processors)	TX	2, 7	Rugen v. Interactive Business Sys. Inc.	864 S.W.2d 548 (Tex.Ct.App.—Dallas 1993)
Manager	Employment agency (technical division)	MN	2	Walker Employment Serv. v. Parkhurst	300 Minn. 264, 219 N.W.2d 437 (1974)
Manager	Employment agency (temporary)	NC	3d, 9, 14, AT-42	Manpower of Guilford County v. Hedgecock	42 N.C.App. 515, 257 S.E.2d 109 (1979)
Manager	Finance	AL	3f	Stokes v. Moore	262 Ala. 59, 77 So.2d 331 (1955)

Manager	Metal welding	CT	2, 3, 3d, 3f, 3g, 14	Scott v. General Iron & Welding Co.	171 Conn. 132, 368 A.2d 111 (1976)
Manager	Oil company	NC	3a	Seaboard Indus. v. Blair	10 N.C.App. 323, 178 S.E.2d 781 (1971)
Manager	Oil company	NH	3	Seaboard Indus. v. Blair	10 N.C.App. 323, 178 S.E.2d 781 (1971)
Manager	Pest control	AL	1, 3f, 4, 10	Dobbins v. Getz Exterminators of Ala.	382 So.2d 1135 (Ala.Civ.App. 1980)
Manager	Pest control	AR	2, 3d, 3f, 3g, 7	Orkin Exterminating Co. v. Murrell	212 Ark. 449, 206 S.W.2d 185 (1947)
Manager	Pest control	FL	3f, AT-42	Capelouto v. Orkin Exterminating Co. of Fla.	183 So.2d 532 (Fla.), appeal dismissed, 385 U.S. 11, reh'g denied, 385 U.S. 964 (1966)
Manager	Pest control	IL	3c	Smithereen Co. v. Renfroe	325 Ill. App. 229, 59 N.E.2d 545 (1st Dist. 1945)
Manager	Pest control	NE	2, 3g, 4	Ecolab, Inc. v. Morrisette	879 F.2d 325 (8th Cir. 1989) (applying Nebraska law)
Manager	Produce brokerage	AZ	2, 3b, 3d, 3e, 3g, 14	Amex Distrib. Co. v. Mascari	150 Ariz. 510, 724 P.2d 596 (App. 1986)
Manager	Produce brokerage	WY	3f	Amex Distrib. Co. v. Mascari	150 Ariz. 510, 724 P.2d 596 (App. 1986)
Manager	Propane	TX	3b	B. Cantrell Oil Co. v. Hino Gas Sales	756 S.W.2d 648 (Tex.Ct.App.—Corpus Christi 1988)
Manager	Property management	GA	2, 3, 3d, 3g, 4	Lane Co. v. Taylor	174 Ga.App. 356, 330 S.E.2d 112 (1985)
Manager	Property management	IL	5, 7, AT-23	Hamer Holding Group v. Elmore	202 Ill.App.3d 994, 148 Ill.Dec. 310, 560 N.E.2d 907 (1st Dist. 1990)

Manager (branch)	Finance	WV	3, 9, 10	Household Fin. Corp. v. Sutton	130 W.Va. 277, 43 S.E.2d 144 (1947)
Manager (branch)	Fur processing	NJ	6, 10	A. Hollander & Son v. Imperial Fur Blending Corp.	2 N.J. 235, 66 A.2d 319 (1949)
Manager (branch)	Insurance industry survey and audit service	KS	4, 5, 6, 12	Equifax Servs. v. Hitz	905 F.2d 1355 (10th Cir. 1990)
Manager (branch)	Insurance underwriting, inspection, auditing, and loss-control	FL	9	Insurance Field Servs. v. White & White Inspection	384 So.2d 303 (Fla. 3d Dist.Ct.App. 1980)
Manager (branch)	Jewelry (fashion)	GA	4	Harrison v. Sarah Coventry, Inc.	228 Ga. 169, 184 S.E.2d 448 (1971)
Manager (branch)	Liquefied petroleum gas/appliance	AL	3a, 3c, 3f, AT-43	Daughtry v. Capital Gas	285 Ala. 89, 229 So.2d 480 (1969)
Manager (branch)	Motor products	GA	3	Watkins v. Avnet, Inc.	122 Ga.App. 474, 177 S.E.2d 582 (1970)
Manager (branch)	Pest control	LA	3, 3f, AT-32, AT-42	Allied Bruce Terminix Cos. v. Ferrier	634 So.2d 44 (La.App. 1st Cir. 1994)
Manager (branch)	Pest control	LA	1, 3a	Orkin Exterminating Co. v. Foti	287 So.2d 569 (La.App. 3d Cir. 1973)
Manager (branch)	Pest control	LA	1, 2, 3, 3e, 14	Orkin Exterminating Co. v. Foti	302 So.2d 593 (La. 1974)
Manager (business)	Supplies	WA	8	Parsons Supply v. Smith	22 Wash.App. 520, 591 P.2d 821 (1979)

Manager (division)	Electrical/electronic connector manufacturing	IL	3	AMP, Inc. Fleischhacker	823 F.2d 1199, 3 IER Cases 73 (7th Cir. 1987)
Manager (division)	Employee benefits (insurance, annuities)	VA	AT-8	Hilb, Rogal, & Hamilton Co. v. DePew	440 S.E.2d 918 (Va. 1994)
Manager (division)	Insurance and annuities (employee benefits)	VA	AT-8	Hilb, Rogal, & Hamilton Co. v. DePew	440 S.E.2d 918 (Va. 1994)
Manager (division)	Janitorial products	IL	3, 4	North Am. Paper Co. v. Unterberger	172 Ill.App.3d 410, 122 Ill.Dec. 362, 526 N.E.2d 621, 3 IER Cases 1057 (1st Dist. 1988)
Manager (field)	Photocopier	FL	1, 3, 3f, 4, 6, 9, 14	Xerographics, Inc. v. Thomas	537 So.2d 140 (Fla. 2d Dist.Ct.App. 1988)
Manager (general)	Automobile dealership	TN	AT-29	Dobbs v. Guenther	846 S.W.2d 270 (Tenn.App. 1992)
Manager (general)	Boot and belt manufacturing	TX	13	Justin Belt Co. v. Yost	502 S.W.2d 681 (Tex. 1973)
Manager (general)	Brick industry equipment manufacturing	NC	3, 3c, 3f	Forrest Paschal Mach. Co. v. Milholen	27 N.C.App. 678, 220 S.E.2d 190 (1975)
Manager (general)	Building supplies	MS	3, 3c, 3f, 8, 9, 14	Frierson v. Sheppard Bldg. Supply Co.	247 Miss. 157, 154 So.2d 151 (1963)
Manager (general)	Fund-raising (police groups)	IN	3g, 5, 9, 14	JAK Productions, Inc. v. Wiza	986 F.2d 1080 (7th Cir. 1993)
Manager (general)	Insurance claims adjustment	IL	8	C.G. Caster Co. v. Regan	43 Ill.App.3d 663, 357 N.E.2d 162 (1st Dist. 1976)
Manager (general)	Laxative manufacturing	DC	3f, 4, 9	Burton, Parsons & Co. v. Parsons	146 F.Supp. 114 (D.D.C. 1956)

Manager (office)	Financial services	GA	3	Landmark Fin. Servs. v. Tarpley	236 Ga. 586, 224 S.E.2d 736 (1976)
Manager (office)	Insurance adjustment investigation	NH	12, 14	Allied Adjustment Serv. v. Heney	125 N.H. 698, 484 A.2d 1189 (1984) (applying Massachusetts law)
Manager (office)	Medical record procurement service (legal community)	TX	10	Champion v. Wright	740 S.W.2d 848 (Tex.Ct.App.—San Antonio 1987)
Manager (office)	Not specified	GA	3c	Baker v. National Credit Ass'n	211 Ga. 635, 88 S.E.2d 19 (1955)
Manager (office)	Prosthetic devices	IA	2, 3f, 4	Lamp v. American Prosthetics	379 N.W.2d 909 (Iowa 1986)
Manager (office)	Real estate brokerage	TX	3, 3a	Gill v. Guy Chipman Co.	681 S.W.2d 264 (Tex.Ct.App.—San Antonio 4th Dist. 1984)
Manager (office)	Tool and die steels	IL	2	Cincinnati Tool Steel Co. v. Breed	136 Ill.App.3d 267, 90 Ill.Dec. 463, 482 N.E.2d 170 (2d Dist. 1985)
Manager (office)	Veterinary medicine	TX	2, 3f	Cukjati v. Burkett	772 S.W.2d 215 (Tex.Ct.App.—Dallas 1989)
Manager (office)	Veterinary medicine	TX	3b	Cukjati v. Burkett	772 S.W.2d 215 (Tex.Ct.App.—Dallas 1989)
Manager (operations)	Glass (automobile) installation	MO	2, 3, 3f, 5, 6, 9, 14, AT-21	Osage Glass, Inc. v. Donovan	693 S.W.2d 71 (Mo. 1985)
Manager (plant)	Coffee/tea processing	LA	1	Standard Brands, Inc. v. Zumpe	264 F.Supp. 254 (E.D.La. 1967)
Manager (plant)	Portable building manufacturing	AR	12, AT-83	Nelms v. Morgan Portable Building Corp.	305 Ark. 284, 808 S.W.2d 314 (1991)
Manager (plant)	Railroad car axle rebuilding	NE	2, 4	CAE Vanguard, Inc. v. Newman	246 Neb. 334, 518 N.E.2d 652 (1994)
Manager (plant)	Textiles	SC	7	Lowndes Prods. v. Brower	259 S.C. 322, 191 S.E.2d 761 (1972)

Manager (senior accounts)	Awards program planning	IL	2, 3, 3c, 3d, 3f, 3g, 4, 5, 6, 11, 14	McRand, Inc. v. van Beelen	138 Ill.App.3d 1045, 93 Ill.Dec. 471, 486 N.E.2d 1306 (1st Dist. 1985)
Manager (senior accounts)	Incentive awards program planning	NY	3c	McRand, Inc. v. van Beelen	138 Ill.App.3d 1045, 93 Ill.Dec. 471, 486 N.E.2d 1306 (1985)
Manager (senior accounts)	Paper	NY	2, 3, 3f, 14	Scott Paper Co. v. Finnegan	101 A.D.2d 787, 476 N.Y.S.2d 316 (1st Dep't 1984)
Manager (senior regional)	Courier service	MO	3d, 3e	Gelco Express Corp. v. Ashby	689 S.W.2d 790 (Mo.App. 1985)
Manager (service)	Car wash building, supplies, and repair service	TX	3f, 7, AT-21, AT-41	Car Wash. Sys. of Tex., Inc. v. Brigance	856 S.W.2d 853 (Tex.Ct.App.—Fort Worth 1993)
Manager (service and branch)	Fire prevention equipment	PA	3b, 3c	George W. Kistler, Inc. v. O'Brien	464 Pa. 475, 347 A.2d 311 (1975)
Manager (store)	Beauty products	LA	3	Sally Beauty Co. v. Barney	442 So.2d 820 (La.App. 4th Cir. 1983)
Manager (store)	Clothing/jewelry	DE	3f	Livingston v. Macher	30 Del.Ch. 94, 54 A.2d 169 (1947)
Manager (store)	Hardware retailing	TN	3f	Suggs v. Glenn	1989 Tenn.App., No. 837, Jan. 20, 1989
Manager (store)	Liquefied petroleum gas retailing	MS	3, 3d, 3e, 3f, 7, 8	Empiregas, Inc. of Kosciusko v. Bain	599 So.2d 971 (Miss. 1992)
Manager (store)	Rentals	GA	3d, AT-55	Colquitt v. Network Rental	195 Ga.App. 244, 393 S.E.2d 28 (1990)
Manager (store, partner)	Not specified	IN	2	Slisz v. Munzenreider Corp.	411 N.E.2d 700 (Ind.App. 1980)
Manager (trainee)	Loan (small)	IA	2, 3f	Mutual Loan Co. v. Pierce	245 Iowa 1051, 65 N.W.2d 405 (1954)
Manager (unit)	Food services	IL	12	American Food Mgmt. v. Henson	105 Ill.App.3d 141, 434 N.E.2d 59 (5th Dist. 1982)

Manager (yard)	Lumber retailing	WI	4	*Fullerton Lumber Co. v. Torborg*	270 Wis.2d 133, 70 N.W.2d 585 (1955)
Manager, sales	Advertising	AL	1	*Parker v. EBSCO Indus.*	282 Ala. 98, 209 So.2d 383 (1968)
Manager, sales	Advertising	MI	1	*Thompson Recruiting Advertising, Inc. v. Wedes*	651 F.Supp. 107 (E.D.La 1986)
Manager, sales	Barbecue and fireplace accessories	MO	5, 10, AT-12, AT-21	*Jackes-Evans Mfg. Co. v. Christen*	848 S.W.2d 553, 8 IER Cases 469 (Mo.App. 1993)
Manager, sales	Building industry products and services	PA	3c, 3f, 5	*Harsco Corp. v. Klein*	395 Pa.Super. 212, 576 A.2d 1118 (1990)
Manager, sales	Cable television equipment	UT	3, 3b, 3c, 3d, 3f, 5, 6, 7, 10	*System Concepts, Inc. v. Dixon*	669 P.2d 421 (Utah 1983)
Manager, sales	Cable television equipment	WY	3f	*Systems Concepts, Inc. v. Dixon*	669 P.2d 421 (Utah 1983)
Manager, sales	Chemicals	FL	3f, 5, 6	*State Chem. Mfg. Co. v. Lopez*	642 So.2d 1127 (Fla.App. 3 Dist. 1994)
Manager, sales	Chemicals	TN	3f	*Dearborn Chem. Co. v. Rhodes*	(Tenn.Ct.App. April 19, 1985) (LEXIS, Employ library, Tenn. file)
Manager, sales	Coffee supply	GA	2, 3, 3c, 3d, 4	*Wiley v. Royal Cup*	258 Ga. 357, 370 S.E.2d 744 (1988)
Manager, sales	Cooling tower heat-exchange film pack	TX	2, 3a, 5, 8	*Bertotti v. C.E. Sheppard Co.*	752 S.W.2d 168 (Tex.Ct.App.—Houston 1988)
Manager, sales	Dairy	AL	3f	*White Dairy Co. v. Davidson*	283 Ala. 63, 214 So.2d 416 (1968)
Manager, sales	Debt collection	AZ	2, 3, 7, 8, 14	*American Credit Bureau v. Carter*	11 Ariz.App. 145, 462 P.2d 838 (1969)
Manager, sales	Insurance	IL	4	*L&R Ins. Agency v. McPhail*	92 Ill. App. 2d 107, 235 N.E.2d 153 (5th Dist.), appeal denied, 39 Ill.2d 626 (1986)

Manager, sales	Insurance	OH	AT-12	Hilb, Rogal & Hamilton Agency of Dayton v. Reynolds	81 Ohio App.3d 330, 610 N.E.2d 1102 (Ohio App. 3d Dist. 1992)
Manager, sales	Insurance	SD	4, 14	First Am. Sys. v. Rezatto	311 N.W.2d 51 (S.D. 1981)
Manager, sales	Intraocular lens manufacturing	MN	12	Surgidev Corp. v. Eye Technology, Inc.	648 F.Supp. 661 (D.Minn. 1986), aff'd, 828 F.2d 452 (8th Cir. 1987)
Manager, sales	Lawn care products	IL	2, 3, 3f, 5	Tyler Enters. of Elwood v. Shafer	214 Ill.App.3d 145, 158 Ill.Dec. 50, 573 N.E.2d 863 (3d Dist. 1991)
Manager, sales	Media firm	TN	2, 3f, 5	William B. Tanner Co. v. Taylor	530 S.W.2d 517 (Tenn.Ct.App. 1974)
Manager, sales	Medical devices (angioplasty products)	MA	14	C.R. Bard, Inc. v. Boden	D.C. Mass., No. 89-0088-Z, May 9, 1989
Manager, sales	Metal	MS	10	Tricon Metals & Serv. v. Topp	537 So.2d 1331 (Miss. 1989)
Manager, sales	Monuments and mausoleums	AL	3	McNeel Marble Co. v. Robinette	259 Ala. 66, 65 So.2d 221 (1953)
Manager, sales	Not specified	AL	1	Industrial Corp. v. Marlow	292 Ala. 407, 295 So.2d 396 (1976)
Manager, sales	Not specified	VA	3f, 3g, 12	Rochester v. Rochester Corp.	316 F.Supp. 139 (E.D.Va. 1970)
Manager, sales	Pipe and tube inspection service (oil field industry)	TX	3f	AMF Tuboscope v. McBryde	618 S.W.2d 105 (Tex.Ct.App. 1981)
Manager, sales	Printing materials	IL	2	Image Supplies v. Hilmert	71 Ill.App.3d 710, 28 Ill.Dec. 86, 390 N.E.2d 68 (1979)
Manager, sales	Rubber handgrips	AR	2	Allen v. Johar Inc.	823 S.W.2d 824 (Ark. 1992)
Manager, sales	Television installations (hospital sites)	GA	11	Shandor v. Wells Nat'l Serv. Corp.	478 F.Supp. 12 (N.D.Ga. 1979)

Position	Industry/Product	State	Sections	Case	Citation
Manager, sales (regional)	Carburetion equipment	MO	3g	Empire Gas Corp. v. Graham	654 S.W.2d 329 (Mo.App. 1983)
Manager, sales (regional)	Insulation	IL	3d, 3g, 4	Dryvit Sys. v. Rushing	132 Ill.App.3d 9, 477 N.E.2d 35 (1st Dist. 1985)
Manager, sales (regional)	Mutual funds	PA	3	Pennsylvania Funds Corp. v. Vogel	399 Pa. 1, 159 A.2d 472 (1960)
Manager, sales (regional)	Printing (check imprinting)	NJ	10	Knollmeyer v. Rudco Indus.	154 N.J. Super. 309, 381 A.2d 378 (App.Div. 1977)
Manager, sales and general	Plastic piece goods	MA	3, 3c, 3d	Novelty Bias Binding Co. v. Shevrin	342 Mass. 714, 175 N.E.2d 374 (1961)
Manager, sales, overseas	Airline customers	OH	14	Evans v. Duracote Corp.	13 Ohio App.2d 63, 233 N.E.2d 873 (1968)
Manager trainee	Alarms (fire and burglar)	GA	3d, 3f, 4, 14, AT-55	Rollins Protective Servs. Co. v. Palermo	249 Ga. 138, 287 S.E.2d 546 (1982)
Manager trainee	Pest control	GA	4, 8	Orkin Exterminating Co. v. Gill	222 Ga. 760, 152 S.E.2d 411 (1966)
Manicurist	Beauty	MO	3, 3a, 5	Nail Boutique v. Church	758 S.W.2d 206 (Mo.App. 1988)
Manufacturer's representative	Appliances	IL	5	Peterson-Jorwic Group v. Pecora	224 Ill.App.3d 460, 166 Ill.Dec. 718, 586 N.E.2d 676 (1st Dist. 1991)
Manufacturer's representative	Jewelry	GA	1, AT-20	Klovis, Inc. v. Kinsler	239 Ga. 569, 238 S.E.2d 344 (1977)
Manufacturer's representative	Not specified	GA	3, 3d, 3f, 4	Jarrett v. Hamilton	179 Ga.App. 422, 346 S.E.2d 875 (1986)
Manufacturer's representative	Not specified	WY	3d, 7	Jarrett v. Hamilton	179 Ga.App. 422, 346 S.E.2d 875 (1986)

Profession	Industry	State	Sections	Case	Citation
Nurse	Health care (Nursing service (home))	MS	3, 7	Sta-Home Health Agency v. Umphers	562 So.2d 1258 (Miss. 1990)
Nurse (visiting)	Home health care	NY	3f	Tender Loving Care v. Franzese	131 A.D.2d 747, 517 N.Y.S.2d 50 (2d Dep't 1987)
Nurse (vocational, licensed)	Weight loss	TX	8	Kees v. Medical Directors, Inc.	583 S.W.2d 475 (Tex.Civ.App. 1979)
Nurse's aide (geriatric)	Nursing services (geriatric)	OH	3b, 3c, AT-21, AT-39	Chrysalis Health Care, Inc. v. Brooks	65 Ohio Misc.2d 32, 640 N.E.2d 915 (Ohio Mun. 1994)
Operator	Car repair	MO	3d, 10	Herrington v. Hall	624 S.W.2d 148 (Mo.App. 1981)
Optician	Health care (Optical)	WA	3c	Schneller v. Hayes	176 Wash. 115, 28 P.2d 273 (1934)
Optician	Ophthalmic dispensing	NY	2	Carpenter & Hughes v. De Joseph	10 N.Y.2d 925, 224 N.Y.S.2d 9, 179 N.E.2d 854 (1961)
Optometrist	Health care (Optometry)	ME	2, 3, 3c, 3f, 10, 11	Brignull v. Albert	666 A.2d 82, 11 IER Cases 319 (Me. 1995)
Optometrist	Health care (Optometry)	NC	2, 3d	Beasley v. Banks	90 N.C.App. 458, 368 S.E.2d 885 (1988)
Optometrist	Health care (Optometry)	PA	3f, 9, 10	Hayes v. Altman	424 Pa. 23, 225 A.2d 670 (1967)
Orthodontist (apprentice)	Health care (Dentistry)	DC	3e, 3f, 7, 9, 14	Erikson v. Hawley	56 App.D.C. 268, 12 F.2d 491 (1926)
Osteopath	Health care (Osteopathic)	OH	3f, 7, 14	Williams v. Hobbs	9 Ohio App.3d 331, 460 N.E.2d 287 (1983)
Performer	Performing arts (Vaudeville)	NY	14	Shubert Theatrical Co. v. Gallagher	206 A.D. 514, 201 N.Y.S. 577 (1923)
Performer (theatrical)	Performing arts	NY	2	Nazzaro v. Washington	81 N.Y.S.2d 769 (Sup.Ct. 1948)

Occupation	Industry	State	Restrictions	Case	Citation
Personality	Broadcasting (Television)	OH	3f, 7, 14	Clooney v. Scripps-Howard Broadcasting Co. WCPO Television Div.	35 Ohio App.2d 124, 300 N.E.2d 256 (1973)
Pharmacist	Pharmaceutical services	UT	2, 3, 3a, 3d, 3f, 5, 8, 14	Allen v. Rose Park Pharmacy	237 P.2d 823 (Utah 1951)
Phlebotomist	Medical lab	IL	2, 3b, 5, 6, 7, 14	Southern Ill. Medical Business Assocs. v. Camillo	190 Ill.App.3d 664, 138 Ill.Dec. 4, 546 N.E.2d 1059 (5th Dist. 1989)
Photographer	Photographic services (school yearbook and pictures)	SC	3e, 3f, 5, 14	Delmar Studios of the Carolinas v. Kinsey	233 S.C. 313, 104 S.E.2d 338 (1958)
Photographer	Publishing (shoppers' guide)	AL	3, 3f, 9, 14	Tyler v. Eufala Tribune Publishing Co.	500 So.2d 1005 (Ala. 1986)
Photographer	School pictures	WI	4, 12	Bush v. National School Studios, Inc.	139 Wis 2d 635, 407 N.W.2d 883 (1987)
Photographer (portrait)	Photographic services	NV	3f, 4	Haig v. Gittings	260 S.W.2d 311 (Tex. 1953)
Physician	Health care	CA	1	Bosley Medical Group v. Abramson	161 Cal.App.3d 284, 207 Cal.Rptr. 477 (1984)
Physician	Health care	CO	3f	Freudenthal v. Espey	45 Colo. 488, 102 P.2d 280 (1909)
Physician	Health care	FL	11, 14, AT-75	Humana Medical Plan v. Jacobson	1992 WL 385412 (Fla. 3d Dist.Ct.App., No. 91-1396, Dec. 29, 1992)
Physician	Health care	FL	14, AT-86	Tannenbaum v. Biscayne Osteopathic Hosp., Inc.	190 So.2d 777 (Fla. 1966)
Physician	Health care	GA	3f	Dominy v. National Emergency Servs.	215 Ga.App. 537, 451 S.E.2d 472 (1994)

Physician	Health care	GA	AT-42	Gynecology Oncology, P.C. v. Weiser	212 Ga.App. 858, 443 S.E.2d 526 (1994)
Physician	Health care	GA	3f	McAlpin v. Coweta Fayette Surgical Assocs., P.C.	458 S.E.2d 499 (Ga.App. 1995)
Physician	Health care	GA	3f	McMurray v. Bateman	221 Ga. 240, 144 S.E.2d 345 (1965)
Physician	Health care	GA	3, 3d, 3f, 12, AT-22, AT-65	Pittman v. Harbin Clinic Professional Ass'n	210 Ga.App. 767, 437 S.E.2d 619 (1993)
Physician	Health care	GA	3, AT-22	Roberts v. Tifton Medical Clinic	206 Ga.App. 612, 426 S.E.2d 188 (1992)
Physician	Health care	IL	3, 4	Akhter v. Shah	199 Ill.App.3d 131, 74 Ill.Dec. 730, 456 N.E.2d 232 (1st Dist. 1983)
Physician	Health care	IL	2, 3, 3d, 3f	Canfield v. Spear	44 Ill.2d 49, 254 N.E.2d 433 (1969)
Physician	Health care	IL	3	Frazier & Dallas v. Dettman	212 Ill.App.3d 139, 155 Ill.Dec. 771, 659 N.E.2d 1382 (1991)
Physician	Health care	IL	3d, 3f	Storer v. Brock	351 Ill. 643, 184 N.E. 868 (1933)
Physician	Health care	IL	2, 4	Total Health Physicians, S.C. v. Barrientos	151 Ill.App.3d 726, 104 Ill.Dec. 580, 502 N.E.2d 1240 (1986)
Physician	Health care	IN	8, 10, 11, 14	Gomez v. Chua Medical Corp.	510 N.E.2d 191, 2 IER Cases 490 (Ind.App. 1987)
Physician	Health care	IN	3f, AT-75	Medical Specialists, Inc. v. Sleweon	652 N.E.2d 517, 10 IER Cases 1202 (Ind.App. 1995)
Physician	Health care	IN	3f, 10, 14	Raymundo v. Hammond Clinic Ass'n	449 N.E.2d 276 (Ind.App. 1983)
Physician	Health care	KY	11	Daniel Boone Clinic, P.S.C. v. Dahhan	734 S.W.2d 488 (Ky.Ct.App. 1987), disc. rev. denied (August 26, 1987)
Physician	Health care	KY	3e, 6	Lareau v. O'Nan	355 S.W.2d 679 (Ky.Ct.App. 1962)

Physician	Health care (Cardiovascular and thoracic surgery)	IL	8	Rao v. Rao	718 F.2d 219, 1 IER Cases 267 (7th Cir. 1983)
Physician	Health care (Cardiology)	FL	1, 3, 5, 6, 14	Chandra v. Gadodia	610 So.2d 15, 17 Fla. L. Weekly D2603 (Fla. 5th Dist.Ct.App. 1992), review denied, 621 So.2d 432 (Fla. 1993)
Physician	Health care (Cardiology)	MI	1, 14	Cardiology Assocs. of SW Mich. v. Zencka	155 Mich.App. 632 400 N.W.2d 606 (1986)
Physician	Health care (Cardiology)	MO	2, 3f, 7, 8, AT-39	Ballesteros v. Johnson	812 S.W.2d 217 (Mo.App. 1991)
Physician	Health care (Dermatology)	GA	AT-65	Karlin v. Weinberg	77 N.J. 408, 390 A.2d 1161 (1978)
Physician	Health care (Dermatology)	NJ	2, 3, 3b, 3d, 3f	Karlin v. Weinberg	77 N.J. 408, 390 A.2d 1161 (1978)
Physician	Health care (Emergency medicine)	GA	3f	Dominy v. National Emergency Servs.	215 Ga.App. 537, 451 S.E.2d 472 (1994)
Physician	Health care (Emergency medicine)	LA	1, AT-6, AT-75	Emergency Physicians Ass'n v. Our Lady of the Lake Regional Medical Center	635 So.2d 1148 (La.App. 1st Cir. 1994)
Physician	Health care (Endocrinology)	NC	3, 3d, 3f, 5, 6, 7, 14	Nalle Clinic Co. v. Parker	101 N.C.App. 341, 399 S.E.2d 363, 6 IER Cases 158 (1991)
Physician	Health care (Endocrinology)	NC	3, 3d, 3f, 7	Statesville Medical Group, P.A. v. Dickey	106 N.C.App. 669, 418 S.E.2d 256, 7 IER Cases 1095 (1992)
Physician	Health care (Gastroenterology)	IN	3, 3d, 3f, 5, 6, 7, 14	Fumo v. Medical Group of Mich. City	590 N.E.2d 1103 (Ind.App. 3d Dist. 1992)

Physician	Health care (Obstetrics and gynecology)	MA	1, 11, AT-21, AT-50, AT-75, AT-94	*Falmouth Ob-Gyn Assocs., Inc. v. Abisla*	417 Mass. 176, 629 N.E.2d 291 (1994)
Physician	Health care (Obstetrics and gynecology)	NM	3	*Marshall v. Covington*	81 Idaho 199, 339 P.2d 504 (1959)
Physician	Health care (Obstetrics and gynecology)	NY	2, 3f, 10	*Novendstern v. Mt. Kisco Medical Group*	177 A.D.2d 623, 576 N.Y.S.2d 329 (2d Dep't 1991)
Physician	Health care (Obstetrics, gynecology, endocrinology and *in vitro* fertilization)	VA	3	*Lifesource Inst. of Fertility & Endocrinology v. Gianfortoni*	18 Va.Cir. 330 (Henrico County 1989)
Physician	Health care (Oncology)	GA	AT-42	*Gynecology Oncology, P.C. v. Weiser*	212 Ga.App. 858, 443 S.E.2d 526 (1994)
Physician	Health care (Oncology)	GA	2, 3f, 4, AT-23	*Osta v. Moran*	208 Ga.App. 544, 430 S.E.2d 837 (1993)
Physician	Health care (Ophthalmology)	GA	AT-5	*Jones v. Solomon*	207 Ga.App. 592, 428 S.E.2d 637 (1993)
Physician	Health care (Ophthalmology)	IL	2, 3, 3d, 3f, 4, 7	*Gillespie v. Carbondale & Marion Eye Centers, Ltd.*	251 Ill.App.3d 625, 190 Ill.Dec. 950, 622 N.E.2d 1267 (5th Dist. 1993)
Physician	Health care (Ophthalmology)	IL	2, 3d, 3f, 4	*House of Vision, Inc. v. Hiyane*	37 Ill.2d 32, 225 N.E.2d 21 (1967)
Physician	Health care (Ophthalmology)	IL	2, 3d, 3f, 7, 14	*Retina Servs. v. Garoon*	182 Ill.App.3d 851, 131 Ill.Dec. 276, 538 N.E.2d 651 (1st Dist. 1989)
Physician	Health care (Ophthalmology)	LA	3f, AT-10	*Medivision, Inc. v. Germer*	617 So.2d 69 (La.App. 4th Cir. 1993)
Physician	Health care (Ophthalmology)	MO	8, 14, AT-17	*McKnight v. Midwest Eye Inst. of Kan. City*	799 S.W.2d 909 (Mo.App. 1990)
Physician	Health care (Ophthalmology)	NY	3, 3c, 3f, 11, 14	*Zellner v. Stephen D. Conrad, M.D. P.C.*	183 A.D.2d 250, 589 N.Y.S.2d 903, 8 IER Cases 4 (2d Dep't 1992)

Physician	Health care (Orthopedic surgery)	AR	2, 3, 3f, 14	*Duffner v. Alberty*	19 Ark.App. 137, 718 S.W.2d 111 (1986)
Physician	Health care (Orthopedic surgery)	AZ	3, 3f, 4, 5, 6, 7, 8, 11, 13, 14	*Phoenix Orthopedic Surgeons v. Peairs*	790 P.2d 752 (Ariz.App. 1989)
Physician	Health care (Orthopedic surgery (hands))	FL	1, 3, 5, 6, AT-75	*Jewett Orthopaedic Clinic, P.A. v. White*	629 So.2d 922, 18 Fla. L. Weekly D2548 (Fla. 5th Dist.Ct.App. 1993)
Physician	Health care (Orthopedic surgery)	IA	3f, 14	*Cogley Clinic v. Martini*	253 Iowa 541, 112 N.W.2d 678 (1962)
Physician	Health care (Orthopedic surgery)	MI	1, 14	*Burns Clinic Medical Center, P.C. v. Vorenkamp*	165 Mich.App. 224, 418 N.W.2d 393 (1987)
Physician	Health care (Orthopedic surgery)	NV	2, 3, 3d, 3f, 4, 9, 14	*Ellis v. McDaniel*	95 Nev. 455, 596 P.2d 222 (1979)
Physician	Health care (Orthopedic surgery)	WY	3	*Duffner v. Alberty*	19 Ark.App. 137, 718 S.W.2d 111 (1986)
Physician	Health care (Osteopathic (pain management clinic))	WI	2, 3, 3f, 3g, 11	*Pollack v. Calimag*	157 Wis.2d 222, 458 N.W.2d 591 (Wis.Ct.App. 1990)
Physician	Health care (Osteopathic)	OH	3f, 7, 14	*Williams v. Hobbs*	9 Ohio App.3d 331, 460 N.E.2d 287 (1983)
Physician	Health care (Osteopathic radiology)	FL	14, AT-86	*Tannenbaum v. Biscayne Osteopathic Hosp., Inc.*	190 So.2d 777 (Fla. 1966)
Physician	Health care (Otolaryngology)	AL	1, 14	*Odess v. Taylor*	282 Ala. 389, 211 So.2d 805 (1968) (per curiam)
Physician	Health care (Otolarynology)	MN	2, 3c, 8	*Granger v. Craven*	159 Minn. 296, 199 N.W. 10 (1924)
Physician	Health care (Pathology)	KS	3b	*Ferraro v. Lattimore Fink Labs.*	191 Kan. 53, 379 P.2d 266 (1981)

Physician	Health care (Pediatric endocrinology)	NC	3, 3d, 3f, 5, 6, 7, 14	*Nalle Clinic Co. v. Parker*	101 N.C.App. 341, 399 S.E.2d 363, 6 IER Cases 158 (1991)
Physician	Health care (Pediatrics and neonatology)	ID	2, 3, 3f, 7, 9, 14	*Dick v. Geist*	107 Idaho 931, 693 P.2d 1133 (Ct.App. 1985)
Physician	Health care (Pediatrics)	FL	8	*Hefelfinger v. David*	305 So.2d 823 (Fla. 1st Dist.Ct.App. 1975
Physician	Health care (Physical medicine and rehabilitation)	IL	2, 3, 3f, 5, 11	*Sarah Bush Lincoln Health Center v. Perket*	238 Ill.App.3d 958, 178 Ill.Dec. 819, 605 N.E.2d 613 (4th Dist. 1992)
Physician	Health care (Podiatry)	NV	1, 2, 3, 3a, 3f, 5, 7, 9, 10, 13, 14	*Hansen v. Edwards*	83 Nev. 189, 426 P.2d 792 (1967)
Physician	Health care (Podiatry)	NY	2	*Smith v. Hurley*	634 N.Y.S.2d 334 (App.Div. 4th Dep't 1995)
Physician	Health care (Psychiatry)	GA	AT-65	*Shankman v. Coastal Psychiatric Assocs.*	258 Ga. 294, 368 S.E.2d 753 (1988)
Physician	Health care (Psychiatry)	LA	11, 14	*McCray v. Cole*	259 La. 646, 251 So.2d 161 (1971)
Physician	Health care (Radiology, osteopathic)	FL	14, AT-86	*Tannenbaum v. Biscayne Osteopathic Hosp., Inc.*	190 So.2d 777 (Fla. 1966)
Physician	Health care (Surgery)	AL	1	*Associated Surgeons, P.A. v. Watwood*	295 Ala. 229, 326 So.2d 712 (1976)
Physician	Health care (Surgery)	GA	3f	*McAlpin v. Coweta Fayette Surgical Assocs., P.C.*	438 S.E.2d 499 (Ga.App. 1995)
Physician	Health care (Surgery)	KS	2, 3f, 4	*Foltz v. Struxness*	168 Kan. 714, 215 P.2d 133 (1950)
Physician	Health care (Surgery)	MN	2, 3c, 8	*Granger v. Craven*	159 Minn. 296, 199 N.W. 10 (1924)
Physician	Health care (Surgery)	WI	3, 3e, 3f	*Geocaris v. Surgical Consultants*	100 Wis.2d 387, 302 N.W.2d 76 (Wis.Ct.App. 1981)

Position	Industry	State	Sections	Case	Citation
Physician (partner)	Health care	OR	3f, 8	*McCallum v. Ashbury*	238 Or. 257, 393 P.2d 774 (1964)
Physician (partner)	Health care (Medicine, surgery, and obstetrics)	NH	3	*Rakestraw v. Lanier*	104 Ga. 188, 30 S.E. 735 (1898)
Physician (partner)	Health care (Radiology)	CA	1	*South Bay Radiology Medical Assocs. v. W.M. Asher, M.D., Inc.*	220 Cal.App.3d 1074, 269 Cal. Rptr. 15 (1990)
Physician (partner)	Health care (Radiology)	TX	2, 3f, 4, 7, 14, AT-66	*Isuani v. Manske-Sheffield Radiology Group*	798 S.W.2d 346 (Tex.Ct.App.—Beaumont 1990), *reversed,* 802 S.W.2d 235 (Tex.) *on remand,* 805 S.W.2d 602 (Tex.Ct.App.—Beaumont 1991)
Physicist	Computer equipment	MN	3c	*Modern Controls, Inc. v. Andreakis*	578 F.2d 1264 (8th Cir. 1978)
Pilot	Crop spraying (aerial)	AR	3f, 4	*Brown v. Devine*	240 Ark. 838, 402 S.W.2d 669 (1966)
Pilot	Crop spraying (aerial)	NE	2, 3, 3a, 3f, 4, 14	*Boisen v. Petersen Flying Serv.*	222 Neb. 239, 383 N.W.2d 29 (1986)
Pilot	Flying service	AR	AT-3, AT-29	*Tidwell Flying Serv. v. Smith Corp.*	1992 WL 70302 (Ark.App. No. CA-91-429, Apr. 1, 1992)
Pilot (helicopter)	Agricultural spraying (aerial)	OH	12	*S&S Chopper Serv. v. Scripter*	59 Ohio App.2d 311, 394 N.E.2d 1011 (1977)
Pilot (helicopter)	Oil exploration	TX	3	*Recon Exploration, Inc. v. Hodges*	798 S.W.2d 848 (Tex.Ct.App.—Dallas 1990)
Private investigator	Private investigation	DE	AT-12	*Hilb, Rogal & Hamilton Agency of Dayton v. Reynolds*	69 Ohio.App.3d 753, 591 N.E.2d 1265 (10th Dist. 1990)
Programmer	Computer software (dairy cattle feed)	FL	2, 3f, 4, 6	*Marshall v. Gore*	506 So.2d 91, 1 IER Cases 318 (Fla. 2d Dist.Ct.App. 1987)
Programmer	Computer systems	TX	2, 5, 7	*Electronic Data Sys. Corp. v. Powell*	524 S.W.2d 343 (Tex.Civ.App.—Dallas 1975, writ ref'd n.r.e.)

Realtor	Real estate	GA	2	Mike Bajalia, Inc., v. Pike	226 Ga. 131, 172 S.E.2d 676 (1970)
Realtor	Real estate	NY	5	Merrill Lynch Realty Assocs. v. Burr	140 A.D.2d 745, 528 N.Y.S.2d 857 (2d Dep't 1988)
Realtor	Rental agency	DE	8	East Coast Resorts v. Lynch	1975 WL 1956 (Del.Ch. 1987)
Recharger	Fire fighting equipment	NC	3a, 3f	Safety Equip. Sales & Serv. v. Williams	22 N.C.App. 410, 206 S.E.2d 745 (1974)
Recording artist (musical vocalist)	Record company	NY	2	King Records, Inc. v. Brown	21 A.D.2d 593, 252 N.Y.S.2d 988 (1964)
Recruiter	Employment agency	CO	2, 3f	Gulick v. A. Robert Strawn & Assocs.	477 P.2d 489 (Colo.App. 1970)
Recruiter	Employment agency	CO	1, 2, 3b, 3f, 3g, 4, 7, 8, 10, 11, 14	Management Recruiters of Boulder v. Miller	762 P.2d 763, 3 IER Cases 1265 (Colo.App. 1988)
Recruiter	Employment agency	CO	3f	Wagner v. A&B Personnel Sys.	473 P.2d 179 (Colo.App. 1970)
Recruiter	Employment agency	DE	3f, 5	Bernard Personnel Consultants v. Mazarella	1990 WL 124969 (Del.Ch. No. 11660, Aug. 28, 1990)
Recruiter	Employment agency	DE	8	Caldwell Flexible Staffing v. Mays	1976 WL 1716 (Del.Ch., Nos. 5204 & 5205, Nov. 26, 1976)
Recruiter	Employment agency	DE	3, 3d, 5	Lewmor, Inc. v. Fleming	1986 WL 1244 (Del.Ch. No. 8335, Jan. 29, 1986)
Recruiter	Employment agency	FL	3d	Availability, Inc. v. Riley	336 So.2d 668 (Fla. 2d Dist.Ct.App. 1976)
Recruiter	Employment agency	GA	3g	Windsor-Douglas Assocs. v. Patterson	179 Ga.App. 674, 347 S.E.2d 362 (1986)
Recruiter	Employment agency	LA	1	Jon Bet & Assocs. v. Tyer	550 So.2d 673 (La.App. 2d Cir. 1989)
Recruiter	Employment agency	LA	6	Melway, Inc. v. Wesley	290 So.2d 454 (La.App. 2d Cir. 1974)
Recruiter	Employment agency	MD	2, 3e	Silver v. Goldberger	231 Md. 1, 188 A.2d 155 (1963)

Recruiter	Employment agency	MN	3b, 3c	National Recruiters v. Cashman	323 N.W.2d 736 (Minn. 1982)
Recruiter	Employment agency	MS	2, 3, 3f	Donahoe v. Tatum	242 Miss. 253, 134 So.2d 442 (1961)
Recruiter	Employment agency	NH	2, 3, 3f, 4, 10, AT-21, AT-95	Technical Aid Corp. v. Allen	591 A.2d 262 (N.H. 1991)
Recruiter	Employment agency	OH	3f, 5	Gobel v. Laing	41 Ohio Op.2d 175, 12 Ohio App.2d 93, 231 N.E.2d 341 (1967)
Recruiter	Employment agency	PA	3d, 3f	Robert Clifton Assocs. v. O'Connor	338 Pa.Super. 246, 487 A.2d 947 (1985)
Recruiter	Employment agency	TX	11	Eberts v. Businesspeople Personnel Servs.	620 S.W.2d 861 (Tex.Ct.App.—Dallas 1981)
Recruiter	Employment agency (data processors)	TX	3f, 4	Diversified Human Resources Group v. Levinson-Polakoff	752 S.W.2d 8 (Tex.Ct.App.—Dallas 1988)
Recruiter	Employment agency (data processors)	TX	2, 7	Rugen v. Interactive Business Sys. Inc.	864 S.W.2d 548 (Tex.Ct.App.—Dallas 1993)
Recruiter	Employment agency (environmental, health, safety, and clinical health care industries)	DE	2, 5, 10	Meyer Ventures, Inc. v. Barnak	1990 WL 172648 (Del.Ch. No. 11502, Nov. 2, 1990)
Recruiter	Employment agency (executive)	FL	6	Grant v. Robert Half, Int'l	597 So.2d 801, 7 IER Cases 1367, 17 Fla. L. Weekly D1160 (Fla. 3d Dist.Ct.App. 1992)
Recruiter	Employment agency (office support)	IL	2, 5	Office Mates 5, North Shore, Inc. v. Hazen	234 Ill.App.3d 557, 175 Ill.Dec. 58, 599 N.E.2d 1072 (1st Dist. 1992)

Recruiter	Employment agency (physicians)	GA	1, 3g, 4, 11	Hart v. Jackson & Coker (Hart I)	5 IER Cases 1441 (Ga.Super.Ct., DeKalb County, No. 90-5654-3, Sept. 7, 1990)
Recuiter	Employment agency (physicians)	GA	1, 2, 3, 3d, 3f, 3g, 4, 8, 9, 11, AT-20	Jackson & Coker v. Hart (Hart II)	261 Ga. 371, 405 S.E.2d 253, 6 IER Cases 1000 (1991)
Recruiter	Employment agency (printing industry)	PA	3g	Gordon Wahls Co. v. Linde	306 Pa.Super. 64, 452 A.2d 4 (1982)
Recruiter	Employment agency (telecommunications)	MN	2, 3f, 3g, 4, 5, 6, 7	Management Recruiters Int'l v. Professional Placement Servs.	1992 WL 61542 (Minn.Ct.App. No. C6-91-2055, Mar. 31, 1992)
Recruiter	Employment agency (temporary, nurses)	AL	AT-57	McSlain v. Nursefinders of Mobile	598 So.2d 853 (Ala. 1992)
Recruiter	Employment agency (temporary)	PA	11	Bettinger v. C. Berke Assocs.	455 Pa. 100, 314 A.2d 296 (1974)
Rental agent	Medical equipment	OH	3b, 3d, 3f, 10, 14	Columbus Medical Equip. Co. v. Watters	13 Ohio App.3d 149, 468 N.E.2d 343 (1983)
Rental agent	Vehicle leasing	NC	3, 3e, 3f, 4, 5	Triangle Leasing v. McMahon	385 S.E.2d 360 (N.C.App. 1989), aff'd in part and rev'd in part, 327 N.C. 224, 393 S.E.2d 854 (1990)
Repair person	Car repair (automobile frame)	PA	3a, 4	Barb-Lee Mobile Frame Co. v. Hoot	416 Pa. 222, 206 A.2d 59 (1965)
Repair person	Medical equipment	TX	3, 3d, 3g	Picker Int'l, Inc. v. Blanton	756 F.Supp. 971 (N.D.Tex. 1990)
Repair person	Photocopier	WA	2, 3	Copier Specialists, Inc. v. Gillen	776 Wash.App. 771, 887 P.2d 919 (1995)
Repair person	Seals (industrial)	IL	5, 6, 7	Hydroaire, Inc. v. Sager	98 Ill.App.3d 758, 53 Ill.Dec. 928, 424 N.E.2d 719 (1st Dist. 1981)
Repair wedger	Metal industry	OR	2, 3e, 14	Rem Metals Corp. v. Logan	278 Or. 715, 565 P.2d 1080 (1977)

Sales supervisor	Roofing (commercial and industrial)	VA	4	*Consolidated Indus. Roofing v. Williams*	17 Va.Cir. 341 (City of Roanoke 1989)
Sales trainer	Advertising	AL	1	*Parker v. EBSCO Indus.*	282 Ala. 98, 209 So.2d 383 (1968)
Salesperson	Accounting	MD	AT-86	*Friedman & Fuller, P.C. v. Funkhouser*	107 Md. App. 91, 666 A.2d 1298 (1995)
Salesperson	Advertising (magazine)	TN	3, 3d, 3f, 4, AT-8	*Dabora, Inc. v. Kline*	884 S.W.2d 475 (Tenn.App. 1994)
Salesperson	Advertising (movie-theater intermission)	LA	2	*Theatre Time Clock v. Stewart*	276 F.Supp. 593 (E.D.La. 1967)
Salesperson	Advertising (radio air time)	TX	2, 3, 3c, 3e, 4	*Daytona Group of Tex. v. Smith*	800 S.W.2d 285 (Tex.Ct.App.—Corpus Christi 1990)
Salesperson	Advertising (television time)	AL	2, 3, 3c, 3f	*Birmingham Television Corp. v. DeRamus*	502 So.2d 761 (Ala.Civ.App. 1986)
Salesperson	Advertising (television time)	AL	2, 3f	*Booth v. WPMI Television Co.*	553 So.2d 209, 3 IER Cases 1799 (Ala. 1988)
Salesperson	Advertising broker-age (newspaper)	TN	2	*Arkansas Dailies, Inc. v. Dan*	36 Tenn.App. 633, 260 S.W.2d 200 (1953)
Salesperson	Air brakes	LA	3, 3f, 4, 14	*Comet Indus. v. Lawrence*	600 So.2d 85 (La.App. 2d Cir. 1992)
Salesperson	Air filters (computer, custom-made)	CA	2, 14	*Cambridge Filter Corp. v. International Filter*	548 F.Supp. 1301 (D. Nev. 1982) (applying California law)
Salesperson	Alarms	CT	3c	*Alarm Sec. Protection v. Karasevich*	12 Conn. L. Tribune No. 14 at 30 (Super.Ct, Dec. 24, 1985)
Salesperson	Alarms (fire and burglar)	GA	3d, 3f, 4, 14, AT-55	*Rollins Protective Servs. Co. v. Palermo*	249 Ga. 138, 287 S.E.2d 546 (1982)
Salesperson	Artwork	GA	3g, AT-42	*Paul Robinson, Inc. v. Haege*	218 Ga.App. 578, 462 S.E.2d 396 (1995)

Salesperson	Business forms	VA	2, 3, 3f, 8, 12	*Lehman v. Standard Forms, Inc.*	1995 Del. Ch. LEXIS 11 (Del.Chanc., C.A. No. 13688, Jan. 12, 1995) (applying Virginia law)
Salesperson	Candy, cigarettes, and tobacco	OH	AT-11	*Safier's, Inc. v. Bialer*	59 Ohio Law Abs. 292, 42 Ohio Op. 209, 93 N.E.2d 734 (Ohio C.P. 1950)
Salesperson	Cellular car phones and air time	TX	2, 5	*Unitel Corp. v. Decker*	731 S.W.2d 654 (Tex.Ct.App.—Dallas 1992)
Salesperson	Cellular phones	KY	9	*Cellular One, Inc. v. Boyd*	653 So.2d 30 (La.App. 1st Cir. 1995)
Salesperson	Cellular phones	LA	1, 3, 3c, 3f, 5, 6, 8, 11, AT-32, AT-40A, AT-51	*Cellular One, Inc. v. Boyd*	653 So.2d 30 (La.App. 1st Cir. 1995)
Salesperson	Cellular phones	TX	AT-90	*Centel Cellular Co. v. Light*	899 S.W.2d 343 (Tex.App.—Tyler 1995)
Salesperson	Cellular phones	TX	1, 3, 3a, 3b, 3c, 14, AT-4	*Light v. Centel Cellular Co.*	883 S.W.2d 642 (Tex. 1994)
Salesperson	Chemical cleaners	GA	AT-42	*Arrow Chem. Corp. v. Pugh*	490 S.W.2d 628 (Tex.Civ.App. 1972)
Salesperson	Chemical cleaners	LA	1	*NCH Corp. v. Broyles*	749 F.2d 247 (5th Cir. 1985)
Salesperson	Chemical cleaners	TX	1, AT-4	*Miller Paper Co. v. Robert Paper Co.*	901 S.W.2d 593 (Tex.Ct.App.—Amarillo 1995)
Salesperson	Chemical processing equipment	VA	8, 14	*Grant v. Carotek, Inc.*	737 F.2d 410 (4th Cir. 1984)
Salesperson	Chemical products	IN	12	*Mantek Div. of NCH Corp. v. Share Corp.*	780 F.2d 702 (7th Cir. 1986)
Salesperson	Chemical products	LA	1	*Napasco Int'l Western Div. v. Maxson*	420 So.2d 1276 (La.App. 3d Cir. 1982)
Salesperson	Chemical products	MO	3a	*USA Chem. v. Lewis*	557 S.W.2d 15 (Mo.App. 1977)

Salesperson	Clothing (custom-printed, promotional)	NY	2, 3	Primo Enter. v. Bachner	148 A.D.2d 350, 539 N.Y.S.2d 320 (1st Dep't 1989)
Salesperson	Clothing (men's, custom)	TX	2, 5, 6, 7	Tom James Co. v. Mendrop	819 S.W.2d 251 (Tex.Ct.App.—Fort Worth 1991)
Salesperson	Clothing (wholesale)	MN	6	Thermorama, Inc. v. Buckwold	267 Minn. 551, 125 N.W.2d 844 (1964)
Salesperson	Coal industry equipment and supplies	WV	2, 3e, 3f, AT-90	Voorhees v. Guyan Machinery Co.	191 W.Va. 450, 446 S.E.2d 672 (1994)
Salesperson	Coating, cleaning and antiseptic compounds	LA	2	W.R. Grace & Co. v. Savoie	322 F.Supp. 790 (E.D.La. 1970)
Salesperson	Coffee	AL	3f	Dixon v. Royal Cup	386 So.2d 481 (Ala.Civ.App. 1980)
Salesperson (route)	Coffee	LA	2	Daigle v. Standard Coffee Serv. Co.	479 So.2d 469 (La.App. 3d Cir. 1985)
Salesperson (route)	Coffee	LA	1, 2, 3, 3a, 3b, 3c, 5, 6	Landry v. William B. Reily & Co.	524 So.2d 750 (La.App. 3d Cir. 1988)
Salesperson	Coffee and tea	NY	2, 5	Greenwich Milis Co., Inc. v. Barrie House Coffee Co.	91 A.D.2d 398, 459 N.Y.S.2d 454 (1983)
Salesperson	Computer power supply equipment design, manufacture, and marketing	VA	3f, AT-2, AT-21	Power Distribution, Inc. v. Emergency Power Eng'g Inc.	569 F.Supp. 54, 1 IER Cases 239 (E.D. Va. 1983)
Salesperson	Computers	IL	2, 3, 3d, 3f, 3g, 5, 7, 10	PCx Corp. v. Ross	168 Ill.App.3d 1047, 119 Ill.Dec. 474, 522 N.E.2d 1333 (1st Dist. 1988)
Salesperson	Computers	MN	7	Ensco Int'l v. Blegen	410 N.W.2d 11 (Minn.Ct.App. 1987)
Salesperson	Computers	MO	3b, 3c	Computer Sales Int'l v. Collins	723 S.W.2d 450 (Mo.App. 1986)
Salesperson	Computers	NY	2, 5, 7	Data Sys. Computer Centre v. Tempesta	171 A.D.2d 724, 566 N.Y.S.2d 957 (2d Dep't 1991)

Salesperson	Connectors (electrical)	CA	2, 3, 3a, 5, 9, 12, 14	*Hollingsworth Solderless Terminal Co. v. Turley*	622 F.2d 1324 (9th Cir. 1980) (applying California law)
Salesperson	Construction industry supplies and equipment	MO	7, 14, AT-38, AT-91	*Luketich v. Goedecke, Wood & Co.*	835 S.W.2d 504, 7 IER Cases 1033 (Mo.App. 1992)
Salesperson	Cookware (aluminum)	NC	3c	*Super-Maid Cook-Ware Corp. v. Hamil*	50 F.2d 830 (5th Cir. 1931)
Salesperson	Credit insurance	CA	2, 3g	*American Credit Indemnity Co. v. Sacks*	213 Cal.App.3d 622, 262 Cal.Rptr. 92 (1989)
Salesperson	Debt collection	RI	4	*Central Adjustment Bureau, Inc. v. Ingram*	678 S.W.2d 28 (Tenn. 1984)
Salesperson	Debt collection	VT	12	*International Collection Serv. v. Gibbs*	510 A.2d 1325 (Vt. 1986)
Salesperson	Delicatessen products	CT	3c, 3f	*Roessler v. Burwell*	119 Conn. 289, 176 A. 126 (1934)
Salesperson	Delicatessen products	SC	3c	*Roessler v. Burwell*	119 Conn. 289, 176 A. 126 (1934)
Salesperson	Dental lab	NJ	3d, 3f, 8	*Hogan v. Bergen Brunswig Corp.*	153 N.J. Super. 37, 378 A.2d 1164 (App.Div. 1977) (per curiam)
Salesperson	Dental lab supplies	NY	3c	*Hogan v. Bergen Brunswig Corp.*	153 N.J.Super. 37, 378 A.2d 1164 (App. Div. 1977) (per curiam)
Salesperson	Depilatories (animal skins)	NJ	10	*Stone v. Grasselli Chem. Co.*	65 N.J. Eq. 776, 55 A. 736 (E.&A. 1903)
Salesperson	Design (kitchens (appliances))	VT	2, 3, 3b, 3e, 3f, 5, 7, 8, 10	*Vermont Elec. Supply Co. v. Andrus*	132 Vt. 195, 315 A.2d 456 (1974)
Salesperson	Disinfectants (Catholic institution customers)	OH	3f	*Federal Sanitation Co. v. Frankel*	34 Ohio App. 331, 171 N.E. 339 (1929)
Salesperson	Electrical contracting	DE	3c	*Comfort, Inc. v. McDonald*	1984 WL 8216 (Del.Ch., No. 1066(S), Jun. 1, 1984)

Salesperson	Electronic products	GA	3d	*Barry v. Stanco Communications Prods.*	243 Ga. 68, 252 S.E.2d 491 (1979)
Salesperson	Employee benefits (insurance, annuities)	VA	AT-8	*Hilb, Rogal, & Hamilton Co. v. DePew*	440 S.E.2d 918 (Va. 1994)
Salesperson	Employment agency (temporary)	OR	3c	*Olsten Corp. v. Sommers*	534 F.Supp. 395 (D. Ore. 1982)
Salesperson	Envelopes (business)	OR	3b, 6, 14	*Mail-Well Envelope Co. v. Saley*	262 Or. 143, 497 P.2d 364 (1972)
Salesperson	Fall-protection equipment	DE	2, 3, 3c, 3f, 3g, 5, 8, 9, 10, AT-12, AT-38	*Research & Trading Corp. v. Pfuhl*	1992 WL 345465 (Del.Ch., No. 12527, Nov. 18, 1992)
Salesperson	Fall-protection equipment	DE	3c, 3f, 14	*Research & Trading Corp. v. Powell*	468 A.2d 1301 (Del.Ch. No. 12527, Nov. 18, 1983)
Salesperson	Farm and industrial equipment, nuts, bolts, and tools	GA	3f	*Smith v. HBT, Inc.*	213 Ga.App. 560, 445 S.E.2d 315 (1994)
Salesperson	Fasteners	IL	3, 3f, 3g, 4, AT-55	*Abbott-Interfast Corp. v. Harkabus*	250 Ill.App.3d 13, 189 Ill.Dec. 288, 619 N.E.2d 1337 (2d Dist. 1993)
Salesperson	Fasteners (stainless steel)	MA	2, 3f, 4, 14, AT-52	*All Stainless v. Colby*	364 Mass. 773, 308 N.E.2d 481 (1974)
Salesperson	Food (frozen)	MO	3a	*Renwood Food Prods. v. Schaefer*	240 Mo.App. 939, 223 S.W.2d 144 (1949)
Salesperson	Food (wholesale)	DE	3, 14	*Burris Foods, Inc. v. Razzano*	1984 WL 8230 (Del.Ch. 1984)
Salesperson	Food and paper supplies	CO	3, 3d, 3f	*Knoebel Mercantile Co. v. Siders*	165 Colo. 393, 439 P.2d 355 (1968)
Salesperson	Food products	AR	2, 3f	*Borden, Inc. v. Huey*	261 Ark. 313, 547 S.W.2d 760 (1977)

	Industry	State	Sections	Case	Citation
Salesperson	Graphics and printing	VA	2, 3, 3f, 8, 12	Lehman v. Standard Forms, Inc.	1995 Del. Ch. LEXIS 11 (Del.Chanc., C.A. No. 13688, Jan. 12, 1995) (applying Virginia law)
Salesperson	Grocery (wholesale)	KY	2, 3, 3a, 3b, 3g, 8, 14	Higdon Food Serv. v. Walker & Kesterson Meat Co.	641 S.W.2d 750 (Ky. 1982)
Salesperson	Hardware	AK	3	Barnes Group v. Harper	653 F.2d 175 (5th Cir. 1981), cert. denied, 455 U.S. 921 (1982)
Salesperson	Hardware	FL	3	Foster & Co. v. Snodgrass	333 So.2d 521 (Fla. 2d Dist.Ct.App. 1976)
Salesperson	Hardware	GA	3d	Barnes Group v. Harper	653 F.2d 175 (5th Cir. 1981) cert. denied, 455 U.S. 921 (1982)
Salesperson	Hardware, home improvement products, tools	AL	3f, 4, 5, 14	Mason Corp. v. Kennedy	286 Ala. 639, 244 So.2d 383 (1968)
Salesperson	Hearing aids	MA	2, 14	National Hearing Aid Centers v. Avers	2 Mass.App.Ct. 285, 311 N.E.2d 573 (1974)
Salesperson	Hearing aids	NH	10	Matthal v. Proskowetz	537 S.W.2d 320 (Tex.Civ.App. 1976)
Salesperson	Hearing aids	TN	2	Levy v. Baker	528 S.W.2d 558 (Tenn.Ct.App. 1973)
Salesperson	Hearing aids	UT	2, 3, 3e, 5, 10, 14	Robbins v. Finlay	645 P.2d 623 (Utah 1982)
Salesperson	Heating systems (radiant)	PA	3, 3f	Jacobson & Co. v. International Inv't Corp.	427 Pa. 439, 235 A.2d 612 (1967)
Salesperson	Homes	PA	3, 4	Albee Homes v. Caddie Homes	417 Pa. 177, 207 A.2d 768 (1965)
Salesperson	Industrial and farm equipment, nuts, bolts, and tools	GA	3f	Smith v. HBT, Inc.	213 Ga.App. 560, 445 S.E.2d 315 (1994)
Salesperson	Industrial gases and welding products	TN	2, 3	Selox, Inc. v. Ford	675 S.W.2d 474 (Tenn. 1984)

Occupation	Description	State	Numbers	Case	Citation
Salesperson	Industrial material-lifting equipment	PA	2, 3e, 3f 4, 5, 6, 14	John G. Bryant Co. v. Sling Testing & Repair	471 Pa. 1, 369 A.2d 1164 (1977)
Salesperson	Insulation	KS	14	Nenow v. L.C. Cassidy & Son of Fla., Inc.	141 So.2d 636 (Fla. Dist.Ct.App. 1962)
Salesperson	Insulation	NJ	14	Ellis v. Lionikis	162 N.J. Super. 579, 394 A.2d 116 (App.Div. 1978)
Salesperson	Insurance	AL	2, 3, 3c, 3f, 10, AT-33	Clark v. Liberty Nat'l Life Ins. Co.	592 So.2d 564 (Ala. 1992)
Salesperson	Insurance	AL	AT-83	Cornwall & Stevens Se., Inc. v. Stewart	887 F.Supp. 1490 (M.D. Ala. 1995)
Salesperson	Insurance	AL	3f	Himes v. Masonic Mut. Life Ass'n of DC	215 Ala. 183, 110 So. 133 (1926)
Salesperson	Insurance	AL	1, 3	Hoppe v. Preferred Risk Mut. Ins. Co.	470 So.2d 1161 (Ala. 1985)
Salesperson	Insurance	AL	2, 3, 10, 14	James S. Kemper & Co. SE v. Cox & Assocs.	434 So.2d 1380 (Ala. 1983)
Salesperson	Insurance	AL	2, 3, 3f, 5, 14	Sheffield v. Stoudenmire	553 So.2d 125, 4 IER Cases 1872 (Ala. 1989)
Salesperson	Insurance	AR	2, 3, 3f, 4, 14	Federated Mut. Ins. Co. v. Bennett	36 Ark.App. 99, 818 S.W.2d 596 (1991)
Salesperson	Insurance	AR	2, 3, 3c, 3d, 3g, 9, 10, 14	Girard v. Rebsamen Ins. Co.	14 Ark.App. 154, 685 S.W.2d 526 (1985)
Salesperson	Insurance	AR	AT-12	Marsh & McLennan of Ark v. Herget	900 S.W.2d 195 (Ark. 1995)
Salesperson	Insurance	AR	2, 3, 3f	Owens v. Penn Mut. Life Ins. Co.	851 F.2d 1053, 3 IER Cases 1144 (8th Cir. 1988)
Salesperson	Insurance	AR	3	Rebsamen Ins. Co. v. Milton	269 Ark. 737, 600 S.W.2d 441 (App. 1980)

Salesperson	Insurance	AR	3f	United Ins. Agency v. Martin	258 Ark. 916, 529 S.W.2d 871 (1975)
Salesperson	Insurance	AZ	2, 3d, 3e, 3f, 4, 8, 14	Olliver/Pilcher Ins. v. Daniels	148 Ariz. 530, 715 P.2d 1218 (1986)
Salesperson	Insurance	CA	2, 3g	American Credit Indemnity Co. v. Sacks	213 Cal.App.3d 622, 262 Cal. Rptr. 92 (1989)
Salesperson	Insurance	CA	2, 3f	State Farm Mut. Auto Ins. Co. v. Dempster	174 Cal.App.2d 418, 344 P.2d 821 (1959)
Salesperson	Insurance	CO	3f	Colonial Life & Accident Ins. Co. v. Kappers	488 P.2d 96 (Colo.App. 1971)
Salesperson	Insurance	CT	3	New England Ins. Agency v. Miller	No. CV-89-0285030-S, 1991 WL 65766 (Conn. Super.Ct. April 16, 1991)
Salesperson	Insurance	CT	1, 3, 3d, 3f, 3g, 8, 10	Robert S. Weiss & Assocs. v. Wiederlight	208 Conn. 525, 546 A.2d 216 (1988)
Salesperson	Insurance	CT	3g	Tuttle v. Riggs-Warfield-Roloson, Inc.	251 Md. 45, 246 A.2d 588 (1968)
Salesperson	Insurance	DC	10	Group Ass'n Plans v. Colquhoun	151 App.D.C. 298, 466 F.2d 469 (1972)
Salesperson	Insurance	DE	2, 3g, 5	C. Edgar Wood, Inc. v. Clark	1986 WL 1160 (Del.Ch. 1986)
Salesperson	Insurance	FL	3f, 3g, 5, 6	Joseph U. Moore v. Howard	534 So.2d 935, 4 IER Cases 46 (Fla. 2d Dist.Ct.App. 1988)
Salesperson	Insurance	FL	2, 3f, 3g, 4, 5	Joseph U. Moore, Inc. v. Neu	500 So.2d 561, 1 IER Cases 1710 (Fla. 2d Dist.Ct.App. 1986), review denied, 508 So.2d 15 (Fla. 1987)
Salesperson	Insurance	FL	5, 7	Sabina v. Dahlia Corp.	650 So.2d 96 (Fla. 2d Dist.Ct.App. 1995)

Salesperson	Insurance	ID	2, 3, 3f, 4	Insurance Center, Inc. v. Taylor	94 Idaho 896, 499 P.2d 1252 (1972)
Salesperson	Insurance	IL	3, 3c, 3f, 3g, 4, 14	Corroon & Black of Ill. v. Magner	145 Ill.App.3d 151, 98 Ill.Dec. 663, 494 N.E.2d 785 (1st Dist. 1986)
Salesperson	Insurance	IL	4	L&R Ins. Agency v. McPhail	92 Ill.App.2d 107, 235 N.E.2d 153 (5th Dist.), appeal denied, 39 Ill.2d 626 (1986)
Salesperson	Insurance	IL	2, 4	Lee O'Keefe Ins. Agency, Inc. v. Ferega	163 Ill.App.3d 997, 114 Ill.Dec. 919, 516 N.E.2d 1313 (1987)
Salesperson	Insurance	IL	2	Lincoln Towers Ins. Agency v. Farrell	90 Ill.App.3d 353, 54 Ill.Dec.817, 425 N.E.2d 1034 (1st Dist. 1981)
Salesperson	Insurance	IL	3, 4	Prudential Ins. Co. of Am. v. Sempetrean	171 Ill.App.3d 810, 121 Ill.Dec. 709, 525 N.E.2d 1016 (1st Dist. 1988)
Salesperson	Insurance	IL	2, 14	Rapp Ins. Agency v. Baldree	231 Ill.App.3d 1038, 173 Ill.Dec. 962, 597 N.E.2d 936 (5th Dist. 1992)
Salesperson	Insurance	IL	3f, 11, 14	Tomei v. Tomei	235 Ill.App.3d 166, 176 Ill.Dec. 716, 602 N.E.2d 23 (1st Dist. 1992)
Salesperson	Insurance	IN	2, 3d, 3g, 4, 5, 6, 7, 11	College Life Ins. Co. of Am. v. Austin	466 N.E.2d 738 (Ind.App. 1984)
Salesperson	Insurance	IN	2, 3d, 3f, 3g	Commercial Bankers Life Ins. Co. of Am. v. Smith	516 N.E.2d 110 (Ind.App. 1987)
Salesperson	Insurance	IN	3d, 3g, 14	Field v. Alexander & Alexander of Ind.	503 N.E.2d 627 (Ind.App. 1987)
Salesperson	Insurance	IN	5, 7	Harvest Ins. Agency v. Inter-Ocean Ins. Co.	492 N.E.2d 686 (Ind. 1986)
Salesperson	Insurance	IN	3c, 3f	Leatherman v. Management Advisors	448 N.E.2d 1048 (Ind. 1983)

Salesperson	Insurance	IN	Rollins v. American State Bank	3c	487 N.E.2d 842 (Ind.App. 1986)
Salesperson	Insurance	LA	Commonwealth Life Ins. Co. v. Neal	1, 2, 3a	521 F.Supp. 812 (M.D.La. 1981) aff'd, 669 F.2d 300 (5th Cir. 1982)
Salesperson	Insurance	MD	Hebb v. Stump, Harvey & Cook, Inc.	4	25 Md.App. 478, 334 A.2d 563, cert. denied, 275 Md. 749 (1975)
Salesperson	Insurance	MD	Massachusetts Indem. & Life Ins. Co. v. Dresser	11	269 Md. 364, 306 A.2d 213 (1973)
Salesperson	Insurance	MD	Nationwide Mut. Ins. Co. v. Hart	4, 5, 7, 14	73 Md.App. 406, 534 A.2d 999 (1988)
Salesperson	Insurance	MD	Tuttle v. Riggs-Warfield-Roloson, Inc.	3c, 3d, 3f, 3g, 9, 10	251 Md. 45, 246 A.2d 588 (1968)
Salesperson	Insurance	ME	Chapman & Drake v. Harrington	2, 3, 3a, 3d, 3f, 3g, 4, 10, 14	545 A.2d 645, 3 IER Cases 1146 (Me. 1988)
Salesperson	Insurance	MI	Follmer, Rudzewicz & Co. v. Kosko	3g	420 Mich. 394, 362 N.W.2d 676 (1984)
Salesperson	Insurance	MN	Davies & Davies Agency v. Davies	3b, 3c, 3d, 4	298 N.W.2d 127 (Minn. 1980)
Salesperson	Insurance	MN	Overholt Crop Ins. Serv. Co. v. Bredeson	3a, 3e, 3f, 3g, 5, 7	437 N.W.2d 698 (Minn.Ct.App. 1989)
Salesperson	Insurance	MO	Adrian N. Baker & Co. v. Demartino	3g, 8	733 S.W.2d 14 (Mo.App. 1987)
Salesperson	Insurance	MO	C.M. Brown & Assocs. v. King	9	680 S.W.2d 365 (Mo.App. 1984)
Salesperson	Insurance	MO	Financial Guardian, Inc. v. Kutter	AT-41	630 S.W.2d 197 (Mo.App. 1982)
Salesperson	Insurance	MS	Thames v. Davis & Goulet Ins.	3e	420 So.2d 1041 (Miss. 1982)

Salesperson	Insurance	MT	2, 3, 3d, 3e, 3f	First Am. Ins. Agency v. Gould	203 Mont. 217, 661 P.2d 451 (1983)
Salesperson	Insurance	MT	1, 3d, 3e, 3f, 14	J.T. Miller Co. v. Madel	176 Mont. 49, 575 P.2d 1321 (1978)
Salesperson	Insurance	NC	2	Asheville Assocs. v. Berman	255 N.C. 400,121 S.E.2d 593 (1981)
Salesperson	Insurance	NC	3a, 5, 7	Robins & Weil v. Mason	70 N.C.App. 537, 320 S.E.2d 693, disc. rev. denied, 312 N.C. 495, 322 S.E.2d 559 (1984)
Salesperson	Insurance	ND	3f, 11, 14, AT-49	Geiss v. Northern Ins. Agency	153 N.W.2d 688 (N.D. 1967)
Salesperson	Insurance	ND	1, 3f, 11, 14, AT-49	Werlinger v. Mutual Serv. Casualty Ins. Co.	496 N.W.2d 26 (N.D. 1993)
Salesperson	Insurance	NE	2, 3, 3g, 7, 10, AT-66	Chambers-Dobson, Inc. v. Squier	238 Neb. 748, 472 N.W.2d 391, 6 IER Cases 1127 (1991)
Salesperson	Insurance	NE	2	Farmers Underwriters Ass'n v. Eckel	185 Neb. 531, 177 N.W.2d 274 (1970)
Salesperson	Insurance	NE	3f	National Farmer's Union Serv. Corp. v. Edwards	220 Neb. 231, 369 N.W.2d 76 (1985)
Salesperson	Insurance	NE	3d	Peterson v. Don Peterson & Assocs.	234 Neb. 651, 452 N.W.2d 517 (1990)
Salesperson	Insurance	NE	2, 12	Rain & Hail Ins. Serv. v. Casper	902 F.2d 699, 5 IER Cases 571 (8th Cir. 1990) (applying Nebraska law)
Salesperson	Insurance	NM	8	Danzer v. Professional Insurors	101 N.M. 178, 679 P.2d 1276 (1984)
Salesperson	Insurance	NY	5, 10	Atlantic Mutual Ins. Co. v. Noble Van & Storage Co.	537 N.Y.S.2d 213 (App.Div. 1989)
Salesperson	Insurance	NY	3f	Brewster-Allen-Wichert v. Kiepler	131 A.D.2d 620, 516 N.Y.S.2d 949 (2d Dep't 1987)

Salesperson	Insurance	TX	4, 10	Franiewicz v. National Comp Assocs.	633 S.W.2d 505 (Tex. 1982)
Salesperson	Insurance	TX	3, 5, 7, AT-76	Hilb, Rogal & Hamilton Co. of Tex. v. Wurzman	861 S.W.2d 30 (Tex.Ct.App.—Dallas 1993)
Salesperson	Insurance	TX	2, 3, 4, AT-72, AT-96	Murco Agency v. Ryan	800 S.W.2d 600 (Tex.Ct.App.—Dallas 1990)
Salesperson	Insurance	TX	1, 3	Wabash Life Ins. Co. v. Garner	732 F.Supp. 692 (N.D. Tex. 1989)
Salesperson	Insurance	VA	AT-8	Hilb, Rogal, & Hamilton Co. v. DePew	440 S.E.2d 918 (Va. 1994)
Salesperson	Insurance	WA	8	Comfort & Fleming Ins. Brokers v. Hoxsey	26 Wash.App. 172, 613 P.2d 138 (1980)
Salesperson	Insurance	WI	2, 3, 3d, 3f, 3g, 3g, 14	Rollins Burdick Hunter of Wis. v. Hamilton	101 Wis.2d 460, 304 N.W.2d 752 (1981)
Salesperson	Insurance	WI	4	Streiff v. American Family Mut. Ins. Co.	118 Wis.2d 602, 348 N.W.2d 505 (1984)
Salesperson	Insurance	WV	3f, 3g, 14	Wyckoff v. Painter	145 W.Va. 310, 115 S.E.2d 80 (1960)
Salesperson	Insurance	WY	8	Adrian N. Baker & Co. v. Demartino	733 S.W.2d 14 (Mo.App. 1987)
Salesperson	Insurance	WY	4	Insurance Center, Inc. v. Taylor	94 Idaho 896, 499 P.2d 1252 (1972)
Salesperson	Insurance (car racing)	FL	2, 3f	Auto Club Affiliates v. Donahey	281 So.2d 239 (Fla. 2d Dist.Ct.App. 1973)
Salesperson	Insurance adjusting	MO	2	Ibur & Assocs. Co. v. Walsh	595 S.W.2d 33 (Mo.App. 1980)
Salesperson	Insurance and annuities (employee benefits)	VA	AT-8	Hilb, Rogal, & Hamilton Co. v. DePew	440 S.E.2d 918 (Va. 1994)

Salesperson	Insurance and bonds	NM	3c, 3g, 9, 10, 14	Manuel Lujan Ins. v. Jordan	100 N.M. 573, 673 P. 1306 (1983)
Salesperson	Insurance and real estate	NH	2, 3d, 3f, 14	Dunfey Realty Co. v. Enwright	101 N.H. 195, 138 A.2d 80 (1957)
Salesperson	Investigation service (charitable solicitation scams)	CA	2	California Intelligence Bureau v. Cunningham	83 Cal.App.2d 197, 188 P.2d 303 (1948)
Salesperson	Janitorial products	IL	2, 3, AT-42	Jefco Laboratories, Inc. v. Carroo	136 Ill.App.3d 793, 91 Ill.Dec. 513, 483 N.E.2d 999 (1985)
Salesperson	Janitorial products	GA	AT-42	Arrow Chem. Corp. v. Pugh	490 S.W.2d 628 (Tex.Civ.App. 1972)
Salesperson	Janitorial service	OH	3, 3f, 4	American Bldg. Servs. v. Cohen	78 Ohio App.3d 29, 603 N.E.2d 432 (Ohio App. 12th Dist. 1992)
Salesperson	Janitorial supplies	GA	3, 3f	Puritan/Churchill Chem. Co. v. Eubank	245 Ga. 334, 265 S.E.2d 16 (1980)
Salesperson	Janitorial supplies	NC	3	Wilmar, Inc. v. Corsillo	24 N.C.App. 271, 210 S.E.2d 427 (1974), cert. denied, 286 N.C. 421, 211 S.E.2d 802 (1975)
Salesperson	Janitorial supplies, chemicals, and paper	TX	1, AT-4	Miller Paper Co. v. Robert Paper Co.	901 S.W.2d 593 (Tex.Ct.App.—Amarillo 1995)
Salesperson	Labels (customized pressure-sensitive)	IL	AT-12	Label Printers v. Pflug (Label Printers II)	246 Ill.App.3d 435, 186 Ill.Dec. 516, 616 N.E.2d 706 (2d Dist. 1993)
Salesperson	Labels (customized pressure-sensitive)	IL	2, 3, 7	Label Printers v. Pflug (Label Printers I)	206 Ill.App.3d 483, 151 Ill.Dec. 720, 564 N.E.2d 1382, 6 IER Cases 214 (2d Dist. 1991)
Salesperson	Laundry	KS	14	Avenue Z Wet Wash Laundry Co. v. Yarmush	129 Misc. 427, 221 N.Y.S. 506 (N.Y.Sup.Ct. 1927)
Salesperson	Lawn care products	IL	2, 3, 3f, 5	Tyler Enters. of Elwood v. Shafer	214 Ill.App.3d 145, 158 Ill.Dec. 50, 573 N.E.2d 863 (3d Dist. 1991)

Salesperson	Linen service (hospitals)	TX	3, 3e, 3f, 4, 6, 14	Martin v. Linen Sys. for Hosps.	671 S.W.2d 706 (Tex.Ct.App.—Houston [1st Dist.] 1984)
Salesperson	Liquor (wholesale)	KS	2, 3, 3f, 3g, 4, 14	Eastern Distrib. Co. v. Flynn	222 Kan. 666, 567 P.2d 1371 (1977)
Salesperson	Litigation support services	LA	3c, 3f, 14, AT-32	Litigation Reprographics & Support Servs. v. Scott	599 So.2d 922 (La.App. 4th Cir. 1992)
Salesperson	Livestock feed additives	IL	2, 14	Agrimerica, Inc. v. Mathes	199 Ill.App.3d 435, 145 Ill.Dec. 587, 557 N.E.2d 357 (1990)
Salesperson	Livestock feed additives	IL	2, 3, 3f, 3g, 5	Agrimerica, Inc. v. Mathes	170 Ill.App.3d 1025, 120 Ill.Dec. 765, 524 N.E.2d 947 (1st Dist. 1988)
Salesperson	Lubricants (industrial)	IL	10	Tower Oil & Technology Co. v. Buckley	99 Ill.App.3d 637, 425 N.E.2d 1060 (1st Dist. 1981)
Salesperson	Lumber	PA	3c, 10	Ruffing v. 84 Lumber Co.	600 A.2d 545 (Pa.Super. 1991)
Salesperson	Lumber (wholesale)	OH	3c, 3f, 14	Morgan Lumber Sales Co. v. Toth	41 Ohio Misc. 17, 321 N.E.2d 907 (1974)
Salesperson	Machinery and tools (industrial)	PA	2	Boldt Mach. & Tools v. Wallace	469 Pa. 504, 366 A.2d 902 (1976)
Salesperson	Magazine subscriptions	AL	1, 3f, 10, 12	Blalock v. Perfect Subscription Co.	458 F.Supp. 123 (S.D.Ala. 1978), aff'd, 599 F.2d 743 (5th Cir. 1979) (per curiam)
Salesperson	Maintenance products	AL	1	C&C Prod. v. Fidelity & Deposit Co.	512 F.2d 1375 (5th Cir. 1975)
Salesperson	Maintenance supplies (industrial)	AL	3f	Premier Indus. Corp. v. Marlow	292 Ala. 407, 295 So.2d 396, cert. denied, 419 U.S. 1033 (1974)
Salesperson	Manufacturer's representative	CT	3a, 3f, 5, 6, 7	Hart, Nininger, Campbell Assocs. v. Rogers	16 Conn.App. 619, 548 A.2d 758 (1988)
Salesperson	Manufacturer's representative	NY	10	Gimper v. Giacchetta	633 N.Y.S.2d 614 (App.Div. 3d Dep't 1995)

Salesperson	Medical equipment (home)	PA	2, 3, 3a, 4, 10	Morgan's Home Equip. v. Martucci	390 Pa. 618, 136 A.2d 838 (1957)
Salesperson	Medical equipment (oxygen/allied health care supply)	MT	1, 3, 3d, 3e, 14	State Medical Oxygen & Supply v. American Medical Oxygen Co.	240 Mont. 70, 782 P.2d 1272 (1989)
Salesperson	Medical equipment (pacemakers)	MN	4	Medtronic, Inc. v. Gibbons	684 F.2d 565 (8th Cir. 1982)
Salesperson	Medical equipment (pacemakers)	MS	2, 3, 3d, 3e, 3f, 3g, 4, 5, 6, 14	Taylor v. Cordis Corp.	634 F.Supp. 1242 (S.D. Miss. 1986)
Salesperson	Medical equipment (surgical supplies)	LA	1	Standard-Crescent City Surgical Supplies, Inc. v. Mouton	535 So.2d 1301 (La.App. 5th Cir. 1988)
Salesperson	Medical records management, billing, and bookkeeping	PA	3a, 3f, 3g, 14	Records Center, Inc. v. Comprehensive Management, Inc.	363 Pa.Super. 79, 525 A.2d 433 (1987)
Salesperson	Medical records management, billing and bookkeeping	WY	3b	Records Center, Inc. v. Comprehensive Management, Inc.	363 Pa.Super. 79, 525 A.2d 433 (1987)
Salesperson	Medical supplies	WI	2, 3, 3f, 3g, 4, 12, 14, AT-89	General Medical Corp. v. Koobs	179 Wis.2d 422, 507 N.W.2d 381, 8 IER Cases 1409 (Wis.Ct.App. 1993)
Salesperson	Metal-hardness testing equipment	NY	10	Special Prods. Mfg., Inc. v. Douglass	169 A.D.2d 891, 564 N.Y.S.2d 615 (3d Dep't 1991)
Salesperson	Mobile homes	MO	2, 3, 3d, 3f, 7	Cape Mobile Mart v. Mobley	780 S.W.2d 116 (Mo.App. 1989)
Salesperson	Mobile homes and offices	CT	3c, 3f, 4	Timenterial, Inc. v. Dagata	29 Conn.Supp. 180, 277 A.2d 512 (Super. Ct. Hartford Cty. 1971)
Salesperson	Mortgages (secondary)	MN	6, 14	Rosewood Mortgage Corp. v. Hefty	383 N.W.2d 456 (Minn.Ct.App. 1986)

Salesperson	Not specified	TN	4	Comcast Sound Communications, Inc. v. Hoelke	572 N.Y.S.2d 189 (N.Y.App.Div. 4th Dep't 1991)
Salesperson	Not specified	TX	2, 3f, 3g, 4, 5, 7	Safeguard Business Sys. v. Schaeffer	822 S.W.2d 640 (Tex.Ct.App.—Dallas 1991)
Salesperson	Not specified	VA	3d, 8	Linville v. Servisoft of Va.	211 Va. 53, 174 S.E.2d 785 (1970)
Salesperson	Nursing home sales and leasing	OK	1, 3d, 3f, 4	Cohen Realty v. Marinick	817 P.2d 747, 6 IER Cases 1629 (Okla. Ct. App. 1991)
Salesperson	Nuts, bolts, tools, farm and industrial equipment	GA	3f	Smith v. HBT, Inc.	213 Ga.App. 560, 445 S.E.2d 315 (1994)
Salesperson	Office equipment	MD	3c	Simko, Inc. v. Graymar	55 Md. 561, 464 A.2d 1104 (1983)
Salesperson	Office equipment	OH	3c	Prinz Office Equip. Co. v. Pesko	1990 WL 7996 (Ohio Ct. App. (Summit), No. CA-14155, Jan. 31, 1990) (unreported)
Salesperson	Office supplies	GA	3	Ponders, Inc. v. Norman	246 Ga. 647, 272 S.E.2d 345 (1980)
Salesperson	Office supplies	RI	2, 5, 6, 7, 14	Paramount Office Supply v. MacIsaac, Inc.	524 A.2d 1099 (R.I. 1987)
Salesperson	Office supplies (inked ribbons and carbon paper)	NY	2, 3, 3d, 3f, 5, 14	Columbia Ribbon & Carbon Mfg. Co. v. A-1-A Corp.	42 N.Y.2d 496, 398 N.Y.S.2d 1004, 369 N.E.2d 4 (1977)
Salesperson	Oil and gas	WI	3f, 5, 6	Lakeside Oil Co. v. Slutsky	8 Wis.2d 157, 98 N.W.2d 415 (1959)
Salesperson	Oil field equipment	TX	2, 3, 3f, 4, 10	Weatherford Oil Tool Co. v. Campbell	161 Tex. 310, 340 S.W.2d 950 (1960)
Salesperson	Oil well drill bits, stabilizers, and cement mills	TX	3f	Gillen v. Diadrill, Inc.	624 S.W.2d 259 (Tex.Ct.App. 1981)

Salesperson	Photocopier	OH	3c	Copeco, Inc. v. Caley	91 Ohio App.3d 474, 632 N.E.2d 1299 (1992), *motion to certify record overruled,* 69 Ohio St.3d 79, 630 N.E.2d 662 (1994)
Salesperson	Photographic services (school pictures)	LA	4	National School Studios v. Barrios	236 So.2d 309 (La.App. 4th Cir. 1970)
Salesperson	Photographic services (school pictures)	WA	3, 10	National School Studios v. Superior School Photo Serv., Inc.	40 Wash.2d 263, 242 P.2d 756 (Sup.Ct. 1st Dep't 1952)
Salesperson	Photographic services (school pictures and yearbook)	SC	3e, 3f, 5, 14	Delmar Studios of the Carolinas v. Kinsey	233 S.C. 313, 104 S.E.2d 338 (1958)
Salesperson	Physician billing service	IL	3	Perman v. ArcVentures, Inc.	554 N.E.2d 982, 5 IER Cases 338 (Ill.App. 1st Dist. 1990)
Salesperson	Picture frames and molding (wholesale)	TX	3g	Toch v. Eric Schuster Corp.	490 S.W.2d 618 (Tex.Ct.App.—Dallas 1972)
Salesperson	Pipe and tube inspection service (oil field industry)	TX	3f	AMF Tuboscope v. McBryde	618 S.W.2d 105 (Tex.Ct.App. 1981)
Salesperson	Polyethylene products	NC	2, 3, 5, 7, 12	A.E.P. Indus., Inc.. v. McClure	308 N.C. 393, 302 S.E.2d 754 (1983)
Salesperson	Polyethylene products	WY	2, 3, 3d	A.E.P. Indus., Inc. v. McClure	308 N.C. 393, 302 S.E.2d 754 (1983)
Salesperson	Portable restrooms	MN	3c, 4, 6, 10	Satellite Indus. v. Keeling	396 N.W.2d 635 (Minn.Ct.App. 1986)
Salesperson	Printing	IL	3c, 12	Curtis 1000, Inc. v. Suess	24 F.3d 941 (7th Cir. 1994)
Salesperson	Printing	IL	8	Wessel Co. v. Busa	28 Ill.App.3d 686, 329 N.E.2d 414 (1st Dist. 1975)

Salesperson	Printing (commercial)	IL	2, 7	Reinhardt Printing Co. v. Feld	142 Ill.App.3d 9, 96 Ill.Dec. 97, 490 N.E.2d 1302 (1st Dist. 1986)
Salesperson	Printing (commercial)	IL	2, 3c, 5	Shapiro v. Regent Printing Co.	192 Ill.App.3d 1005, 140 Ill.Dec. 142, 549 N.E.2d 793 (1st Dist. 1989)
Salesperson	Printing and graphics	VA	2, 3, 3f, 8, 12	Lehman v. Standard Forms, Inc.	1995 Del. Ch. LEXIS 11 (Del.Chanc., C.A. No. 13688, Jan. 12, 1995) (applying Virginia law)
Salesperson	Printing equipment	CO	3f	Addressograph Multigraph Corp. v. Kelley	146 Colo. 550, 362 P.2d 184 (1964)
Salesperson	Printing plate materials	OH	3, 3g, 4, 14	Extine v. Williamson Midwest	176 Ohio St.2d 403, 200 N.E.2d 297 (1964) (overruled)
Salesperson	Printing services	MD	2, 3g, 4, 10, 14	Fowler v. Printers II	89 Md.App. 448, 598 A.2d 794 (1991)
Salesperson	Propane gas	CO	3f	Suburban Gas of Grand Junction v. Bockelman	157 Colo. 78, 401 P.2d 268 (1965)
Salesperson	Propane gas	DE	14	Gas Oil Prods. of Del. v. Kabino	1987 WL 19,279 (Del. Super. Ct., 1987)
Salesperson	Publishing (custom)	MN	2, 3, 3f, 3g, 6, 8, 14	Webb Publishing Co. v. Fosshage	426 N.W.2d 445 (Minn.Ct.App. 1985)
Salesperson	Radio pagers	TX	AT-90	Centel Cellular Co. v. Light	899 S.W.2d 343 (Tex.Ct.App.—Tyler 1995)
Salesperson	Real estate	AR	3f	Miller v. Fairfield Bay, Inc.	247 Ark. 565, 446 S.W.2d 660 (1969)
Salesperson	Real estate	AR	2, 3f, 4, 14	Rector-Phillips-Morse v. Vroman	253 Ark. 750, 489 S.W.2d 1 (1973)
Salesperson	Real estate	CT	3f, 5, 6, 9	Welles v. O'Connell	23 Conn.Supp. 335, 183 A.2d 287 (1962)
Salesperson	Real estate	MA	14	Albramson v. Blackman	340 Mass. 714, 166 N.E.2d 729 (1960)

Salesperson	Real estate	MA	2	Blackwell v. E.M. Helides, Jr., Inc.	368 Mass. 225, 331 N.E.2d 54 (1975)
Salesperson	Real estate	ME	2, 3, 3a, 3e, 3f, 5, 8, 14	Roy v. Bolduc	140 Me. 103, 34 A.2d 479 (1943)
Salesperson	Real estate	MN	2	Jim w. Miller Constr. v. Schaefer	298 N.W.2d 455 (Minn. 1980)
Salesperson	Real estate, mortgage loan, and fire insurance	WV	3, 3f, 8, 14	Pancake Realty Co. v. Harber	137 W.Va. 605, 73 S.E.2d 438 (1952)
Salesperson	Records storage and retrieval (medical)	IL	2	Service Centers of Chicago v. Minogue	180 Ill.App.3d 447, 129 Ill.Dec. 367, 535 N.E.2d 1132 (1st Dist. 1989)
Salesperson	Refrigeration equipment	MO	2, 5, 10	Refrigeration Indus., Inc. v. Nemmers	880 S.W.2d 912 (Mo.App. S.D. 1994)
Salesperson	Road machinery	VT	2, 3c, 3d, 3f, 14	Dyar Sales & Mach. Co. v. Bleiler	106 Vt. 425, 175 A. 27 (1934)
Salesperson	Roofing (commercial and industrial)	VA	4	Consolidated Indus. Roofing v. Williams	17 Va.Cir. 341 (City of Roanoke 1989)
Salesperson	Satellite equipment	FL	1, 6	Satellite Indus., Inc. v. Stutz	437 So.2d 222 (Fla. 4th Dist.Ct.App. 1988)
Salesperson	School rings, diplomas and other school items	IL	3, 11, 14	Callahan v. L.G. Balfour	179 Ill.App.3d 372, 534 N.E.2d 565 (1st Dist. 1989)
Salesperson	School supplies	AR	2, 3f, 10, 11, 14	All-State Supply v. Fisher	252 Ark. 962, 483 S.W.2d 210 (1972)
Salesperson	School yearbooks	NY	5	American Yearbook Co. v. St. Pierre	56 A.D.2d 832, 392 N.Y.S.2d 66 (2d Dep't 1977)
Salesperson	Seals (industrial)	IL	5, 6, 7	Hydroaire, Inc. v. Sager	98 Ill.App.3d 758, 53 Ill.Dec. 928, 424 N.E.2d 719 (1st Dist. 1981)

Occupation	Business	State	Sections	Case	Citation
Salesperson	Tobacco (wholesale)	CT	3, 3f, 14	New Haven Tobacco Co. v. Perelli (New Haven Tobacco II)	18 Conn.App. 531, 559 A.2d 715 (1989)
Salesperson	Tobacco (wholesale)	CT	3, 14	New Haven Tobacco Co. v. Perelli (New Haven Tobacco I)	11 Conn.App. 636, 528 A.2d 865 (1987)
Salesperson	Tools, nuts, bolts, and farm and industrial equipment	GA	3f	Smith v. HBT, Inc.	213 Ga.App. 560, 445 S.E.2d 315 (1994)
Salesperson	Trailers	CO	3e	Sprague's Aetna Trailer Sales v. Hruz	172 Colo. 469, 474 P.2d 216 (1970)
Salesperson	Tree care	MA	2, 14	New England Tree Expert Co. v. Russell	306 Mass. 504, 28 N.E.2d 907 (1940)
Salesperson	Uniform rentals	CT	3g	Uniform Rental Div., Inc. v. Moreno	83 A.D.2d 629, 441 N.Y.S.2d 538 (2d Dep't 1981)
Salesperson	Uniform rentals	GA	3c, 3f	Thomas v. Coastal Indus. Servs.	214 Ga. 832, 108 S.E.2d 328 (1959)
Salesperson	Uniform rentals	NY	3f	Uniform Rental Div., Inc. v. Moreno	83 A.D.2d 629, 441 N.Y.S.2d 538 (2d Dep't 1981)
Salesperson	Vending services	NY	2	Briskin v. All Seasons Servs., Inc.	615 N.Y.S.2d 166 (App.Div. 4th Dep't 1994)
Salesperson	Veterinary drugs and other products	HI	3b	Ramsey v. Mutual Supply Co.	58 Tenn.App. 164, 427 S.W.2d 849 (1968)
Salesperson	Veterinary drugs and other products	TN	2, 3a, 9	Ramsey v. Mutual Supply Co.	58 Tenn.App. 164, 427 S.W.2d 849 (1968)
Salesperson	Water purifier manufacturing	GA	4	Water Servs. v. Tesco Chems.	410 F.2d 163 (5th Cir. 1969)

Role	Industry	State	Clauses	Case	Citation
Salesperson (independent contractor)	Chemicals	TX	3d, 3f, 9	Wilson v. Chemco Chem. Co.	711 S.W.2d 265 (Tex.Ct.App., Dallas 1986)
Salesperson (independent contractor)	Confection	FL	1	Junior Salesman of Fla. v. Bogeais	541 So.2d 676 (Fla. 5th Dist.Ct.App. 1989), reh'g denied (April 19, 1989)
Salesperson (independent contractor)	Insurance	FL	1	Ware v. Money-Plan Int'l	467 So.2d 1072 (Fla. 2d Dist.Ct.App. 1985)
Salesperson (independent contractor)	Securities	FL	1	Economic Research Analysts v. Brennan	232 So.2d 219 (Fla. 4th Dist.Ct.App. 1970)
Salesperson (partner)	Insurance	TX	AT-12, AT-40	Herrman & Andreas Ins. Agency v. Appling	800 S.W.2d 312 (Tex.Ct.App.—Corpus Christi 1990)
Salesperson (partner, limited)	Insurance	VA	2, 3d, 3f, 3g, 5, 14	Meissel v. Finley	198 Va. 577, 95 S.E.2d 186 (1956)
Salesperson (primary)	Computer software systems	TX	1, 3, 4	B.J. Software Sys. v. Osina	827 S.W.2d 543 (Tex.Ct.App.—Houston [1st Dist.] 1992)
Salesperson (route)	Coffee	DE	3	Take-A-Break Coffee Serv., Inc. v. Grose	(Del.Ch. C.A. No. 11217, May 14, 1990)
Salesperson (route)	Coffee	IN	3d, 3f	4408, Inc. v. Losure	175 Ind.App. 658, 373 N.E.2d 899 (1978)
Salesperson (route)	Coffee	LA	1, 2	In re Stanford Coffee Serv. Co.	499 So.2d 1314 (La.App. 4th Cir. 1986) writ denied, 501 So.2d 232 (La. 1987)
Salesperson (route)	Coffee and tea	CO	3f	Jewel Tea Co. v. Watkins	26 Colo.App. 494, 145 P. 719 (1915)

Salesperson (route)	Laundry	NM	3f	*Excelsior Laundry Co. v. Diehl*	32 N.M. 169, 252 P. 991 (1927)
Salesperson (route)	Laundry	NM	2, 3, 3a, 3d, 3f, 3g, 10, 14	*Nichols v. Anderson*	43 N.M. 296, 92 P.2d 781 (1939)
Salesperson (route)	Laundry	PA	3a, 3b	*Modern Laundry & Dry Cleaning Co. v. Farrer*	536 A.2d 409 (Pa.Super. 1988)
Salesperson (route)	Laundry	SC	3, 3b, 3f, 7, 10, AT-82	*Rental Uniform Serv. of Florence v. Dudley*	278 S.C. 274, 301 S.E.2d 142 (1983)
Salesperson (route)	Laundry, linen, uniform rentals	LA	4, 14	*Buckeye Garment Rental Co. v. Jones*	276 F.Supp. 560 (E.D.La. 1967)
Salesperson (route)	Linen	AR	3a, 3f, 5, 8	*Bailey v. King*	240 Ark. 245, 398 S.W.2d 906 (1966)
Salesperson (route)	Linen service	MA	5	*Suburban Coat, Apron & Linen Supply Co. v. LeBlanc*	300 Mass. 509, 15 N.E.2d 828 (1938)
Salesperson (route)	Liquor (wholesale)	RI	4	*Eastern Distrib. Co. v. Flynn*	222 Kan. 666, 567 P.2d 1371 (1977)
Salesperson (route)	Lunch truck	FL	3b, 3c	*Tasty Box Lunch v. Kennedy*	121 So.2d 52 (Fla. 5th Dist.Ct.App. 1960)
Salesperson (route)	Milk	LA	2	*Peltier v. Hebert*	245 So.2d 511 (La.App. 1971)
Salesperson (route)	Mobile food service (lunch truck)	TN	2	*Kaset v. Combs*	58 Tenn.App. 559, 434 S.W.2d 838 (1968)
Salesperson (route)	Tea	MI	2	*Grand Union Tea Co. v. Dodds*	164 Mich. 50, 128 N.W. 1090 (1910)
Salesperson (supervisor)	Janitorial service	CA	5	*Aetna Bldg. Maintenance Co. v. West*	39 Cal.2d 198, 246 P.2d 11 (1952)
Scientist	Medical diagnostic kit manufacturing	UT	2	*Microbiological Research Corp. v. Muna*	625 P.2d 690 (Utah 1981)

Service technician	Photocopiers	LA	AT-10	Louisiana Office Sys., Inc. v. Bodreaux	298 So.2d 341 (La.App.), remanded, 302 So.2d 37 (La. 1974), dismissed, 309 So.2d 779 (La.App. 1975)
Service technician	Photocopiers, micro-fiche equipment, and offset printing equipment	IL	2, 5, 6	A.B. Dick Co. v. American Pro-Tech	159 Ill.App.3d 786, 112 Ill.Dec. 649, 514 N.E.2d 45, 4 IER Cases 600 (1st Dist. 1987)
Serviceperson	Medical equipment (critical care and anesthesia equipment)	VA	1, 3, 3a, 3d, 3f, 9	Blue Ridge Anesthesia & Critical Care v. Gidick	239 Va. 369, 389 S.E.2d 467, 5 IER Cases 292 (1990)
Singer	Record company	NY	2	King Records, Inc. v. Brown	21 A.D.2d 593, 252 N.Y.S.2d 988 (1964)
Social worker (clinical, licensed)	Health care (social work)	VA	4	Northern Va. Psychiatric Group, P.C. v. Halpern	19 Va.Cir. 279 (Fairfax County 1990)
Speech therapist	Health care	LA	1, 3, 3f	LaFourche Speech & Language Servs., Inc. v. Juckett	652 So.2d 679 (La.App. 1st Cir. 1995)
Stock broker	Securities	CA	12	Frame v. Merrill Lynch, Pierce, Fenner & Smith, Inc.	20 Cal.App.3d 668, 97 Cal. Rptr. 811 (1971)
Stock broker	Securities	DE	3, 3f	Merrill Lynch Pierce, Fenner & Smith v. Price	(Del.Ch. C.A. No. 11097, Sept. 13, 1989)
Stock broker	Securities	IA	2	Dain Bosworth, Inc. v. Brandhorst	356 N.W.2d 590 (Iowa App. 1984)
Stock broker	Securities	NY	8, 14	Post v. Merrill, Lynch, Pierce, Fenner & Smith	48 N.Y.2d 84, 421 N.Y.S.2d 847, 397 N.E.2d 358 (1979)

Team leader	Heating element manufacturing	KN	3b, 5	*Heatron v. Shackelford*	898 F.Supp. 1491, 10 IER Cases 1736 (D. Kan. 1995)
Technician	Tree care	MD	3b, 3c, 3f, 8, 14	*Ruhl v. F.A. Bartlett Tree Expert Co.*	245 Md. 118, 225 A.2d 288 (1967)
Telephone secretary	Answering service	FL	3	*Answer All Tel. Secretarial Serv. v. Call 24*	381 So.2d 281 (Fla. 5th Dist.Ct.App. 1980)
Theatrical booking agent	Theatrical booking	NY	2	*Frederick Bros. Artists Corp. v. Yates*	271 A.D. 69, 62 N.Y.S.2S 714 (1946), *aff'd* 296 N.Y. 820, 72 N.E.2d 13 (1947) (per curiam)
Theatrical performer (histrionics)	Performing arts	NY	2	*Nazzaro v. Washington*	81 N.Y.S.2d 769 (Sup.Ct. 1948)
Therapist	Health care (Occupational therapy)	MN	2	*Rehabilitation Specialists v. Koering*	404 N.W.2d 301 (Minn.Ct.App. 1987)
Trader (wood products)	Lumber	OR	3d, 3f, 4	*Lavey v. Edwards*	264 Or. 331, 505 P.2d 342 (1973)
Travel agent	Travel	TX	2, 3, 3a, 3c, 3f, 4, 13, AT-90	*Travel Masters v. Star Tours*	742 S.W.2d 837 (Tex.Ct.App., Dallas 1987)
Treasurer	Supplies	WA	8	*Parsons Supply v. Smith*	22 Wash.App. 520, 591 P.2d 821 (1979)
Truck driver	Transportation	GA	3	*Stein Steel & Supply Co. v. Tucker*	219 Ga. 844, 136 S.E.2d 355 (1964)
Truck driver	Truck driver leasing	TN	1, 2, 3, 14	*Hasty v. Rent-A-Driver*	671 S.W.2d 471 (Tenn. 1984)
Trust officer	Bank	WV	1, 3, 3f, 7	*Torbett v. Wheeling Dollar Sav. & Trust Co.*	314 S.E.2d 166 (W.Va. 1983)
Undertaker	Undertaking	MA	3f, 3g	*Folsom Funeral Serv. v. Rodgers*	6 Mass.App. 843, 372 N.E.2d 532 (1978)

Veterinarian	Veterinary medicine	SD	1, 3c, 4, 14	*Loescher v. Policky*	84 S.D. 447, 173 N.W.2d 50 (1969)
Veterinarian	Veterinary medicine	TX	2, 3f	*Cukjati v. Burkett*	722 S.W.2d 215 (Tex.Ct.App.—Dallas 1989)
Veterinarian	Veterinary medicine	WY	3b	*Cukjati v. Burkett*	772 S.W.2d 215 (Tex.Ct.App.—Dallas 1989)
Veterinarian	Veterinary medicine	WY	2, 3, 3a, 3b, 3c, 3d, 3e, 3f, 4, 6, 7, 8, 9, 10, 13, AT-4, AT-21, AT-73, AT-82, AT-93	*Hopper v. All Pet Animal Clinic, Inc.*	861 P.2d 531, 9 IER Cases 554 (Wyo. 1993)
Veterinarian	Veterinary medicine	WY	3b	*Stevenson v. Parsons*	96 N.C.App 93, 384 S.E.2d 291 (1989)
Veterinarian	Veterinary medicine	WY	3, 3e, 4, 10, 14	*Tench v. Weaver*	374 P.2d 27 (Wyo. 1962)
Water analyst	Water analysis	WV	2, 3f, 14	*Appalachian Laboratories v. Bostic*	359 S.E.2d 614 (W.Va. 1987) (per curiam)
Writer	Magazine (horse)	TN	3, 3d, 3f, 4, AT-8	*Dabora, Inc. v. Kline*	884 S.W.2d 475 (Tenn.App. 1994)
Writer	Technical writing	MN	2	*Sandstorm v. Douglas Mach. Corp.*	372 N.W.2d 89 (Minn.Ct.App. 1985)

Index of Employment Covenant Cases Not Specifying Occupation

For the "State" column, see the list of state abbreviations on page xviii if necessary. For the "Question Nos." column:

- *See the "List of General Questions" beginning at page xvi of this volume for the meaning of question numbers and page numbers for particular states.*
- *An "AT-" followed by a number (e.g., AT-1) indicates information is contained in a discussion of an Additional Topic; see the "Finding List of Additional Topics" beginning at page xxx of this volume to identify the topic concerned if necessary, and for page numbers for particular states.*

For the "Citation" column, where the state is noted and it varies from that listed in the "State" column, this indicates a discussion of a case decided in another state. Cases not listed here are included in other indexes as follows:

- *Cases in which an occupation was mentioned in the court decision are listed by occupation in the "Index of Employment Covenant Cases Specifying Occupation."*
- *Cases which involved a sale of business rather than an occupation are listed by industry in the "Index of Sale-of-Business Covenant Cases."*
- *Cases involving covenants relating to other types of transactions are listed by transaction/relationship in the "Index of Covenant Cases Not Involving Employment or Sale of Business."*
- *Cases not involving covenants are listed by state in the "Index of Cases Not Involving Covenants."*

Cases listed either in this index or in the "Index of Employment Covenant Cases Specifying Occupation" may be searched together by industry, using the "Index of Employment Covenant Cases by Industry." In that index, the term "Not specified" in the "Occupation" column is a signal to consult this index rather than the "Index of Employment Covenant Cases Specifying Occupation" for additional information.

Editor's Note: Cases decided by the Texas Court of Appeals before September 1, 1981, are cited as "Tex. Civ. App." After that date, cases are cited as "Tex. Ct. App." The change in the court's name and the rules for proper citation in documents submitted to Texas courts are explained in the Texas Rules of Form.

Industry	State	Question	Case Name	Citation
Advertising	NY	AT-59	Kennedy v. Kennedy	195 A.D.2d 229, 607 N.Y.S.2d 773 (4th Dep't 1994)
Agricultural equipment design and manufacturing	KS	2, 3b	Evco Distrib. v. Brandau	6 Kan.App.2d 53, 626 P.2d 1192 (1981)
Air ambulance service	FL	6	Air Ambulance Network, Inc. v. Floribus	511 So.2d 702 (Fla. 3d Dist.Ct.App. 1987)
Alarms	GA	3g	Specialized Alarm Servs. v. Kauska	189 Ga.App. 863, 377 S.E.2d 703 (1989), reh'g denied (Jan. 19, 1989)
Automotive manufacturing	FL	10, 11, 14	Brannon v. Auto Center Mfg. Co.	393 So.2d 75 (Fla. 5th Dist.Ct.App. 1981)
Beverage	GA	3d	Southeastern Beverage Co. v. Dillard	233 Ga. 346, 211 S.E.2d 299 (1974)
Box manufacturing	NJ	2, 3, 4, 9, 10, 12	Raven v. A. Klein & Co.	195 N.J. Super. 209, 478 A.2d 1208 (App.Div. 1984)
Broadcasting	MA	2, 6	Knowles Broadcasting Co. v. Oreto	3 Mass.App. 707, 322 N.E.2d 791 (1975)
Chemical	FL	3f	Kenco Chem. & Mfg. Co. v. Railey	286 So.2d 272 (Fla. 1st Dist.Ct.App. 1973)
Computer aided design equipment	OH	11, 14	Cad Cam, Inc. v. Underwood	36 OhioApp.3d 90, 521 N.E.2d 498 (1987)
Computer services	FL	5, 6	AGS Computer Servs. v. Rodriguez	592 So.2d 801, 17 Fla. L. Weekly D398 (Fla. 4th Dist.Ct.App. 1992)
Computing service	AK	2, 3, 3a, 3d, 3e, 3f, 4, 11, 14	Data Management v. Greene	757 P.2d 62, 3 IER Cases 796 (Alaska 1988)

Industry	State	Provisions	Case	Citation
Country club management	TX	5, 7	Rimes v. Club Corp. of Am.	542 S.W.2d 909 (Tex.Civ.App.—Dallas 1976)
Credit	GA	AT-7	Norman v. Nationwide Credit	202 Ga.App. 732, 415 S.E.2d 293, cert. denied (Feb. 10, 1992)
Data processing	NY	2, 3f, 4, 14	Purchasing Assocs., Inc. v. Weitz	13 N.Y.2d 267, 246 N.Y.S.2d 600, 196 N.E.2d 245 (1963)
Diamond wholesaling	KS	14	Abramov v. Royal Dallas, Inc.	536 S.W.2d 388 (Tex.Civ.App. 1976)
Electrical equipment manufacturing	IL	3f	G&W Elec. Co. v. Joslyn Mfg. & Supply Co.	127 Ill.App.3d 44, 468 N.E.2d 449 (3d Dist. 1984)
Electronics	NC	3, 3f, 4, 5, 7	Electronical S. v. Lewis	385 S.E.2d 352 (N.C.App. 1989)
Employment agency (temporary)	GA	3f	Crowe v. Manpower Temporary Serv.	256 Ga. 239, 347 S.E.2d 560 (1986)
Exterior wall panel manufacturing	NY	5	Composite Panel Fabricators, Inc. v. Webb	118 A.D.2d 615, 499 N.Y.S.2d 765 (2d Dep't 1968)
Farming (hydroponic)	MD	3c	Waterfall Farm Sys. Inc. v. Craig	1995 U.S. App. LEXIS 17181 (D. Md., No. H-94-1247, Sept. 23, 1995)
Fasteners	IA	5	Diversified Fastening Sys. v. Rogge	786 F.Supp. 1486 (N.D. Iowa 1991)
Finance	LA	11	Beneficial Fin. Co. of Monroe v. Aldridge	200 So.2d 681 (La. 1967)
Fire extinguisher sales and service	AL	2, 3, 3e, 3f	Calhoun v. Brendle, Inc.	502 So.2d 689 (Ala. 1986)
Food brokerage	SC	10	Gathings v. Robertson Brokerage Co.	367 S.E.2d 423 (S.CApp. 1988)
Food products	DE	3f, 8	Caras v. American Original Corp.	1987 WL 15533 (Del.Ch. 1987)
Graphics	CO	3, 4	National Graphics Co. v. Dilley	681 P.2d 546 (Colo.App. 1984)
Hotel	MO	7	Suiter v. Holiday Inn Southwest	864 S.W.2d 436 (Mo.App. 1993) (per curiam)

FL	3, 3d, 4, 6	Miller Mechanical v. Ruth	300 So.2d 11 (Fla. 1974)	Not specified
FL	7, 10, AT-67	Ross v. Champion Computer Corp.	582 So.2d 152, 16 Fla. L. Weekly D1893 (Fla. 4th Dist.Ct.App. 1991)	Not specified
FL	3	Suave Shoe Corp. v. Fernandez	390 So.2d 799 (Fla. 3d Dist.Ct.App. 1980) (per curiam)	Not specified
FL	5, 6, 9, 11	Sun Elastic Corp. v. O.B. Indus.	603 So.2d 516 (Fla. 3d Dist.Ct.App. 1992)	Not specified
FL	7	United Marine v. Raill	584 So.2d 1137 (Fla. 3d Dist.Ct.App. 1991)	Not specified
GA	2, 3, 3d, 4	Durham v. Stand-by Labor of Ga.	230 Ga. 558, 198 S.E.2d 145 (1973)	Not specified
GA	3g	Kirschbaum v. Jones	206 Ga. 192, 56 S.E.2d 484 (1949)	Not specified
GA	3	McNeill Group v. Restivo	252 Ga. 112, 311 S.E.2d 831 (1984)	Not specified
GA	AT-23	S. Hammond Story Agency v. Baer	202 Ga.App. 281, 414 S.E.2d 287 (1991), reconsideration denied (Dec. 19, 1991), cert. denied (Feb. 4, 1992)	Not specified
IL	5	Buzz Barton & Assocs. v. Giannone	108 Ill.2d 373, 91 Ill.Dec. 636, 483 N.E.2d 1271 (1985)	Not specified
LA	10, 11, AT-66	G.T. Michelli Co. v. McKey	599 So.2d 355 (La.App. 1st Cir. 1992)	Not specified
LA	8	Johnston v. Alloy Distribs.	536 So.2d 526 (La.App. 1st Cir. 1988)	Not specified
LA	8	Neal v. Superior Enters.	552 So.2d 1047 (La.App. 1st Cir. 1989)	Not specified
NY	10	Barone v. Marcisak	96 A.D.2d 816, 465 N.Y.S.2d 561 (2d Dep't 1983)	Not specified
NY	9, 10	National Survival Game of N.Y., Inc. v. NSG of LI Corp.	169 A.D.2d 760, 565 N.Y.S.2d 127 (2d Dep't 1991)	Not specified
NY	5, 10, 11	Pencom Sys., Inc. v. Shapiro	193 A.D.2d 561, 598 N.Y.S.2d 212 (1st Dep't 1993)	Not specified

Studio (not specified as to type)	WI	3f	*Holsen v. Marshall & Lisley Bank*	52 Wis.2d 281, 190 N.W.2d 189 (1971)
Telephone interconnect equipment sales and service	IA	3f, 4, 14, AT-69	*Phone Connection v. Harbst*	494 N.W.2d 445, 7 IER Cases 570 (Iowa App. 1992)
Title insurance	DE	AT-12	*Townsend v. Collord*	575 S.W.2d 422 (Tex.Civ.App., Fort Worth 1978)
Towel rentals	LA	3e, 6	*Target Rental Towel v. Byrd*	341 So.2d 600 (La.App. 2d Cir. 1975)
Vertical blinds manufacturing	NY	10	*Spielvogel v. Zitofsky*	175 A.D.2d 830, 573 N.Y.S.2d 198 (2d Dep't 1991)
Video surveillance system sales and service	DE	2	*Custom Video v. N.A., Video*	Del.Ch., CA No. 9261, Hartnett, V.C. (Sept. 25, 1987) (applying New Jersey substantive law)

Index of Employment Covenant Cases by Industry

Once the industry at issue is located in this Index:

- *If an occupation is listed in the "Occupation" column, consult the appropriate listing in the "Index of Employment Covenant Cases Specifying Occupation" above for additional information.*
- *If an occupation is not listed, and instead the term "Not specified" appears in the "Occupation" column, consult the appropriate listing in the "Index of Employment Covenant Cases Not Specifying Occupation" above for additional information.*

Industry	Occupation
Accounting	Accountant
Accounting	Accountant (partner)
Accounting	Manager
Accounting	Manager (office)
Accounting	Salesperson
Accounting	Supervisor (bookkeeping)
Accounting (tax)	Accountant
Accounting software	Computer programmer
Actuarial services	Actuary
Ad valorem property tax lowering service	Appraiser
Ad valorem property tax lowering service	Attorney
Adhesives (industrial)	Manager, sales (district)
Admixtures (concrete drying and setting additives)	Manager, sales (regional)
Advertising	Account executive
Advertising	Advertising executive
Advertising	Corporate officer (vice president)
Advertising	Hostess
Advertising	Manager, sales
Advertising	Not specified
Advertising	Sales trainer
Advertising (magazine)	Salesperson
Advertising (movie-theater intermission)	Salesperson
Advertising (personnel recruitment)	Manager, sales (regional)
Advertising (radio air time)	Salesperson
Advertising (television)	Creative director
Advertising (television time)	Salesperson
Advertising brokerage (newspaper)	Manager (office)
Advertising brokerage (newspaper)	Salesperson
Aeronautical engineering	Engineer
Agricultural consulting	Consultant (crop and soil)
Agricultural equipment design and manufacturing	Not specified

Agricultural spraying (aerial)	Pilot (helicopter)
Air ambulance service	Not specified
Air brakes	Salesperson
Air compressors	Manager (marketing)
Air conditioning and heating equipment	Installer
Air conditioning and heating equipment	Installer's helper
Air filters (computer, custom-made)	Salesperson
Airline customers	Manager (sales, overseas)
Airplane parts manufacturing	Research and development coordinator
Alarm (burglar and fire) systems	Salesperson
Alarm (fire) systems	Service technician
Alarms	Installer
Alarms	Not specified
Alarms	Salesperson
Alarms (fire and burglar)	Manager trainee
Alarms (fire and burglar)	Salesperson
Answering service	Telephone secretary
Appliances	Manufacturer's representative
Appliance and furniture retailing	Salesperson
Architecture	Architect
Artwork	Salesperson
Asbestos abatement	Asbestos-abatement technician
Audio engineering (recording studio)	Engineer
Auditing (credit unions)	Auditor
Automated system design	Engineer
Automobile air conditioners	Installer
Automobile dealership	Corporate officer (director)
Automobile dealership	Corporate officer (vice president)
Automobile dealership	Manager (general)
Automobile glass	Manager (district)
Automobile glass installation	Manager
Automobile glass replacement service	Corporate officer
Automobile insurance club	Manager (district)

Automobile lubricating	Salesperson
Automobile roof	Installer
Automobile tag and title	Courier
Automobiles	Salesperson
Automotive additives	Subdistributor
Automotive and janitorial supplies	Salesperson
Automotive manufacturing	Not specified
Automotive parts (after-market)	Salesperson
Automotive repair	Foreman
Automotive repair	Mechanic
Aviation service	Corporate officer (chairman)
Aviation service	Corporate officer (president)
Awards program planning	Corporate officer (vice president)
Awards program planning	Manager (senior)
Awards program planning	Manager (senior accounts)
Bagels	Baker
Baked goods	Salesperson (house-to-house)
Bakery	Baker
Bakery	Manager
Balloon bouquets	Salesperson
Bank	Bank officer (loan)
Bank	Corporate officer (executive)
Bank	Corporate officer (vice president)
Bank	Corporate officer (vice president, assistant)
Bank	Trust officer
Bar	Bartender
Barbecue and fireplace accessories	Manager, sales
Barber/beauty shop equipment	Salesperson
Beauty	Cosmetologist
Beauty	Electrologist
Beauty	Esthetician
Beauty	Hair stylist

Beauty	Manicurist
Beauty (facial spa salon)	Esthetician
Beauty pageants	Corporate officer (director, state)
Beauty products	Manager (store)
Beauty products	Salesperson
Beverage	Not specified
Beverages (alcoholic, wholesale)	Salesperson
Bolts, nuts, tools, farm and industrial equipment	Salesperson
Bond sales	Corporate officer (vice president)
Book retailing	Bookseller (partner)
Boot and belt manufacturing	Manager (general)
Bowling equipment	Salesperson
Box manufacturing	Not specified
Brick industry equipment manufacturing	Manager (general)
Broadcasting	Not specified
Broadcasting (Radio (hillbilly entertainment))	Disc jockey
Broadcasting (Radio)	Broadcaster
Broadcasting (Radio)	Disc jockey
Broadcasting (Radio)	News director
Broadcasting (Television)	Broadcaster
Broadcasting (Television)	Host (show)
Broadcasting (Television)	Meteorologist
Broadcasting (Television)	Personality
Brush excavation	Manager
Building demolition	Supervisor
Building industry products and services	Manager, sales
Building maintenance	Corporate officer (director, regional)
Building maintenance service	Account executive (senior)
Building products manufacturing	Corporate officer (director)
Building supplies	Corporate officer
Building supplies	Corporate officer (director)

Building supplies	Corporate officer (executive)
Building supplies	Manager (general)
Building supplies	Salesperson
Bumper rechroming	Corporate officer (vice president)
Business	Consultant
Business forms	Corporate officer (president)
Business forms	Sales manager
Business forms	Salesperson
Cable television equipment	Manager, sales
Candy, cigarettes, and tobacco	Salesperson
Car rental	Counter person
Car repair	Operator
Car repair (automobile frame)	Repair person
Car wash building, supplies, and repair service	Manager (service)
Carburetion equipment	Manager, sales (regional)
Cassette tape manufacturing	Corporate officer (vice president)
Cellular car phones and air time	Salesperson
Cellular phones	Salesperson
Chair	Designer
Chair manufacturing	Corporate officer
Check cashing	Corporate officer (chief executive officer)
Chemical	Manager
Chemical	Not specified
Chemical (industrial) manufacturing	Chemist
Chemical cleaners	Salesperson
Chemical engineering	Engineer
Chemical processing equipment manufacturing	Corporate officer (vice president)
Chemical processing equipment manufacturing	Manager
Chemical processing equipment	Salesperson
Chemical products	Manager, sales (district)

Chemical products	Salesperson
Chemical products (commercial)	Salesperson
Chemical products (industrial maintenance)	Salesperson
Chemical products (plating-on-plastics chemicals)	Salesperson
Chemicals	Manager, sales
Chemicals	Salesperson
Chemicals	Salesperson (independent contractor)
Chemicals (ceramic)	Salesperson
Chemicals (industrial)	Salesperson
Civil (concrete aggregates testing) engineering	Engineer
Civil (soil and foundation) engineering	Engineer
Civil engineering	Engineer
Cleaning material	Manager, sales (assistant)
Cleaning service	Salesperson
Cleaning supplies	Salesperson
Clothing	Salesperson
Clothing (custom-printed, promotional)	Salesperson
Clothing (men's, custom)	Salesperson
Clothing (wholesale)	Salesperson
Clothing (women's retail)	Buyer
Clothing/jewelry	Manager (store)
Clothing retailing	Debt collector
Clothing retailing	Delivery person
Coal industry equipment and supplies	Salesperson
Coating, cleaning and antiseptic compounds	Salesperson
Coffee	Salesperson
Coffee	Salesperson (route)
Coffee and tea	Salesperson
Coffee and tea	Salesperson (route)
Coffee supply	Manager, sales

Construction (mining equipment manufacturer) engineering	Engineer
Construction and remodeling (retail space)	Manager (project)
Construction industry supplies and equipment	Salesperson
Consulting	Consultant
Consulting (employment)	Psychologist
Consulting (professional management and accounting)	Management consultant
Conveyer belt sales and service	Manager (division)
Cookware (aluminum)	Salesperson
Cooling tower heat-exchange film pack	Manager, sales
Corrugated box manufacturing	Corporate officer (president)
Country club management	Not specified
Courier service	Manager (senior regional)
Court reporting	Court reporter
Court reporting	Court reporter (independent contractor)
Credit	Not specified
Credit insurance	Salesperson
Crop spraying (aerial)	Pilot
Dairy	Manager
Dairy	Manager, sales
Dairy	Salesperson (route)
Dance	Instructor
Data processing	Corporate officer (chief executive officer)
Data processing	Corporate officer (president)
Data processing	Not specified
Debt collection	Chief operating officer
Debt collection	Corporate officer (president)
Debt collection	Debt collector
Debt collection	Manager
Debt collection	Manager (collections)
Debt collection	Manager (district)

Debt collection	Manager (regional)
Debt collection	Manager, sales
Debt collection	Public relations director
Debt collection	Salesperson
Debt collection (cable television industry)	Corporate officer (vice president)
Delicatessen products	Salesperson
Dental lab	Dental lab technician
Dental lab	Salesperson
Dental lab supplies	Salesperson
Depilatories (animal skins)	Salesperson
Design (kitchens (appliances))	Salesperson
Developer (office park)	Corporate officer (executive)
Diamond wholesaling	Not specified
Direct marketing (mailing lists)	Corporate officer (vice president, senior)
Disinfectants (Catholic institution customers)	Salesperson
Drafting and engineering (industrial) service	Draftsperson
Dry cleaning	Manager (production)
Education (Dance)	Instructor
Education (Driving (truck))	Instructor
Education (Music)	Instructor
Education (Physical)	Instructor
Education (Piano)	Instructor
Electrical	Engineer
Electrical contracting	Attorney (general counsel)
Electrical contracting	Corporate officer (secretary)
Electrical contracting	Manager
Electrical contracting	Salesperson
Electrical/electronic connector manufacturing	Manager (division)
Electrical equipment manufacturing	Not specified
Electronic products	Salesperson

Electronics	Not specified
Electronics engineering	Engineer
Electronics manufacturing	Corporate officer (president)
Employee benefits	Consultant
Employee benefits (insurance, annuities)	Manager (division)
Employee benefits (insurance, annuities)	Salesperson
Employee benefits consulting	Attorney
Employment agency	Recruiter
Employment agency (data processors)	Manager
Employment agency (data processors)	Manager (branch)
Employment agency (data processors)	Recruiter
Employment agency (environmental, health, safety, and clinical health care industries)	Recruiter
Employment agency (executive)	Recruiter
Employment agency (office support)	Recruiter
Employment agency (physicians)	Recruiter
Employment agency (printing industry)	Recruiter
Employment agency (technical division)	Manager
Employment agency (technical service firm)	Job shopper
Employment agency (telecommunications)	Recruiter
Employment agency (temporary)	Account manager
Employment agency (temporary)	Manager
Employment agency (temporary)	Manager (account)
Employment agency (temporary)	Manager (branch)
Employment agency (temporary)	Not specified
Employment agency (temporary)	Recruiter
Employment agency (temporary)	Salesperson
Employment agency (temporary, nurses)	Recruiter
Engineering	Engineer
Entertainment	Disc jockey (mobile)
Entertainment	Disc jockey (mobile, independent contractor)
Entertainment (musical)	Agent (booking)

Entertainment (theatrical)	Agent (booking)
Envelopes (business)	Salesperson
Excavation contracting	Subcontactor's agreement
Exterior wall panel manufacturing	Not specified
Fall-protection equipment	Salesperson
Farm and industrial equipment, nuts, bolts, and tools	Salesperson
Farming (hydroponic)	Not specified
Fasteners	Not specified
Fasteners	Salesperson
Fasteners (stainless steel)	Salesperson
Finance	Manager
Finance	Manager (branch)
Finance	Manager (office)
Finance	Not specified
Finance (business and personal)	Consultant
Finance and insurance consulting	Manager (district)
Finance and small loan	Supervisor
Financial management	Counsellor
Financial services	Manager (office)
Fire detection and extinguishing equipment	Engineer
Fire detection and extinguishing equipment	Estimator
Fire extinguisher sales and service	Not specified
Fire fighting equipment	Recharger
Fire prevention equipment	Manager (service and branch)
Fireproofing	Fireproofing technician
Flying service	Pilot
Food	Corporate officer
Food	Corporate officer (president)
Food	Salesperson (route)
Food (frozen)	Salesperson
Food (wholesale)	Salesperson
Food and paper supplies	Salesperson

Food brokerage	Not specified
Food label regulation	Lobbyist
Food products	Not specified
Food products	Salesperson
Food service management	Corporate officer (chief executive officer)
Food service management	Corporate officer (president)
Food service management	Corporate officer (vice president, sales)
Food services	Manager (unit)
Foreign currency exchange and precious metal firms	Corporate officer (vice president, senior)
Forms (business)	Salesperson
Forms (business) and equipment	Salesperson
Freight forwarding	Corporate officer (director)
Freight forwarding	Corporate officer (president)
Freight forwarding	Manager
Fuel	Salesperson
Fund-raising	Fund-raiser
Fund-raising (police groups)	Corporate officer (vice president)
Fund-raising (police groups)	Manager (general)
Fund-raising products	Salesperson
Fur processing	Manager (branch)
Furniture	Salesperson
Furniture and appliances (retail)	Salesperson
Games (coin-operated soccer)	Salesperson
Garbage collection	Garbage collector
Gas (bulk)	Delivery person
Gearbox manufacturing	Corporate officer (chief executive officer)
Gearbox manufacturing	Corporate officer (president)
Gifts and stationery	Buyer (assistant)
Glass (automobile) installation	Manager (operations)
Glue applicator equipment manufacturing	Manager (production)

Grain	Exclusive purchase contact
Grant application preparation	Consultant
Grant application preparation	Corporate officer (vice president)
Graphics	Not specified
Graphics and printing	Salesperson
Grocery	Corporate officer (chief executive officer)
Grocery	Manager (meat department)
Grocery (wholesale)	Salesperson
Grocery and discount pharmacy chain retailing	Corporate officer (vice president)
Grocery chain	Corporate officer (chief executive officer)
Grocery store	Manager
Hair brush importing	Manager, sales (import department)
Hardness-testing equipment	Service technician
Hardware	Salesperson
Hardware business	Corporate officer (director)
Hardware, home improvement products, tools	Salesperson
Hardware retailing	Corporate officer (president)
Hardware retailing	Manager (store)
Health care	Physician
Health care	Physician (independent contractor)
Health care	Physician (partner)
Health care	Speech therapist
Health care (Abortion)	Physician
Health care (Cardiology)	Physician
Health care (Cardiovascular and thoracic surgery)	Physician
Health care (Chiropractic)	Chiropractor
Health care (Dentistry (pediatric))	Dentist
Health care (Dentistry)	Dentist

Health care (Dentistry)	Dentist (independent contractor)
Health care (Dentistry)	Orthodontist (apprentice)
Health care (Denturist)	Dentist
Health care (Dermatology)	Physician
Health care (Emergency medicine)	Physician
Health care (Emergency room)	Physician (independent contractor)
Health care (Endocrinology)	Physician
Health care (Gastroenterology)	Physician
Health care (Gastroenterology and internal medicine)	Physician
Health care (General medicine and surgery)	Physician
Health care (Gynecology)	Physician
Health care (Infectious diseases)	Physician
Health care (Internal medicine)	Physician
Health care (Medicine, surgery, and obstetrics)	Physician (partner)
Health care (Neurology)	Physician
Health care (Neurosurgery)	Physician
Health care (Nursing service (home))	Nurse
Health care (Obstetrics)	Physician
Health care (Obstetrics and gynecology)	Physician
Health care (Obstetrics, gynecology, endocrinology and *in vitro* fertilization)	Physician
Health care (Occupational therapy)	Therapist
Health care (Oncology)	Physician
Health care (Ophthalmology)	Physician
Health care (Optical)	Optician
Health care (Optometry)	Optometrist
Health care (Oral surgery)	Dentist
Health care (Orthopedic surgery)	Physician
Health care (Orthopedic surgery)	Physician (independent contaractor)
Health care (Orthopedic surgery (hands))	Physician

Health care (Osteopathic (pain management clinic))	Physician
Health care (Osteopathic)	Osteopath
Health care (Osteopathic radiology)	Physician
Health care (Otolaryngology)	Physician
Health care (Pathology)	Physician
Health care (Pediatric endocrinology)	Physician
Health care (Pediatrics and neonatology)	Physician
Health care (Pediatrics)	Physician
Health care (Physical medicine and rehabilitation)	Physician
Health care (Physical rehabilitation clinic)	Corporate officer (president)
Health care (Podiatry)	Physican
Health care (Psychiatry)	Physician
Health care (Psychology)	Psychologist
Health care (Radiology)	Physician (partner)
Health care (Radiology, osteopathic)	Physician
Health care (Social work)	Social worker (clinical, licensed)
Health care (Speech therapy)	Speech therapist
Health care (Surgery)	Physician
Health care (Vascular surgery)	Physician
Health care cost-containment consulting	Manager (chief project)
Health spa	Manager
Hearing aids	Salesperson
Heat-applied graphics (transfers)	Art supervisor
Heating element manufacturing	Team leader
Heating systems (radiant)	Salesperson
Highway guard rail, sign, and fence erection	Corporate officer
Highway guard rail, sign, and fence erector business	Corporate officer (director)
Home health care	Nurse (visiting)
Home inspection	Inspector (home)
Homes	Salesperson
Horseshoeing	Horseshoer

Horseshoeing	Horseshoer (apprentice)
Hospital	Corporate officer (director)
Hot-melt equipment	Marketing specialist
Hotel	Chief operating officer
Hotel	Not specified
Household goods (installment plan)	Salesperson (door-to-door)
Hydraulics	Corporate officer (vice president)
Ice	Delivery person
Incentive awards program planning	Corporate officer (director)
Incentive awards program planning	Corporate officer (vice president)
Incentive awards program planning	Manager (senior)
Income tax preparation	Income tax preparer
Industrial and farm equipment, nuts, bolts, and tools	Salesperson
Industrial engineering	Engineer
Industrial gases and welding products	Salesperson
Industrial hygiene consulting	Hygienist (industrial)
Industrial hygiene consulting	Industrial hygienist
Industrial material-lifting equipment	Salesperson
Industrial supply	Corporate officer
Insulation	Manager (sales)
Insulation	Manager, sales (regional)
Insulation	Sales manager
Insulation	Salesperson
Insurance	Accountant
Insurance	Adjuster
Insurance	Broker
Insurance	Corporate officer (director)
Insurance	Corporate officer (president)
Insurance	Corporate officer (vice president, sales and marketing)
Insurance	Corporate officer (vice president)

Insurance	Developer (plan)
Insurance	Manager
Insurance	Manager (district)
Insurance	Manager, sales
Insurance	Not specified
Insurance	Salesperson
Insurance	Salesperson (independent contractor)
Insurance	Salesperson (partner)
Insurance	Salesperson (partner, limited)
Insurance (automobile)	Manager (district)
Insurance (car racing)	Salesperson
Insurance adjusting	Salesperson
Insurance adjustment and appraisal	Not specified
Insurance adjustment investigation	Manager (office)
Insurance and annuities (employee benefits)	Manager (division)
Insurance and annuities (employee benefits)	Salesperson
Insurance and bonds	Salesperson
Insurance and real estate	Salesperson
Insurance claims adjustment	Manager
Insurance claims adjustment	Manager (general)
Insurance clean-up and reconstruction	Estimator
Insurance clean-up and reconstruction	Manager
Insurance industry survey and audit service	Manager (branch)
Insurance underwriting, inspection, auditing, and loss-control	Manager (branch)
Intraocular lens manufacturing	Corporate officer (director, sales support)
Intraocular lens manufacturing	Corporate officer (president)
Intraocular lens manufacturing	Manager, sales
Investigation service (charitable solicitation scams)	Salesperson
Investments	Account executive (senior)

Janitorial products	Manager (division)
Janitorial products	Salesperson
Janitorial service	Janitor
Janitorial service	Manager
Janitorial service	Salesperson
Janitorial service	Salesperson (supervisor)
Janitorial supplies	Not specified
Janitorial supplies	Salesperson
Janitorial supplies, chemicals, and paper	Salesperson
Jewelry	Manufacturer's representative
Jewelry (fashion)	Manager (branch)
Kitchens (appliances)	Designer
Labels (customized pressure-sensitive)	Salesperson
Landfill	Supervisor
Laundry	Delivery person
Laundry	Manager
Laundry	Manager (depot)
Laundry	Salesperson
Laundry	Salesperson (route)
Laundry, linen, uniform rentals	Salesperson (route)
Laundry route sales	Supervisor
Laundry, uniform rental	Corporate officer (chief executive officer)
Law	Attorney
Law	Attorney (partner)
Law	Attorney (shareholder)
Law (Insurance defense)	Attorney
Law (Labor)	Attorney
Law (Labor)	Consultant
Law (Patent)	Attorney
Law (Tax)	Attorney (partner, department head)
Lawn care products	Manager, sales
Lawn care products	Salesperson
Laxative manufacturing	Manager (general)

Lighting products (outdoor)	Consultant
Linen and towel supply	Not specified
Linen service	Salesperson (route)
Linen service (hospitals)	Salesperson
Liquefied petroleum gas/appliance	Manager (branch)
Liquefied petroleum gas retailing	Manager (store)
Liquor (wholesale)	Salesperson
Liquor (wholesale)	Salesperson (route)
Litigation support services	Manager
Litigation support services	Salesperson
Livestock feed additives	Salesperson
Loan (small)	Manager (trainee)
Loan company	Cashier
Loan company	Manager
Lubricants (industrial)	Salesperson
Lumber	Millworker
Lumber	Salesperson
Lumber	Trader (wood products)
Lumber (wholesale)	Salesperson
Lumber retailing	Manager (yard)
Lumber wholesaling	Lumber trader (hardwoods specialist)
Lunch truck	Salesperson (route)
Machinery and tools (industrial)	Salesperson
Machinery cleaning service (water-blasting and acidizing)	Not specified
Magazine	Editor
Magazine	Manager (advertising)
Magazine	Publisher
Magazine (horse)	Writer
Magazine subscriptions	Salesperson
Magnetic fluid rotary seal manufacturing	Manager (product)
Mail (pre-sort)	Not specified
Mailing list rentals	List broker

Maintenance product manufacturing	Corporate officer (vice president)
Maintenance products	Salesperson
Maintenance supplies (industrial)	Salesperson
Management	Consultant
Management (medical and dental offices)	Consultant
Management (medical and dental practices)	Consultant (partnership)
Management consulting	Consultant
Manufacturer's representative	Not specified
Manufacturer's representative	Salesperson
Manufacturer's representative (heating and plumbing supplies, electrical appliances)	Salesperson
Manufacturing	Corporate officer (director)
Manufacturing	Electrician
Marine and industrial supplies (chemical)	Salesperson
Marine contracting	Estimator
Marine contracting	Supervisor (field)
Marketing	Corporate officer (vice president, regional)
Marketing research	Not specified
Match books	Salesperson
Meal (preportioned) service	Corporate officer
Meat (mail order)	Chief operating officer
Meat (mail order)	Manager (general)
Meat cutters and grinders	Salesperson
Meat processing	Corporate officer (controller)
Mechanical engineering	Engineer
Mechanical (blast cleaning machine manufacturer) engineering	Engineer
Media firm	Manager, sales
Medical billing	Not specified
Medical cost-containment service	Corporate officer (executive)
Medical/dental office business services	Consultant
Medical devices (angioplasty products)	Manager, sales

Medical devices (angioplasty products)	Sales director
Medical diagnostic kit design	Scientist
Medical diagnostic kit manufacturing	Corporate officer (president)
Medical diagnostic kit manufacturing	Immunologist
Medical diagnostic kit manufacturing	Manager (general)
Medical diagnostic kit manufacturing	Microbiologist
Medical diagnostic kit manufacturing	Scientist
Medical equipment	Rental agent
Medical equipment	Salesperson
Medical equipment (pacemakers)	Salesperson
Medical equipment (oxygen/allied health care supply)	Salesperson
Medical equipment (angiopacemakers)	Salesperson
Medical equipment (critical care and anesthesia equipment)	Salesperson
Medical equipment (critical care and anesthesia equipment)	Serviceperson
Medical equipment (home)	Salesperson
Medical equipment (short wave electrical)	Not specified
Medical equipment (surgical supplies)	Salesperson
Medical lab	Phlebotomist
Medical products	Sales director
Medical products	Sales director (national accounts)
Medical record copying	Manager (area)
Medical record procurement service (legal community)	Manager (office)
Medical records management, billing and bookkeeping	Salesperson
Medical services	Bookkeeper
Medical services	Secretary
Medical supplies	Salesperson
Medical third-party resource service	Financial eligibility worker
Medical third-party resource service	Supervisor
Meeting planning	Account executive
Metal	Manager, sales

Metal buying and selling (scrap, rod and mill products)	Corporate officer (president)
Metal industry	Repair wedger
Metal smelting and melting	Corporate officer
Metal welding	Manager
Metal-hardness testing equipment	Salesperson
Metal-hardness testing equipment	Service person
Metalic castings manufacturing	Superintendent
Microbiological diagnostics research	Scientist
Military and aerospace petrochemical and nuclear power industry products manufacturing	Engineer
Milk	Salesperson (route)
Mining and construction industry equipment manufacturing	Corporate officer (president)
Mobile food service (lunch truck)	Salesperson (route)
Mobile homes	Salesperson
Mobile homes and offices	Salesperson
Monuments and mausoleums	Manager, sales
Mortgage	Not specified
Mortgages (secondary)	Salesperson
Motor club	Salesperson
Motor products	Manager (branch)
Mud (oil well drilling service) engineering	Engineer
Multimedia productions	Manager (project)
Music supplier (telephonic)	Salesperson
Musical instruments	Salesperson
Mutual funds	Manager, sales (regional)
Newspaper	Corporate officer (chairman)
Newspaper	Corporate officer (president)
Newspaper	Corporate officer (vice president)
Newspaper	Editor
Newspaper	Publisher
Not specified	Auditor

Not specified	Auditor (accounts payable)
Not specified	Bookkeeper
Not specified	Corporate officer
Not specified	File clerk
Not specified	Manager (office)
Not specified	Manager (store, partner)
Not specified	Manager, sales
Not specified	Manager, sales (district)
Not specified	Manufacturer's representative
Not specified	Not specified
Not specified	Salesperson
Not specified	Service engineer
Nursery	Horticulturist
Nursing home sales and leasing	Broker
Nursing home sales and leasing	Leasing agent
Nursing home sales and leasing	Salesperson
Nursing services (geriatric)	Nurse's aide (geriatric)
Nuts, bolts, tools, farm and industrial equipment	Salesperson
Office equipment	Not specified
Office equipment	Salesperson
Office supplies	Salesperson
Office supplies (inked ribbons and carbon paper)	Salesperson
Office supply telemarketing	Not specified
Oil and gas	Salesperson
Oil and gas exploration	Geophysicist
Oil company	Manager
Oil exploration	Microwave spectrometer operator
Oil exploration	Pilot (helicopter)
Oil field equipment	Salesperson
Oil well drill bits, stabilizers, and cement mills	Salesperson
Ophthalmic dispensing	Optician

Orthopedic devices	Fitter/fabricator
Orthopedic devices	Metal polisher
Oxygen equipment (aircraft, emergency)	Corporate officer (director, operations)
Packaging material	Salesperson
Paintless car-dent-removal	Not specified
Paints	Salesperson
Paper	Manager (senior accounts)
Paper (printing, low-grade, odd lots of)	Salesperson
Paper and janitorial supplies	Salesperson
Paper and packaging products	Corporate officer (vice president, sales)
Paper and packaging products	Salesperson
Paper products	Salesperson
Parking lot	Corporate officer (vice president)
Performing arts	Actor
Performing arts	Performer (theatrical (histrionics))
Performing arts	Performer (theatrical)
Performing arts (Vaudeville)	Performer
Pest control	Corporate officer (vice president)
Pest control	Exterminator
Pest control	Manager
Pest control	Manager (branch)
Pest control	Manager trainee
Pest control	Not specified
Pest control	Salesperson
Petroleum	Delivery person
Petroleum products	Salesperson
Pharmaceutical services	Pharmacist
Pharmaceuticals	Manager, sales (national)
Pharmaceuticals	Salesperson
Pharmacy service	Corporate officer (director, bioservices)

Photocopier	Leasing agent
Photocopier	Manager (field)
Photocopier	Repair person
Photocopier	Salesperson
Photocopier	Service technician
Photocopier, microfiche equipment, and offset printing equipment	Service technician
Photofinishing	Manager (general, state)
Photographic services	Photographer (portrait)
Photographic services (school pictures)	Salesperson
Photographic services (school pictures)	Salesperson
Photographic services (school pictures and yearbook)	Salesperson
Photographic services (school yearbook and pictures)	Photographer
Photographic silver recovery	Manager (purchasing)
Physician billing service	Salesperson
Picture frames and molding (wholesale)	Salesperson
Pipe	Inspector
Pipe and tube inspection service (oil field industry)	Manager, sales
Pipe and tube inspection service (oil field industry)	Salesperson
Plastic container	Engineer
Plastic molding compounds manufacturing	Chemist
Plastic molding compounds manufacturing	Supervisor (department)
Plastic piece goods	Manager (sales and general)
Polyethylene products	Salesperson
Polyethylene products	Salesperson
Pool supplies service	Not specified
Portable building manufacturing	Manager (plant)
Portable restrooms	Salesperson
Power generator set exporting	Corporate officer (director, division)
Press clipping service	Reader
Printing	Administrator

Printing	Salesperson
Printing (check imprinting)	Manager, sales (regional)
Printing (commercial)	Salesperson
Printing (financial)	Corporate officer
Printing and graphics	Manager (sales)
Printing and graphics	Sales manager
Printing and graphics	Salesperson
Printing equipment	Salesperson
Printing materials	Manager, sales
Printing plate materials	Salesperson
Printing services	Salesperson
Private investigation	Detective
Private investigation	Private investigator
Produce brokerage	Manager
Product packaging	Corporate officer (chief executive officer)
Product packaging	Corporate officer (president)
Propane	Manager
Propane gas	Salesperson
Property management	Manager
Property management	Property manager
Property management (apartment)	Property manager
Prosthetic devices	Manager (office)
Public relations	Account executive
Public stenography	Court reporter
Publisher (microfiche)	Consultant (acquisitions)
Publishing (custom)	Salesperson
Publishing (shoppers' guide)	Bookkeeper
Publishing (shoppers' guide)	Photographer
Pultrusion rods	Draftsperson
Radio	Reporter (traffic)
Radio pagers	Salesperson
Railroad car axle rebuilding	Manager (plant)
Real estate	Realtor
Real estate	Salesperson

Seafood supply	Not specified
Seals (industrial)	Repair person
Seals (industrial)	Salesperson
Securities	Corporate officer
Securities	Money manager
Securities	Salesperson
Securities	Salesperson (independent contractor)
Securities	Stock broker
Securities	Stock broker (discount)
Security	Night watchman
Security guard service	Manager (regional)
Security service	Corporate officer (president)
Security service	Manager (area)
Security service	Manager (regional)
Security service	Not specified
Security service	Supervisor
Seminar production	Psychologist
Septic systems	Designer
Service station	Bookkeeper
Service station	Consultant
Shoe	Not specified
Shrink-wrap machine manufacturing	Corporate officer (vice president, sales and marketing)
Silk screen processing	Salesperson
Silk screening	Not specified
Sound systems	Salesperson
Soup manufacturing	Sales director
Steel polishing	Corporate officer
Steel polishing	Corporate officer (director)
Store shelving manufacturing	Corporate officer (vice president, marketing)
Structured settlement service	Salesperson
Studio (not specified as to type)	Not specified
Supplies	Manager (business)

Supplies	Salesperson
Supplies	Secretary (officer)
Supplies	Treasurer
Tapes and adhesives	Salesperson
Tar products	Manager (regional)
Tax/accounting	Consultant
Tea	Salesperson
Tea	Salesperson (route)
Technical writing	Writer
Telecommunications	Corporate officer (vice president, marketing)
Telecommunications equipment manufacturing	Corporate officer (vice president)
Telecommunications products and services	Salesperson
Telecommunications testing (remote access)	Corporate officer (director, systems engineering)
Telecommunications testing (remote access)	Engineer
Teleindicator manufacturing	Corporate officer (chief executive officer)
Teleindicator manufacturing	Corporate officer (director)
Teleindicator manufacturing	Corporate officer (president)
Telephone interconnect equipment sales and service	Not specified
Telephone systems	Salesperson
Television installations (hospital sites)	Manager, sales
Television station	Manager (general)
Text editing products	Salesperson
Textile	Corporate officer (chief executive officer)
Textile	Corporate officer (president)
Textiles	Installer (equipment, factory)
Textiles	Manager (plant)
Textiles	Sales promoter
Textiles (contract)	Salesperson
Theatrical	Booking agent

Theatrical booking	Theatrical booking agent
Tire store	Manager (assistant)
Title insurance	Not specified
Tobacco (wholesale)	Salesperson
Tool and die steels	Manager (office)
Tool and die steels	Manager, sales
Tools, nuts, bolts, and farm and industrial equipment	Salesperson
Towel rentals	Not specified
Toys	Corporate officer (vice president)
Trailers	Salesperson
Transportation	Truck driver
Travel	Corporate officer (president)
Travel	Travel agent
Tree care	Salesperson
Tree care	Technician
Truck driver leasing	Truck driver
Truck leasing	Manager, sales
Trucks	Broker
Tunnel drilling	Bidding agent
Typography	Corporate officer (executive)
Undertaking	Undertaker
Unemployment and workers' compensation cost-control consulting	Corporate officer (vice president, sales)
Unemployment insurance advice	Consultant
Unemployment law, tax, and employee benefits consulting	Corporate officer (vice president, senior, operations)
Uniform rentals	Driver
Uniform rentals	Supervisor
Vehicle leasing	Rental agent
Vending services	Salesperson
Vertical blinds manufacturing	Not specified
Veterinary drugs and other products	Salesperson
Veterinary medicine	Manager (office)

Veterinary medicine	Veterinarian
Video surveillance system sales and service	Not specified
Vocational aptitude test design	Psychologist
Warehouse services	Corporate officer (chief executive officer)
Waste oil collection	Manager
Waste oil collection	Manager, sales
Water analysis	Water analyst
Water purifier manufacturing	Engineer (field)
Water purifier manufacturing	Salesperson
Water/sewer supplies wholesaling	Corporate officer (director)
Water treatment (chemical) services	Salesperson
Water treatment products (industrial)	Salesperson
Water treatment products and services	Salesperson
Weight loss	Lecturer
Weight loss	Manager
Weight loss	Manager (area)
Weight loss	Nurse (vocational, licensed)
Weight loss	Salesperson
Welders	Salesperson
Welders (electronic arc)	Manager (district)
Welders (electronic arc)	Salesperson
Welding service	Salesperson
Wheels and brakes (automotive)	Salesperson
Windows (replacement)	Salesperson
Windows and doors (aluminum)	Salesperson
Wood moulding manufacturing	Corporate officer (vice president, marketing)
Wood moulding manufacturing	Manager (general, assistant)
Wood moulding manufacturing	Manager (marketing)
Wood veneer manufacturing	Corporate officer (vice president)
Wood veneer manufacturing	Manager (general)

Index of Sale-of-Business Covenant Cases

For the "State" column, see the list of state abbreviations on page xviii if necessary. For the "Question" column:

- *See the "List of General Questions" beginning at page xvi of this volume for the meaning of question numbers and page numbers for particular states.*
- *An "AT-" followed by a number (e.g., AT-1) indicates information is contained in a discussion of an Additional Topic; see the "Finding List of Additional Topics" beginning at page xxx of this volume to identify the topic concerned if necessary, and page numbers for particular states.*

For the "Citation" column, where the state is noted and it varies from that listed in the "State" column, this indicates a discussion of a case decided in another state. Cases not listed here are included in other indexes as follows:

- *Cases in which an occupation was mentioned in the court decision are listed by occupation in the "Index of Employment Covenant Cases Specifying Occupation."*
- *Cases in which no occupation was mentioned in the court decision are listed by industry in the "Index of Employment Covenant Cases Not Specifying Occupation."*
- *Cases involving covenants relating to types of transactions other than sale of business are listed by transaction/relationship in the "Index of Covenant Cases Not Involving Employment or Sale of Business."*
- *Cases not involving covenants are listed by state in the "Index of Cases Not Involving Covenants."*

Cases listed either in the "Index of Employment Covenant Cases Specifying Occupation" or in the "Index of Employment Covenant Cases Not Specifying Occupation" may be searched together by industry, using the "Index of Employment Covenant Cases by Industry." In that index, the term "Not specified" in the "Occupation" column is a signal to consult the "Index of Employment Covenant Cases Not Specifying Occupation" for additional information.

Editor's Note: Cases decided by the Texas Court of Appeals before September 1, 1981, are cited as "Tex. Civ. App." After that date, cases are cited as "Tex. Ct. App." The change in the court's name and the rules for proper citation in documents submitted to Texas courts are explained in the Texas Rules of Form.

Bank (investment)	NY	6	Shearson Lehman Bros. Holdings v. Schmertzler	116 A.D.2d 216, 500 N.Y.S.2d 520 (1st Dep't 1986)
Bar	WY	10	Matter of Isbell	27 B.R. 926 (Bankr. W.D.Wis. 1988)
Barber shop	CT	14	Domurat v. Mazzaccoli	138 Conn. 327, 84 A.2d 271 (1951)
Barber shop	SC	3f	Metts v. Wenberg	158 S.C. 411, 155 S.E. 734 (1930)
Beverage	NH	AT-21	Wilmot H. Simonson Co. v. Green Textile Assocs.	755 F.2d 217 (1st Cir. 1985)
Bicycle shop	NH	AT-21	Bicycle Transit Authority v. Bell	214 N.C. 219, 333 S.E.2d 299 (1985)
Broadcasting (Radio station)	MT	1, 4	Western Media v. Merrick	727 P.2d 547 (Mont. 1986)
Building maintenance services	NY	3d, 5, 14	Mohawk Maintenance Co. v. Kessler	52 N.Y.2d 276, 437 N.Y.S.2d 646, 419 N.E.2d 324 (1981)
Butchering	CA	3d	Brown v. Kling	101 Cal. 295, 3 P. 995 (1894)
Butchering	NH	10	Canady v. Knox	43 Wash. 567, 86 P. 930 (1906)
Cable television system	SC	10	Condon v. Best View Cablevision	292 S.C. 117, 355 S.E.2d 7 (1987)
Car wash	WA	3d	Rippe v. Doran	4 Wash.App. 952, 486 P.2d 107 (1971)
Chemical sales and distribution	ND	14	Hawkins Chem., Inc. v. McNea	321 N.W.2d 918 (N.D. 1982)
Chemicals	ND	4	Hawkins Chem., Inc. v. McNea	321 N.W.2d 918 (N.D. 1982)
Concrete and construction	ND	14	Igoe v. Atlas Ready-Mix, Inc.	134 N.W.2d 511 (N.D. 1965)
Consulting	IN	3d	Fogle v. Shah	539 N.E.2d 500 (Ind.App. 1989)
Consulting	NY	3f, 5, 6, AT-56	Hay Group v. Nadel	170 A.D.2d 398, 566 N.Y.S.2d 616 (1st Dep't 1991)
Convenience store	AL	AT-43	Russell v. Mullis	479 So.2d 727 (Ala. 1985)
Cylinder manufacturing	AL	AT-90	Defco, Inc. v. Decatur Cylinder, Inc.	595 So.2d 1329 (Ala. 1992)
Dairy product retailing	KS	14	Jenson v. Olson	144 Mont. 224, 395 P.2d 465 (1964)

Business	State	Section	Case	Citation
Dental equipment manufacturing	TX	3f	Chandler v. Mastercraft Dental Corp.	739 S.W.2d 760 (Tex.Ct.App.—Fort Worth 1987, writ denied)
Drug store	MO	9	Brown v. Childers	254 S.W.2d 275 (Mo.App. 1989)
Electrical component repair (aircraft)	MO	2, 3, 3d, 3f, 4, 7, 9, 14, AT-7	AEF-EMF, Inc. v. Passmore	906 S.W.2d 714 (Mo.App. 1995)
Flea market	LA	10	Barnett v. Jabusch	649 So.2d 1158 (La.App. 3rd Cir. 1995)
Florist	GA	10	Williamson v. Palmer	199 Ga.App. 35, 404 S.E.2d 131 (1991)
Fuel oil retailer	MA	5	Sulmonetti v. Hayes	347 Mass. 390, 198 N.E.2d 297 (1964)
Furnace	NH	AT-22	Centorr-Vacuum Indus. v. Lavoie	609 A.2d 1213, 7 IER Cases 982 (N.H. 1992)
General merchandising business	AK	10	Fleischman v. Rahmstorf	226 F. 443 (9th Cir. 1915)
Glass (window and plate installation)	MO	9	Kreger Glass Co. v. Kreger	49 S.W.2d 260 (Mo.Ap. 1932)
Graphic arts	IL	4	Stamatakis Indus., Inc. v. King	165 Ill.App.3d 879, 117 Ill. Dec. 419, 520 N.E.2d 770 (1987)
Grocery	KS	14	Jeansonne v. El Hindy	413 So.2d 999 (La.App. 1982)
Grocery	LA	AT-10	Jeansonne v. El Hindy	413 So.2d 999 (La.App. 1982)
Grocery	MO	3d, AT-10	Schmucks Twenty-Five, Inc. v. Bettendorf	595 S.W.2d 279 (Mo.App. 1979)
Grocery (fancy) importing	NY	14	Von Bremen v. MacMonnies	200 N.Y. 41, 93 N.E. 186 (1910)
Grocery/meat market	CT	4	Beit v. Beit	135 Conn. 195 (1948)
Hair stylist	FL	AT-21	Riddick v. Suncoast Beauty College, Inc.	579 So.2d 855 (Fla. 2d Dist.Ct.App. 1991)

	State		Case	Citation
Hand truck manufacturing	CA	3f	Kaplan v. Nalpak Corp.	158 Cal.App.2d 197, 322 P.2d 226 (1958)
Health care (Chiropractic practice)	PA	5, 6, AT-54.1	Dice v. Clinicorp.	887 F.Supp. 803 (W.D.Pa. 1995)
Health care (Dental practice)	CT	3	Cook v. Johnson	47 Conn. 175 (1879)
Health care (Dental practice)	FL	1	Flatley v. Forbes	483 So.2d 483 (Fla. 2d Dist.Ct.App. 1986)
Health care (Dental practice)	NH	3	Cook v. Johnson	47 Conn. 175 (1879)
Health care (Home nursing service; divorce)	MA	2, 14	Wells v. Wells	9 Mass. App. Ct. 321, 400 N.E.2d 1317 (1980)
Health care (Medical practice)	WA	4, 7, AT-9	Boyd v. Davis	897 P.2d 1239 (Wash. 1995)
Health care (Medical practice (anesthesiology))	AL	AT-48	Zickler v. Schultz	603 So.2d 916 (Ala. 1992)
Health care (Nursing service; divorce)	MA	2, 14	Wells v. Wells	9 Mass. App. Ct. 321, 400 N.E.2d 1317 (1980)
Health care (Optometry practice)	CT	10	New England Eyecare of Waterbury, P.C. v. New England Eyecare, P.C	1991 WL 27919 (Conn. Super.Ct. No. 099465, Jan. 18, 1991)
Health Care (Podiatric practice)	NY	2	Smith v. Hurley	634 N.Y.S.2d 334 (App.Div. 4th Dep't 1995)
Home inspection	CT	AT-80	Sassone v. Lepore	226 Conn. 773, 629 A.2d 357 (1993)
Home nursing service (Divorce)	MA	2, 14	Wells v. Wells	9 Mass. App. Ct. 321, 400 N.E.2d 1317 (1980)
Hosiery store	CT	14	Hayes v. Parklane Hosiery Co.	24 Conn.Supp. 218, 189 A.2d 522 (Super.Ct. Hartford Cty. 1963)

Hospital supply company	NY	AT-86, AT-90	*Thur v. IPCO Corp.*	173 A.D.2d 344, 569 N.Y.S.2d 713 (1st Dep't 1991)
Ice	MA	4, 14	*Metropolitan Ice Co. v. Ducas*	291 Mass. 403, 196 N.E. 856 (1935)
Ice cream, hot dog, soft drink shop	ME	2	*La Grange v. Datsis*	142 Me. 48, 46 A.2d 408 (1946)
Insurance agency	AK	10	*National Bank of Alaska v. J.B.L.&K. of Alaska*	546 P.2d 579 (1976)
Insurance agency	IL	2	*Murphy v. Murphy*	28 Ill.App.3d 475, 328 N.E.2d 642 (1975)
Insurance agency	IN	3	*Woodward Ins. v. White*	437 N.E.2d 59 (Ind.App. 1981)
Insurance agency	LA	4, 14	*Moorman & Givens v. Parkerson*	127 La. 835, 54 So. 47 (1911)
Insurance agency	NY	4	*Alexander & Alexander Servs., Inc. v. Maloof*	105 A.D.2d 1066, 482 N.Y.S.2d 386 (4th Dep't 1984)
Insurance agency	NY	4	*Kraft Agency, Inc. v. Delmonico*	110 A.D.2d 177, 494 N.Y.S2d 77 (4th Dep't 1985)
Insurance agency	PA	10, AT-28	*Bauer v. P.A. Cutri Co. of Bradford*	434 Pa. 305, 253 A.2d 252 (1969)
Insurance agency	TX	2, 3g, 5	*Cottingham v. Engler*	178 S.W.2d 148 (Tex.Civ.App.—Dallas 1944)
Jeweler	NC	3e, 3f	*Jewel Box Stores Corp. v. Morrow*	272 N.C. 659, 158 S.E.2d 840 (1968)
Laundry	DC	3e	*Godfrey v. Roessle*	5 App.D.C. 299 (1895)
Laundry	MN	3f	*Southworth v. Davison*	106 Minn. 119, 118 N.W. 363 (1908)
Laundry	WI	3a	*My Laundry Co. v. Schmeling*	129 Wis. 597, 109 N.W. 540 (1906)
Liquefied petroleum gas	MS	3d	*Herring Gas Co. v. Whiddon*	616 So.2d 892 (Miss. 1993)
Liquefied petroleum gas	TX	3f	*Hice v. Cole*	295 S.W.2d 661 (Tex.Civ.App.—Beaumont 1956)

Business	State		Case	Citation
Liquor store	GA	AT-98	Klein v. Williams	212 Ga.App. 39, 441 S.E.2d 270 (1994)
Livestock pavilion (partner)	CO	6	Ditus v. Beahm	232 P.2d 184 (Colo. 1951)
Lumber business	NM	11	Thomas v. Gavin	15 N.M. 660, 110 P.2d 841 (1910)
Medical compound (kidney, liver and bitters)	CA	3d	Gregory v. Spieker	110 Cal. 150, 42 P. 576 (1895)
Medical waste disposal	LA	12	MedX Inc. of Fla. v. Ranger	780 F.Supp. 398 (E.D. La. 1991)
Metal buying and selling (scrap, rod and mill products)	NY	3d, 5, 10	Meteor Indus. v. Metalloy Indus.	149 A.D.2d 483, 539 N.Y.S.2d 972 (2d Dep't 1989)
Metal painting	MN	10	B&Y Metal Painting v. Ball	279 N.W.2d 813 (Minn. 1979)
Metal smelting and melting	NY	2, 14	Anchor Alloys, Inc. v. Non-Ferrous Proscessing Corp.	39 A.D.2d 504, 336 N.Y.S.2d 944 lv. to appeal denied 32 N.Y.2d 612, 346 N.Y.S.2d 1025, 299 N.E.2d 899 (1973)
Motel	NH	AT-21	Goseelin v. Archibald	121 N.H. 1016, 437 A.2d 302 (1981)
Not specified	FL	AT-12	Mendelsohn v. Florida A&M Tape & Packaging	602 So.2d 622, 17 Fla. L. Weekly D1651 (Fla. 4th Dist.Ct.App. 1992)
Not specified	GA	4	Hamrick v. Kelley	260 Ga. 307, 392 S.E.2d 518 (1990)
Not specified	NY	AT-96	Socia v. Trovato	197 A.D.2d 916, 602 N.Y.S.2d 270 (4th Dep't 1993)
Not specified	TX	AT-17	Hanks v. GAB Business Servs.	644 S.W.2d 707 (Tex. 1982)
Nursery (floral, baby's breath)	WA	5, 6, 7, 10, 11	Riverview Florist v. Watkins	51 Wash.App. 658, 754 P.2d 1055 (1988)
Nursing home	DE	10	Tull v. Turek	37 Del.Ch. 190, 139 A.2d 368 (1958)
Nursing service (Divorce)	MA	2, 14	Wells v. Wells	9 Mass. App. Ct. 321, 400 N.E.2d 1317 (1980)

Business	State		Case	Citation
Orchard heater manufacturing	CA	4	*Mahlstedt v. Fugit*	79 Cal.App.2d 562, 180 P.2d 777 (1947)
Orthotic and prosthetic lab	MO	13, AT-10	*Orthotic & Prosthetic Lab, Inc. v. Pott*	851 S.W.2d 633 (Mo.App. 1993)
Peat moss sales	NY	5, 10	*Hyde Park Prods. Corp. v. Maximilian Lerner Corp.*	65 N.Y.S.2d 316, 491 N.Y.S.2d 302, 480 N.E.2d 1084 (1985)
Pension consulting	IN	3d	*Fogle v. Shah*	539 N.E.2d 500 (Ind.App. 1989)
Pet care supplies	GA	AT-21	*Martin v. RocCorp., Inc.*	441 S.E.2d 671 (Ga.App. 1994)
Pharmaceutical business	OK	3d	*Threlkeld v. Steward*	24 Okla. 403, 103 P. 630 (1909)
Phonograph and amusement device (shuffle board and pin alley) sales and service	TN	10	*Coin Automatic Co. v. Estate of Dixon*	213 Tenn. 311, 375 S.W.2d 858 (1963)
Photofinishing	CA	3f	*Consolidated Photographic Indus. v. Marks*	109 Cal.App.2d 310, 240 P.2d 718 (1952)
Photography	IN	10	*Lawrence v. Cain*	144 Ind.App. 210, 245 N.E.2d 663 (1969)
Photography	SC	12	*Reeves v. Sargent*	200 S.C. 494, 21 S.E.2d 184 (1942)
Photography	SC	AT-7	*Skinner v. Elrod*	417 S.E.2d 599 (S.C. 1992)
Plumbing	AR	5	*Wakenight v. Spear & Rogers*	147 Ark. 342, 227 S.W. 419 (1921)
Portable toilet manufacturing	CA	1, 2, 3f, 7, 14	*Monogram Indus. v. SAR Indus.*	64 Cal.App.3d 692, 134 Cal.Rptr. 714 (1976)
Printer	MA	10, 14	*Packquisition Corp. v. Packard Press New England*	1933 WL 15601 (E.D. Pa., No. 91-5966, Nov. 10, 1992)
Product packaging	NY	3f, 5, 8, 10	*Borne Chem. Co. v. Dictrow*	85 A.D.2d 646, 445 N.Y.S.2d 406 (2d Dep't 1981)
Publishing	ID	AT-15	*In re Oseen*	133 B.R. 527 (Bankr. Idaho 1991)

Railroad track maintenance equipment manufacturing	AL	9, 10, AT-42	Knox Kershaw, Inc. v. Kershaw	598 So.2d 1372 (Ala. 1992)
Real estate brokerage	NY	10, AT-25A, AT-36	Time Assocs., Inc. v. Blake Realty, Inc.	212 A.D.2d 879, 622 N.Y.S.2d 816 (3d Dep't 1995)
Repair (aircraft electrical component)	MO	2, 3, 3d, 3f, 4, 7, 9, 14, AT-7	AEE-EMF, Inc. v. Passmore	906 S.W.2d 714 (Mo.App. 1995)
Respiratory therapy (home)	AL	AT-85A, AT-89A	Russell v. Birmingham Oxygen Service, Inc.	408 So.2d 90 (Ala. 1981)
Restaurant	AL	AT-43	Livingston v. Dobbs	559 So.2d 569 (Ala. 1990)
Restaurant	GA	8	Holloway v. Brown	171 Ga. 481, 155 S.E. 917 (1930)
Restaurant	MI	11	Brillhart v. Dannefel	36 Mich.App.359, 194 N.W.2d 63 (1971), leave denied, 387 Mich. 783 (1972)
Restaurant	NH	10	Mead v. Anton	33 Wash.2d 741, 207 P.2d 227 (1949)
Restaurant	SC	3f, 4, AT-21, AT-95	Cafe Assocs. v. Gerngross	406 S.E.2d 162 (S.C. 1991)
Restaurant	WA	10	Mead v. Anton	33 Wash.2d 741, 207 P.2d 227 (1949)
Safety equipment sales	AL	1, 14, AT-88	Wyatt Safety Supply v. Industrial Safety Prods.	566 So.2d 728 (Ala. 1990)
Sand and gravel mining	MS	3d	Cooper v. Gidden	515 So.2d 900 (Miss. 1987)
Securities brokerage (municipal bonds)	NY	5	Titus & Donnelly, Inc. v. Poto	205 A.D.2d 475, 614 N.Y.S.2d 10 (1st Dep't 1994)
Service station (use as)	CA	1	Roughton v. Socony Mobile Oil Co.	231 Cal.App.2d 188, 41 Cal.Rptr. 714 (1964)
Silversmith spinner	SC	3, 3d, 3f, 4, 14	Somerset v. Reyner	233 S.C. 324, 104 S.E.2d 344 (1958)
Sporting goods and trophies	MO	3d, 9	Champion Sports Center, Inc. v. Peters	763 S.W.2d 367 (Mo.App. 1989)

Index of Covenant Cases Not Involving Employment or Sale of Business

For the "State" column, see the list of state abbreviations on page xviii if necessary. For the "Question" column:

- *See the "List of General Questions" beginning at page xvi of this volume for the meaning of question numbers and page numbers for particular states.*
- *An "AT-" followed by a number (e.g., AT-1) indicates information is contained in a discussion of an Additional Topic; see the "Finding List of Additional Topics" beginning at page xxx of this volume to identify the topic concerned if necessary, and page numbers for particular states.*

For the "Citation" column, where the state is noted and it varies from that listed in the "State" column, this indicates a discussion of a case decided in another state. Cases not listed here are included in other indexes as follows:

- *Cases in which an occupation was mentioned in the court decision are listed by occupation in the "Index of Employment Covenant Cases Specifying Occupation."*
- *Cases in which no occupation was mentioned in the court decision are listed by industry in the "Index of Employment Covenant Cases Not Specifying Occupation."*
- *Cases which involved a sale of business rather than an occupation are listed by industry in the "Index of Sale-of-Business Covenant Cases."*
- *Cases not involving covenants are listed by state in the "Index of Cases Not Involving Covenants."*

Cases listed either in the "Index of Employment Covenant Cases Specifying Occupation" or in the "Index of Employment Covenant Cases Not Specifying Occupation" may be searched together by industry, using the "Index of Employment Covenant Cases by Industry." In that index, the term "Not specified" in the "Occupation" column is a signal to consult the "Index of Employment Covenant Cases Not Specifying Occupation" for additional information.

Editor's Note: Cases decided by the Texas Court of Appeals before September 1, 1981, are cited as "Tex. Civ. App." After that date, cases are cited as "Tex. Ct. App." The change in the court's name and the rules for proper citation in documents submitted to Texas courts are explained in the Texas Rules of Form.

Transaction or Relationship	Industry	State	Question	Case Name	Citation
Book publishing contract	Publishing	LA	3, 3f	*Pelican Publishing Co. v. Wilson*	626 So.2d 721 (La.App. 5th Cir. 1993)
Creditors' composition agreement	Mercantile business	NM	3	*Gross, Kelly & Co. v. Bibo*	19 N.M. 495, 145 P. 480 (1914)
Dealership agreement	Hearing aids	IN	3f	*Willis v. Dictograph Sales Corp.*	222 Ind. 523, 54 N.E.2d 774 (1944)
Dealership agreement	Micrographics equipment	MD	10	*National Micrographics v. OCE-Indus.*	55 Md.App. 526, 465 A.2d 862 (1983)
Dealership agreement	Paint distribution	OK	1	*Crown Paint Co. v. Bankston*	640 P.2d 948 (Okla. 1981), *cert. denied*, 455 U.S. 946 (1982)
Distributorship agreement	Heating fuel	NH	2, 3g, 5	*Home Gas Corp. v. Stafford Fuels*	130 N.H. 74, 534 A.2d 390 (1987)
Distributorship agreement	Milk concentrates	GA	3, 3f, 4, 12, AT-23, AT-53A	*Amstell, Inc. v. Bunge Corp.*	443 S.E.2d 706 (Ga.App. 1994)
Distributorship agreement	Not specified	RI	3, 4, 14	*Durapin v. American Prods.*	559 A.2d 1051 (R.I. 1989)
Distributorship agreement	Paint remover	GA	3	*Owens v. RMA Sales*	183 Ga.App. 340, 358 S.E.2d 857 (1990)
Distributorship agreement	Rope	TN	10	*All-Line, Inc. v. Rabar Corp.*	919 F.2d 475 (7th Cir. 1990)

Type	Business	State	Sections	Case	Citation
Distributorship agreement	Water processing equipment	LA	1, 3f, 4	Water Processing Technologies, Inc. v. Ridgeway	618 So.2d 533 (La.App. 4th Cir. 1993)
Exclusive purchase contract	Grain	RI	4	Max Garelick, Inc. v. Leonardo	105 R.I. 142, 250 A.2d 354 (1969)
Franchise	Car rentals	MD	2, 3, 3d, 3f, 14	Budget Rent A Car of Washington v. Raab	268 Md. 478, 302 A.2d 11 (1973)
Franchise	Car rentals	MO	10	Budget Rent-a-Car of Mo. v. B&G Rent-a-Car	619 S.W.2d 832 (Mo.App. 1981)
Franchise	Car trim repairs	TX	1, 3a, 3b, 13, 14	Hill v. Mobile Auto Trim	725 S.W.2d 168 (Tex. 1987)
Franchise	Chicken meal delivery	CA	12	LaFortune v. Ebie	26 Cal.App.3d 72, 102 Cal. Rptr. 588 (1972)
Franchise	Consumer buying club	IN	4	South Bend Consumers Club v. United Consumers Club	572 F.Supp. 209 (N.D.Ind. 1983)
Franchise	Convenience store	IA	3f, 4	Casey's Gen. Stores v. Campbell Oil	441 N.W.2d 758 (Iowa 1989)
Franchise	Ear piercing and earring sales	PA	3	Piercing Pagoda v. Hoffner	465 Pa. 500, 351 A.2d 207 (1976)
Franchise	Employment agency	AZ	2	Snelling & Snelling v. Dupay Enters.	125 Ariz. 362, 609 P.2d 1062 (App. 1980)
Franchise	Employment agency	CA	1, 2, 3f, 12	Scott v. Snelling & Snelling	732 F.Supp. 1034 (N.D.Cal. 1990)
Franchise	Employment agency	GA	4	Rita Personnel Servs. v. Kot	229 Ga. 314, 191 S.E.2d 79 (1972)
Franchise	Ice cream shop	CO	3	Goldammer v. Fay	326 F.2d 268 (10th Cir. 1964)

Type	Business	State	Sections	Case	Citation
Lease	Building	WI	7	Spheeris Sporting Goods v. Spheeris on Capitol	459 N.W.2d 581 (Wis.Ct.App. 1990)
Lease	Food delivery business (lunch wagon route)	WI	2, 3, 3d, 3g, 11, 14	Chuck Wagon Catering v. Raduege	277 N.W.2d 787 (1979)
Lease	Restaurant	GA	3, 4, 14	Watson v. Waffle House	253 Ga. 671, 324 S.E.2d 175 (1985)
Lease	Restaurant	MT	1, 14	O'Neill v. Ferraro	182 Mont. 214, 596 P.2d 197 (1979)
License agreement	Computer equipment	NH	7	Logic Assocs. v. Time Share Corp.	124 N.H. 565, 474 A.2d 1006 (1984)
License agreement	Doll voice devices	NJ	14	Voices, Inc. v. Metal Tone Mfg. Co.	19 N.J. Eq. 324, 182 A. 880 (Ch.Div.), aff'd, 120 N.J. Eq. 618, 187 A. 370 (E.&A. 1936), cert. denied, 300 U.S. 656 (1937)
License agreement	Paintless car-dent removal	IN	3, 5	Seymour v. Buckley	628 So.2d 554 (Ala. 1993) (applying Indiana law)
License agreement	Sandwich shop	TN	10	Sub Station II v. Banasiak	(Tenn.Ct.App. June 15, 1984) (LEXIS, Employ library, Tenn. file)
Management agreement	Health care (Respiratory therapy)	IN	7, 12	OVRS Acquisition Corp. v. Community Health Servs., Inc.	657 N.E.2d 117 (Ind.App. 1995) (applying Indiana procedural law and choice of law rules)
Management agreement	Health care (Respiratory therapy)	KY	3a, 3b, 3d, 3f, 10	OVRS Acquisition Corp. v. Community Health Servs., Inc.	657 N.E.2d 117 (Ind.App. 1995) (applying Kentucky substantive law)

Rivals' agreement	Not specified	FL	3d	U Shop Rite v. Richard's Paint Mfg. Co.	369 So.2d 1033 (Fla. 4th Dist.Ct.App. 1979)
Rivals' agreement	Towing services	OR	3d, 3f	Rensema v. Nichols	83 Or.App. 322, 731 P.2d 1048 (1986) (per curiam)
Sale of land	Service station (use as)	CA	1	Roughton v. Socony Mobile Oil Co.	231 Cal.App.2d 188, 41 Cal.Rptr. 714 (1964)
Sale of steamboat	Transportation	CT	3	Oregon Steam Navigation Co. v. Windsor	87 U.S. (20 Wall.) 64, 22 L.Ed. 315 (1873)
Scholarship loan repayment agreement	Electrical trades	WI	AT-17.1	Milwaukee Area Joint Apprenticeship Training Comm. for the Elec. Indus. v. Howell	67 F.3d 1333 (7th Cir. 1995)
Settlement agreement	Cookie bakers	MN	9	Minnesota Best Maid Cookie Co. v. Flour Pot Cookie Co.	412 N.W.2d 380 (Minn.Ct.App. 1987)
Settlement agreement	Metallic castings manufacturing	VT	3d	Knapp v. S. Jarvis Adams Co.	135 F. 1008 (6th Cir. 1905)
Settlement agreement	Souvenir wholesaler	NV	3c, 5, 14	Las Vegas Novelty v. Fernandez	106 Nev. 113, 787 P.2d 772 (1990) (per curiam)
Settlement agreement	Thermocouple manufacturing and sales	MO	3f, AT-12	Watlow Elec. Mfg. Co. v. Wrob	899 S.W.2d 585 (Mo.App. 1995)
Settlement agreement (shareholder's suit)	Swimming pools	NY	3f, 5	Conlon v. Concord Pools	170 A.D.2d 754, 566 N.Y.S.2d 860 (3d Dep't 1991)
Shareholders' agreement	Souvenir shop	NV	10	Gramanz v. T-Shirts and Souvenirs, Inc.	894 P.2d 342 (Nev. 1995)

Index of Cases Not Involving Covenants

For the "State" column, see the list of state abbreviations on page xviii if necessary. For the "Question" column:

- *See the "List of General Questions" beginning at page xvi of this volume for the meaning of question numbers and page numbers for particular states.*
- *An "AT-" followed by a number (e.g., AT-1) indicates information is contained in a discussion of an Additional Topic; see the "Finding List of Additional Topics" beginning at page xxx of this volume to identify the topic concerned if necessary, and for the page numbers for particular states.*

For the "Citation" column, where the state is noted and it varies from that listed in the "State" column, this indicates a discussion of a case decided in another state. Cases not listed here are included in other indexes as follows:

- *Cases in which an occupation was mentioned in the court decision are listed by occupation in the "Index of Employment Covenant Cases Specifying Occupation."*
- *Cases in which no occupation was mentioned in the court decision are listed by industry in the "Index of Employment Covenant Cases Not Specifying Occupation."*
- *Cases which involved a sale of business rather than an occupation are listed by industry in the "Index of Sale-of-Business Covenant Cases."*
- *Cases involving covenants relating to other types of transactions are listed by transaction/relationship in the "Index of Covenant Cases Not Involving Employment or Sale of Business."*

Cases listed either in the "Index of Employment Covenant Cases Specifying Occupation" or in the "Index of Employment Covenant Cases Not Specifying Occupation" may be searched together by industry, using the "Index of Employment Covenant Cases by Industry." In that index, the term "Not specified" in the "Occupation" column is a signal to consult the "Index of Employment Covenant Cases Not Specifying Occupation" for additional information.

Editor's Note: Cases decided by the Texas Court of Appeals before September 1, 1981, are cited as "Tex. Civ. App." After that date, cases are cited as "Tex. Ct. App." The change in the court's name and the rules for proper citation in documents submitted to Texas courts are explained in the Texas Rules of Form.

State	Question	Case Name	Citation
AL	10	*Aldridge v. Dolbeer*	567 So.2d 1267 (Ala. 1990)
AL	7	*Davis v. Hester*	582 So.2d 538 (Ala. 1991)
AL	7	*Martin v. First Fed. Sav. & Loan Ass'n of Andalusia*	559 So.2d 1075 (Ala. 1990)
AL	2	*Zoecon Indus. v. American Stockman Tag Co.*	713 F.2d 1174 (5th Cir. 1983)
AK	7	*Betz v. China Hot Springs Group*	657 P.2d 831 (Alaska 1982)
AR	AT-89	*Chick-A-Dilly Properties, Inc. of Camden v. Hilyard*	42 Ark.App. 120, 856 S.W.2d 15 (1993) (en banc)
AR	5	*Database Sys., Inc. v. C.L. Sys.*	640 F.2d 109 (8th Cir. 1981)
AR	AT-89	*Schlytter v. Baker*	580 F.2d 848 (5th Cir. 1978)
AR	12	*SD Leasing, Inc. v. Al Spain & Assoc.*	277 Ark. 178, 640 S.W.2d 451 (1982)
AR	12	*Tiffany Indus. v. Commercial Grain Bin Co.*	714 F.2d 799 (8th Cir. 1989)
CA	2, 9	*Continental Car-Na-Var Corp. v. Mosley*	24 Cal.2d 104, 148 P.2d 9 (1944)
CA	10	*Hesse v. Grossman*	152 Cal.App.2d 536, 313 P.2d 625 (1949)
CA	5, 10	*Klamath-Orleans Lumber Inc. v. Miller*	87 Cal.App.3d 458, 151 Cal.Rptr. 118 (1978)
CA	1	*Morse v. Municipal Court*	13 Cal.3d 149, 118 Cal.Rptr. 14, 529 P.2d 46 (1974)
CO	10	*Brehm v. Johnson*	531 P.2d 991 (Colo.App. 1974)
CT	6	*Berin v. Olson*	183 Conn. 337 (1981)
CT	14	*Collins v. Sears, Roebuck & Co.*	164 Conn. 369, 321 A.2d 444 (1973)
CT	3b	*DePova v. Camden Forge Co.*	254 F.2d 248 (3d Cir. 1985)
CT	6	*Hartford Elec. Light Co. v. Levitz*	173 Conn. 15, 376 A.2d 381 (1979)
CT	10	*Loveridge v. Pendleton Woolen Mills*	788 F.2d 914 (2d Cir. 1986)

CT	2	Town & Country House & Homes Serv., Inc. v. Evans	189 A.2d 390 (Conn. 1963)
CT	3f	Triangle Sheet Metal Works v. Silver	154 Conn. 116, 222 A.2d 220 (1966)
CT	14	Twin City Line Co. v. Harding Glass Co.	283 U.S. 353 (1931)
CT	3f	Widowsky v. Dudek	30 Conn.Supp. 288, 310 A.2d 766 (1972)
CT	14	Williams v. Vista Vestra, Inc.	178 Conn. 323, 422 A.2d 274 (1979)
DE	6	Bayard v. Martin	101 A.2d 329 (1953)
DE	12	Cooper v. Ross & Roberts	505 A.2d 1305 (Del.Super. Ct. 1986)
DE	10	Delaware Limousine Serv. v. Royal Limousine Serv.	1991 WL 53449 (Del.Super.Ct. April 5, 1991)
DE	8	Gaines v. Wilmington Trust Co.	(Del.Super. C.A. No. 90C-MR-135, June 3, 1991)
DE	8	Heideck v. Kent Gen. Hosp., Inc.	446 A.2d 1095 (Del.Super. 1982)
DE	10	Lee Builders, Inc. v. Wells	103 A.2d 918 (Del.Ch. 1954)
DE	8	Merrill v. Crothall-American, Inc.	606 A.2d 96 (Del.Super. 1992)
DE	12	Stone & Webster Eng'g Corp. v. Brunswick Pulp & Paper Co.	209 A.2d 890 (Del. Super. Ct. 1965)
DE	10	White v. Metropolitan Merchandise Mart	107 A.2d 892 (Del.Super. 1954)
FL	7	Acquafredda v. Messina	408 So.2d 828 (Fla. 5th Dist.Ct.App. 1982)
FL	6	Anderson v. Souza	38 Cal.2d 825, 243 P.2d 497 (1952)
FL	11	Ashland Oil v. Pickard	269 So.2d 714 (Fla. 3d Dist.Ct.App. 1972)
FL	6	Barberio-Powell v. Bernstein Leibstone Assocs., Inc.	624 So.2d 383, 18 Fla. L. Weekly D2079 (Fla. 4th Dist.Ct.App. 1993)
FL	12	Bushell v. Wackenhut Int'l	731 F.Supp. 1574 (S.D.Fla. 1990)
FL	2	Harlee v. Professional Serv. Indus.	No. 89-2650, 1992 WL 353702, 17 Fla. L. Weekly D2672 (Fla. 3d Dist.Ct.App. 1992)

Joel A. Klarreich

TANNENBAUM HELPERN SYRACUSE & HIRSCHTRITT LLP
900 Third Avenue • New York, NY 10022
Direct Dial: (212) 508-6747
Facsimile: (212) 508-6797
Email: jak@tanhelp.com

IA	6	Kersten v. Pioneer Hi-Bred Int'l	626 F.Supp. 647 (N.D. Iowa 1985)
ID	12	Cerami-Kote v. Energywave Corp.	773 P.2d 1143 (Idaho 1989)
IL	2	ILG Indus., Inc. v. Scott	49 Ill.2d 88, 273 N.E.2d 393 (1971)
IN	4	Brokaw v. Brokaw	398 N.E.2d 1385 (Ind.App. 1980)
IN	12	Dohm & Nelke Div. of Cashin Sys. Corp. v. Wilson Foods Corp.	531 N.E.2d 512 (Ind.App. 1988)
IN	11	Duckwall v. Rees	119 Ind.App. 474, 86 N.E.2d 460 (1949)
IN	7	Kozuch v. Cra-Mar Video Center, Inc.	478 N.E.2d 110 (Ind.App. 1985)
IN	5	Wells v. Auberry	429 N.E.2d 679 (Ind.App. 1982)
IN	7	Whiteco Indus., Inc. v. Nickolick	549 N.E.2d 396 (Ind.App. 1990)
IN	5	Yakus v. United States	321 U.S. 414, 64 S.Ct. 660, 88 L.Ed. 834 (1944)
KS	5, 6	Erie R.R. v. Tompkins	304 U.S. 64 (1938)
KS	12	Interfirst Bank Clifton v. Fernandez	853 F.2d 292 (5th Cir. 1988)
KS	12	Klaxon Co. v. Stentor Elec. Mfg. Co.	313 U.S. 487 (1941)
KS	5	Lundgrin v. Claytor	619 F.2d 61 (10th Cir. 1980)
KS	12	Missouri Pac. R.R. v. Kansas Gas & Elec. Co.	862 F.2d 796 (10th Cir. 1988)
KS	14	Smith & English, Partners v. Board of Educ. of City of Liberal	115 Kan. 155, 222 P. 101 (1924)
KS	12	St. Paul Surplus Lines Ins. Co. v. International Playtex Inc.	245 Kan. 258, 777 P.2d 1259 (1989), cert. denied, 107 L.Ed. 774 (1990)
KS	14	Standard Chautauqua Sys. v. Gift	120 Kan. 101, 242 P. 145 (1926)
KS	6	Wichita Wire, Inc. v. Lenox	11 Kan.App.2d 459, 726 P.2d 287 (1986)
KY	12	Lewis v. American Family Ins. Group	555 S.W.2d 579 (Ky.Ct.App. 1977)
KY	7	Maupin v. Stansbury	575 S.W.2d 695 (Ky.Ct.App. 1978)

MD	12	Goff v. Aamco Auto. Transmissions	313 F.Supp. 667 (Md. 1970)
MD	2	Maryland Metals, Inc. v. Metzner	282 Md. 31, 382 A.2d 564 (1978)
MD	10	Sloane, Inc. v. House & Assocs.	311 Md. 36, 532 A.2d 694 (1987)
MD	2	Space Aero Prods. Co. v. R.E. Darling Co.	238 Md. 93, 208 A.2d 74, reargument denied, 238 Md. 93, 208 A.2d 699, cert. denied, 382 U.S. 843 (1965)
ME	12	Baybutt Constr. Corp. v. Commercial Union Ins. Co.	455 A.2d 914 (Me. 1983)
ME	5	Ingraham v. University of Maine at Orano	441 A.2d 691 (Me. 1982)
ME	7	State v. Maine State Employees Ass'n	482 A.2d 461 (Me. 1984)
MI	AT-73A	BRB Printing, Inc. v. Buchanan	878 F.Supp. 1049 (E.D.Mich. 1995)
MI	AT-73A	Goodwin v. Coe Pontiac	392 Mich. 195, 220 N.W.2d 664 (1974)
MI	12	Morris v. Watsco, Inc.	385 Mass. 672, 433 N.E.2d 886 (1982)
MI	9	Steggles v. National Discount Corp.	326 Mich. 44, 39 N.W.2d 237 (1949)
MN	2, 5, 7	Dahlberg Bros., Inc. v. Ford Motor Co.	272 Minn. 264, 137 N.W.2d 314 (Minn. 1965)
MN	12	Milkovich v. Sarri	295 Minn. 155, 203 N.W.2d 408 (1973)
MN	5	Miller v. Foley	317 N.W.2d 710 (Minn. 1982)
MN	2, 3f	Ring Computer Sys. v. Paradata Computer Networks	1990 WL 132615 (Minn.Ct.App. 1990) (unpublished)
MO	3d	Carboline Co. v. Jarboe	454 S.W.2d 540 (Mo. 1970)
MO	AT-68	Clark-Lami, Inc. v. Cord	440 S.W.2d 737 (Mo.App. 1969)
MO	14, AT-91	Community Title Co. v. Roosevelt Fed. Sav. & Loan Ass'n	796 S.W.2d 369 (Mo. banc 1990)
MO	AT-7	Mashburn v. Tri-State Motor Transit Co.	841 S.W.2d 249 (Mo.App. 1992)
MO	3d	Midland-Ross Corp. v. Yokana	293 F.2d 411 (3d Cir. 1961)

NC	5	Ridge Community Investors, Inc. v. Berry	293 N.C. 688, 239 S.E.2d 566 (1977)
NC	10	Roane-Barker v. Southeastern Hosp. Supply Corp.	99 N.C.App. 30, 392 S.E.2d 663 (1970)
NC	2, AT-92, AT-94	Spartan Leasing v. Pollar	101 N.C.App. 450, 400 S.E.2d 476 (1991)
NC	10, AT-94	United Laboratories v. Kuykendall	87 N.C.App. 296, 361 S.E.2d 292 (1987)
NC	10, AT-94	United Laboratories v. Kuykendall	322 N.C. 643, 370 S.E.2d 375, 5 IER Cases 1346 (1988)
NC	10, AT-94	United Laboratories v. Kuykendall	102 N.C.App. 484, 403 S.E.2d 104 (1991)
NC	AT-71	Zinn v. Walker	87 N.C.App. 325, 361 S.E.2d 314 (1987), disc. rev. denied, 321 N.C. 747, 366 S.E.2d 871 (1988)
ND	1	Glatt v. Bank of Kirkwood Plaza	383 N.W.2d 473 (N.D. 1986)
NE	7	Gottsch v. Bank of Stapleton	235 Neb. 816, 458 N.W.2d 443 (1990)
NE	10	Harmon Cable Communications of Neb. Ltd. Partnership v. Scope Cable Television	237 Neb. 871, 468 N.W.2d 350 (1991)
NE	7	Hughes v. Enterprise Irrigation Dist.	226 Neb. 230, 410 N.W.2d 494 (1987)
NE	2	Jackson v. Caldwell	18 Utah 2d 81, 415 P.2d 667 (1976)
NE	5	Talarico v. United Furniture Workers Pension Fund A	479 F.Supp. 1072 (D.Neb. 1979)
NH	4	Lemire v. Haley	91 N.H. 357, 19 A.2d 436 (1941)
NH	4	Park v. Board of Aviation Trustees for City of Manchester	96 N.H. 331, 76 A.2d 514 (1950)
NH	4	Piper v. Boston & Me. R.R.	75 N.H. 435, 75 A. 1041 (1910)
NJ	14	AGA Aktiebolag v. ABA Optical Corp.	441 F.Supp. 747 (E.D.N.Y. 1977)
NJ	14	Auxton Computer Enters. v. Parker	174 N.J. Super. 418, 416 A.2d 952 (App.Div. 1980)

State	Case	Section	Citation
NY	Headquarters Buick-Nissan v. Michael Oldsmobile	14	149 A.D.2d 745, 539 N.Y.S.2d 355 (1st Dep't 1989)
NY	Kensington Court Assocs. v. Gullo	5	180 A.D.2d 888, 579 N.Y.S.2d 485 (3d Dep't 1992)
NY	Leo Silfen, Inc. v. Cream	2, 3, 3f, 14	29 N.Y.2d 387, 328 N.Y.S.2d 423, 278 N.E.2d 636 (1972)
NY	Long Island Oil Terminals Ass'n, Inc. v. Commissioner of N.Y. State Dept. of Transp.	7	70 A.D.2d 303, 421 N.Y.S.2d 405 (3d Dep't 1979)
NY	Metal & Salvage Ass'n, Inc. v. Siegel	6, 14	121 A.D.2d 200, 503 N.Y.S.2d 26 (1st Dep't 1986)
NY	Nassau Sports v. Peters	2	352 F.Supp. 867 (E.D.N.Y. 1972)
NY	NCN Co., Inc. v. Cavanaugh	5	627 N.Y.S.2d 446 (A.D. 2d Dep't 1995)
NY	Sabetay v. Sterling Drug	3c	69 N.Y.2d 329, 514 N.Y.S.2d 209, 506 N.E.2d 919, 2 IER Cases 150 (1987)
NY	Walter Karl, Inc. v. Wood	2, 3b, 5, 6	137 A.D.2d 22, 528 N.Y.S.2d 94 (2d Dep't 1988), aff'd, 555 N.Y.S.2d 840 (1990)
NY	Weiss v. Miller	10	166 A.D.2d 283, 564 N.Y.S.2d 110 (1st Dep't 1990)
NY	Zurich Depository Corp. v. Gilenson	2	121 A.D.2d 443, 503 N.Y.S.2d 415 (Dep't 1986)
OH	Adams v. Ohio Dep't of Health	7	5 Ohio Op.3d 148, 356 N.E.2d 324 (1976)
OH	McCluskey v. Rob San Servs.	12	443 F.Supp. 65 (S.D.Ohio 1977)
OH	Nichols v. Waterfield Fin. Corp.	3c	62 Ohio App.3d 717, 577 N.E.2d 422, jurisdictional motion overruled, 45 Ohio St.3d 710, 545 N.E.2d 905 (1989)
OH	O'Brien v. Product Eng. Sales Co.	3c	1988 WL 2436 (Ohio Ct.App. (Montgomery), No. 10417, Jan. 8, 1988) (unreported)
OH	Paglia v. Heinbaugh	3c	1994 WL 110892 (Ohio Ct.App. (Trumbull), No. 93-T-4838, Feb. 25, 1994) (unreported)
OH	Perlmuter Printing Co. v. Strome, Inc.	12	436 F.Supp. 409 (N.D.Ohio 1976)

State	No.	Case	Citation
SC	7	Green v. City of Bennettsville	197 S.C. 313, 15 S.E.2d 334 (1941)
SC	3a	Small v. Springs Indus.	292 S.C. 481, 357 S.E.2d 452, 2 IER Cases 266 (1987)
SD	3f	Crescent Elec. Supply Co. v. Nerison	89 S.D. 203, 232 N.W.2d 76 (1975)
TN	7	Baker v. Battershell	(Tenn.Ct.App. April 19, 1985) (LEXIS, Employ library, Tenn. file)
TN	10	Dalton Properties, Inc. v. Jones	683 P.2d 30 (Nev. 1984)
TN	2	Data Processing Equip. Corp. v. Martin	Appeal No. 87-230-II (Tenn.Ct.App. Dec. 30, 1987; LEXIS Employ library, Tenn. file)
TN	10	Goodman v. Motor Prods. Corp.	9 Ill.App.2d 57, 132 N.E.2d 356 (2d Dist. 1956), aff'd after remand, 22 Ill.App.2d 378, 161 N.E.2d 31 (2d Dist. 1959)
TN	10	Goodson Bros. Coffee Co. v. Institutional Jobbers Co.	1992 WL 184685 (Tenn.App., No. 03A01-9111-CH-00415, Sept. 11, 1991)
TN	3	Holt v. Holt	751 S.W.2d 426 (Tenn.App. 1988)
TN	3	Home Beneficial Ass'n v. White	180 Tenn. 585, 177 S.W.2d 545 (1944)
TN	3	Nashville Ry. & Light Co. v. Lawson	144 Tenn. 78, 227 S.W. 741 (1921)
TN	12	Ohio Casualty Ins. Co. v. Travelers Indemnity Co.	493 S.W.2d 465 (1973)
TN	1	Quality Auto Parts Co. v. Bluff City Buick Co.	1992 WL 379077 (Tenn.App., No. 02A01-9205-CV-00138, 1992)
TN	12	Solomon v. Flowarr Mgmt.	1989 Tenn.App. LEXIS 446 (Tenn. App. Jun. 16, 1989)
TN	10	Wunderlich v. Fortas	776 S.W.2d 953 (Tenn. App. 1989)
TX	2	American Precision Vibrator Co. v. National Air Vibrator Co.	764 S.W.2d 274 (Tex.Civ.App., Houston 1st Dist. 1988)
TX	10	Anbeck Co. v. Zapata Corp.	641 S.W.2d 608 (Tex.App. 1982, writ ref'd n.r.e.)

State	Section	Case	Citation
TX	AT-21	*Portland Gasoline Co. v. Superior Mktg. Co.*	150 Tex. 533, 243 S.W.2d 823 (1951)
TX	2, 3a	*Ramos v. Henry C. Beck Co.*	711 S.W.2d 331 (Tex.Ct.App.—Dallas 1986)
TX	3	*Rio Grande Oil Co. v. State*	539 S.W.2d 917 (Tex.Civ.App.—Houston [1st Dist.] 1976)
TX	3c	*Sterner v. Marathon Oil Co.*	767 S.W.2d 686, 4 IER Cases 592 (Tex. 1989)
TX	5	*Sun Oil Co. v. Whitaker*	424 S.W.2d 505 (Tex. 1982)
TX	3	*Texas Farm Bureau Cotton Ass'n v. Stovall*	113 Tex. 273, 253 S.W. 1101 (1923)
TX	5	*Transport Co. of Texas v. Robertson Transports, Inc.*	152 Tex. 551, 261 S.W.2d 549 (1953)
TX	7	*Zmotny v. Phillips*	529 S.W.2d 760 (Tex. 1975)
WA	10	*Larsen v. Walton Plywood Co.*	65 Wash.2d 1, 390 P.2d 677, modified on reh'g, 65 Wash.2d 21, 396 P.2d 879 (1964)
WA	8	*Lea v. Young*	168 Wash. 496, 12 P.2d 601 (1932)
WA	10	*Walter Implement, Inc. v. Focht*	107 Wash.2d 553, 730 P.2d 1340 (1987)
WI	12	*American Standard Casualty Co. of Wis. v. Cleveland*	124 Wis.2d 258, 369 N.W.2d 168 (1985)
WI	8	*Appleton State Bank v. Lee*	33 Wis.2d 690, 148 N.W.2d 1 (1967)
WI	5	*Dillingham Constr. v. Milwaukee Metro. Sewerage Dist.*	629 F.Supp. 406 (E.D.Wis. 1986)
WI	3c	*Hainz v. Shopko Stores, Inc.*	121 Wis.2d 168, 359 N.W.2d 397 (Wis.App. 1984)
WI	12	*Handal v. American Farmers Mut. Casualty Co.*	79 Wis.2d 67, 255 N.W.2d 903 (1977)
WI	8	*Jolin v. Oster*	55 Wis.2d 199, 198 N.W.2d 639 (1972)
WI	AT-17.1	*Milwaukee Area Joint Apprenticeship Training Comm. for the Elec. Indus. v. Howell*	67 F.3d 1333 (7th Cir. 1995)
WI	12	*Ondrasek v. Tenneson*	158 Wis. 690, 462 N.W.2d 915 (Wis.Ct.App. 1990)